MANAGEMENT FOR NEW AND PROSPECTIVE SUPERVISORS

A Program of Study for Professional *3/13/98*
Development and Success in Management

*To Gary Longstreet,
Much continued success in
your academic and professional
Career,
Francis Bridges*

Francis J. Bridges, Ph.D.
with
Libby L. Roquemore, MBA

ESM Books

MANAGEMENT FOR NEW AND PROSPECTIVE SUPERVISORS
A Program of Study for Professional Development and Success in Management

Printing History:
ESM BOOKS paperback trade edition
1st printing February 1994

For information contact:
ESM Books
Educational Services for Management, Inc.
235 East Ponce deLeon Avenue, Suite 307
Decatur, Georgia 30030-3412
Telephone: 404-373-6386
FAX: 404-982-9478

For purchasing information, write or contact:
ESM Books
235 East Ponce deLeon Avenue, Suite 307
Decatur, Georgia 30030-3412
404-373-6386
404-982-9478 (FAX)

ISBN 0-9623126-3-0
Library of Congress Catalog Card Number 94-70076

Printed in the United States of America

PREFACE

Welcome to the world of management! A job in management is the choicest career opportunity available. Take advantage of this opportunity by preparing yourself to be a complete "professional" in management.

Remember that the *great* managers are only a little bit better than the average ones. New or prospective supervisors can get a running start and gain a competitive edge on other managers by learning something about management theory, concepts, principles and practices. You can also enhance your success as a manager by becoming familiar with management jargon.

Management for New and Prospective Supervisors is written especially for the recently promoted or prospective manager who has had little or no training for the world of management.

Employees who are promoted to a supervisory job typically are bright, dependable, motivated and sincere about doing a good job, but their expertise most often is in the functional, nonmanagement position left behind. Moving into management presents a major challenge, even to those who are familiar with the subject. For those who are not prepared for a job in management, the promotion can be the "beginning of the end." Managers work through other people to achieve desired goals and objectives. Knowing how to stimulate and sustain the motivation of his or her employees is the key to management success. A new or prospective supervisor should understand that the only resource he or she will manage is people, and one must make the shift from expertise in a functional area to greater prowess in human and personal skills.

This book is designed and written for self-directed study, or it can be a manual for group training under the direction of a training specialist.

The book is organized into three sections. The first, consisting of four chapters, is entitled Past and Present Management. Section II includes four chapters on Major Management Functions. Finally, Section III consists of four chapters that deal with The Human Side of Administration.

Special Features

Each chapter contains a number of special features designed to strengthen a reader's understanding of management and his or her ability to apply this knowledge to the job of a supervisor:

Knowledge Goals. At the beginning of each chapter, the goals are presented so that one will know what he or she is expected to learn and master.

Summary. A concise written summary of important points discussed in the chapter is included at the end of each chapter.

Review Questions. Discussion questions are presented at the end of each chapter to help supervisors assimilate the material presented and prepare for group discussion.

Assignments for Personal Growth. A special feature in each chapter is the opportunity for readers to apply practical and theoretical concepts studied in the real world of management. These thought-provoking assignments require supervisors to relate the subjects to specific management situations. Two assignments for personal growth accompany each chapter.

Incidents. Critical incidents in management that are set in the organizational world are presented at the end of each chapter. These short cases are structured with two questions to guide the reader's analysis of the situation.

What is a critical incident? A critical incident is a relatively short summary of a problem situation with the pertinent facts and information included. The incidents end with a decision-making condition facing the manager or key person in the setting. The urgency for a decision makes the incident "critical."

Managers often think that a few paragraphs of information are not sufficient material to analyze critically a problem situation. On the contrary, if the information provided is used properly without making assumptions and if the information presented is buttressed by good insights from readings, experience, or perhaps other studies, then there is more than enough information to make sound judgements that lead to decisions.

The critical incident method of teaching and study is one of the most stimulating techniques available. While not new as a pedagogical device, it is not widely used. The traditional forms of teaching, such as the lecture and case method, are excellent for certain purposes and courses, but none excels the incident method when the subject matter is organization behavior and administration. Critical incidents force concentrated attention on immediate issues that demand decisions (action). The effectiveness of the method is directly related to the skill and knowledge of the instructor and the preparation and interest of the group. The basic concerns of this course are the administration of people, employee problems, group behavior, organizational actions, and so forth, and nothing challenges us more than the analysis of our fellow workers within a formal organizational framework. Part of the attraction is based on our understanding of human problems. We have either been exposed to similar problems, observed them, or can empathize with them. Caution should be taken, however, to avoid presenting snap judgements or loose opinions when analyzing incidents. To become proficient as an analyst and to learn lessons from such a study requires a knowledge of organization behavior, a knowledge of management, and the ability to present ideas and findings in a logical and concise manner.

The incident method stimulates study, intense discussion, and a multitude of viewpoints from participants. It provides a ready review and analysis of different problems in different settings. Finally, the student has a laboratory type of exercise in which to apply the scientific approach to problem-solving and decision-making.

Suggested Readings. Those who would like to pursue subjects presented in the chapter in more detail have a list of suggested resources for in-depth examination. Articles and books listed at the end of each chapter are authored by some of the most distinguished researchers and practitioners in the field of management.

Glossary of Key Terms. Another special feature of this text is a list of key topics and their definitions at the end of the text-material. Over 200 terms discussed in the subject presentation are defined or explained for a reader's ready reference.

Special Acknowledgements

Special acknowledgement goes to the thousands of American managers who have shared their work experiences with me over many years. I have worked with these outstanding people, men and women, in seminars, listened to them, spoken with them and learned from them. They are the heroic people who run our organizations, take full responsibility for results, and make the crucial decisions that determine organizational destiny.

Francis J. Bridges

CONTENTS

Internationally. The Rise of Consumerism. Demographic Changes in the U.S. Shift to a Service Economy. Ethics Defined. Current Emphasis on Ethics. Making Ethical Decisions. Ethics and Legality. Social Responsibility of Management. Definition of Social Responsibility. Social Responsibility of Organizations. Critical Problems Facing Management in the 1990s.

Summary and Review Questions

Assignments for Personal Development

Incident: The Ordinary Office

Suggested Readings.

SECTION 2: MAJOR MANAGEMENT FUNCTIONS

Summary and Review Questions

Assignments for Personal Development

Incident: Opportunity Unlimited

Suggested Readings

Summary and Review Questions

Assignments for Personal Development

Incident: Frustrated Supervisor

Suggested Readings.

ganizing. Activating Authority and Responsibility. Barnard's Acceptance Theory of Authority. Meaning of Delegation. Vertical and Horizontal Organization Structures. Graicunas' Theorem and Its Value. Coordination of Organizational Resources.

Summary and Review Questions

Assignments for Personal Development

Incident: Disgruntled Employees

Suggested Readings.

Origin and Meaning of Control. The Control Process. Need for Control. Factors Affecting Need for Control. How Much Control? Quality Control Circles. Planning and Control. Types of Controls. Incoming, In-Process and Final Stage Controls. Characteristics of Effective Control. Employee Resistance to Control. Overcoming Employee Resistance to Control. Organization and Control. Controlling Controls. Current Trends in Controlling. Total Quality Management (TQM).

Summary and Review Questions

Assignments for Personal Development

Incident: A Smoking Gun!

Suggested Readings

SECTION 3: THE HUMAN SIDE OF ADMINISTRATION

Personnel Management and Human Resource Departments. Line and Staff Conflict. Staffing and Personnel Management. Human Resource Planning. Auditing Human Resources. Staffing and the Legal Environment. Major Federal Legislation Which Affects Staffing. Acquiring Human Resources. Inside and Outside Sources. The Recruitment Process. The Selection Process Defined. Steps in the Selection Process. Assessment Centers. New Employee Orientation and Objectives. Benefits of Orientation. Developing Employee Potential. Training Defined. Types of Training. Performance Appraisals. Promotion, Transfers and Disciplinary Action. Maintaining the Work Force. Compensation and Benefits. "The Peter Principle."

Summary and Review Questions

Assignments for Personal Development

Incident: How to Recruit!

Suggested Readings

The Meaning of Motivation. Motivation as a Psychological Process. Theories of Motivation. Traditional Theory. Maslow's Hierarchy of Needs. Herzberg's Motivation—Maintenance Theory. Theory X and Theory Y. Preference-Expectancy Theory. Skinner's Reinforcement Theory. Value of Theory to Practicing Managers. Morale Defined. Morale and Employee Performance. Motivation and Morale. The Hawthorne Studies. Job Satisfaction and Performance. Meaning of Job Enrichment. Leadership Defined. Formal and Informal Leaders. Leaders and Managers Distinguished. Situational Leader-

CHAPTER 1

THE PROFESSIONAL PERSPECTIVE

After studying this chapter, **you will know**:
- What management is all about
- Whether you are sincere about a career in management
- How new managers are selected
- That opportunity is unlimited in management
- Why so many managers fail
- How training in management gives you an edge
- The importance of having a personal philosophy of management
- About the evolution of the management movement
- Something about pioneers in management—theories and techniques

Introduction

Welcome to the world of management!

This chapter introduces the subject of management by asking pertinent questions that relate to you and to the organization. You should find the answers and comments interesting since you are a new manager just beginning your career in this new world. While you may have several years of employment with the organization, your new position in "management" is truly a new world. The duties, responsibilities and expectations thrust upon managers like you are enormous compared to the job responsibilities of a nonmanagement employee. Being a manager can be extremely challenging and rewarding, but—and this is the clear message of Chapter 1—you must get prepared for the world of management!

From a career point of view, probably the most exciting thing you will do in your life is be a manager. Many supervisors fail, but many become the "professionals" who continue to move upward in the ranks. The great managers are not "perfect" performers; instead, they perform their duties more effectively and efficiently than other managers and tend to achieve the desired results more often than others over a sustained period of time.

Enjoy this chapter. As you read the material, list other questions about the management world you want to discuss and consider further.

What's It All About?

The greatest game in the world today is not soccer or baseball. It is being a manager! If you like thrills and risks, success and failure, action, and desire visibility, management is for you.

Of the 125 million people employed in the United States civilian labor force today, approximately thirteen million are managers. These people live with excitement, work long hours, look forward to Monday mornings, and enjoy their work lives to the fullest. Managers who do not feel this way about their jobs are probably hanging on by their fingertips or one step away from unemployment.

Management is an activity of achieving objectives by working through "others." Working through "others" refers to the support personnel (at the first level of management these would be all nonmanagement employees) who report to the "bosses." Management personnel have many different job titles. Some are simply called managers; others carry such titles as supervisors, foremen, directors, executives, administrators, department heads, and many more. Some titles are tailored to the particular industry or type of organization. Whatever the title, all management personnel have the same task: working through support personnel to achieve the objective(s). One example of pure management is the football coach who works through eleven players on the field to achieve the objective—victory!

One point must be made clear now. A manager does not manage time, inventories, sales, money, operations, etc. *People who hold management positions manage only one resource—people.* Most job titles in organizations today are misleading. Such designations as Sales Manager, Inventory Manager, Office Manager, etc. may reflect other resources over which the manager has responsibility and control. But managers only manage people.

Why Should You Go Into Management?

Maybe you shouldn't!

Many workers in the labor force are not qualified for management. They may be the best employees, but they may lose everything quickly if they accept a position in management. Being a manager is *not* for everyone.

The job, the title, more pay, and the added prestige may be a lure for a hardworking nonmanagement employee. Behind that appeal, however, are several traps.

What are the traps? Such things as better title, more pay, greater prestige, increased authority, much more responsibility, and possible even a key to the executive dining room (or restroom).

These are positive incentives if you are prepared for a management career and willing to accept the risks that accompany such "perks." These same benefits, however, spell doom for the unprepared.

If you are not prepared to become a manager, you have three choices: Get prepared; postpone your decision until you are ready, or turn down the opportunity. It is better to have a decent job at which you are competent and highly regarded than to risk everything in a totally new world without proper preparation.

But you are ambitious. You feel your intelligence is not being taxed in your present job, and you desire the benefits of being in management. What should you consider next as you decide about a future in management?

Generally, those who go into management give reasons similar to the following. Check this list and see if you lean toward the challenge of a career in management:

1. If you demonstrate that you are a good manager, the opportunity for advancement is unlimited.
2. You gain greater respect and more status among your colleagues.
3. You get the chance to use more of your talents and skills.
4. Management offers the chance to acquire more authority (power) and responsibility.
5. The pay and fringe benefits are better in management.
6. You are confident you can manage as well as or better than the managers you have observed.

Are You Sincere About a Career in Management?

If you think you are ready for the challenge of a career in management, answer the following questions. If your answers are positive, you are sincere about pursuing a career in management, and you have recognized some of the conditions which make management a challenge. It is a new world for those who have been in nonmanagement positions, and to accept the conditions is not always easy. *It takes a special type of person to succeed and be outstanding in the field of management, the most demanding of professional careers.*

Make this list of questions your starting point as you check your sincerity about that management career:

1. Do you like being in charge of other people?
2. Do you like to have the responsibility for the actions of others?
3. Do you think you could take satisfaction in seeing employees under your supervision succeed?
4. Would you like being judged on results—good and bad?
5. Would you like a job where your bosses have little appreciation for excuses?
6. Do you enjoy being a "team" player?
7. Do you like visibility?
8. Do you think you can lead others positively toward objectives and do so consistently?
9. Would you enjoy setting the model for employee conduct on the job?
10. Could you accept working 50-60 hours per week routinely when nonmanagement employees work 40?
11. Are you confident you know the subject of management and know what managers are supposed to do?
12. Do you thrive under a certain amount of stress caused by unusual demands, deadlines, schedules, and dealing with a multitude of different personalities?
13. Do you enjoy problem-solving and decision-making and the risks that accompany implementing your decisions?
14. Can you put aside personal interests and preferences and do what is best for the organization?

15. Can you handle pressure from your peers, your posses, and your subordinates?

How Are New Managers Selected?

Most new managers are promoted from within the organization from the ranks of nonmanagement employees. A less significant number are recruited from college campuses with an even smaller number of new managers coming from such sources as personnel placement firms.

The majority of new managers are employees who have had several years of work experience with an organization and have demonstrated the following:

1. Steady and dependable work habits;
2. Excellent knowledge and performance of their jobs;
3. The ability to get along well with others;
4. That they are not trouble makers, and
5. Loyalty to the organization.

Higher management would rather promote from within than chance the unknown qualities of newcomers who are strangers to the organization. Also, this provides an incentive to all employees who have a long-run desire to be in management.

Seniority, which is important in making job promotion, layoff, and transfer decisions in nonmanagement employees, is not the most important factor in determining who goes into management positions. It does not dominate promotion considerations in management above the entry level position. *Performance is the key to climbing the management ladder once you are tapped for that first level position.*

Those management employees recruited from colleges normally go into a management training program before being assigned a permanent management job. Management training in these cases is most likely to be a course of several weeks or months designed to familiarize the recruit with all facets of the organization. This is not really management training! It is technical training which is important, but usually little attention is given to the actual subject of management.

You may wonder what recruiters look for in these college candidates. They seek to weed out the undesirable applicants for management jobs and select those who appear to be personable, highly motivated, possess good intelligence, and who show signs of interest in the organization on a long-term basis. They may look at such things as grades, extracurricular activities, employment records, academic major, and personal recommendations. Experience has shown, however, that managerial success is not guaranteed by an outstanding interview or high test scores. Neither can direct correlation be shown between I.Q. and academic success (or lack of it) and management effectiveness. Selection of management candidates also takes into consideration emotional maturity, stability, and whether the applicant is well-adjusted in general. Finding the answers to these questions about characteristics is difficult. Knowing the applicant well does not tell a recruiter if that person will make an effective practicing manager.

Other sources of management applicants are the mail, friends of employees, relatives of executives, and personnel placement services. Despite the questions and reservations about each method of selection all of these have produced good and bad managers.

Regardless of the source of new managers, few are prepared to be successful. The solution to this problem is not being found within American organizations.

All of these routes remain open, however, to those who wish to enter the field of management.

Is the Opportunity Unlimited in Management?

A job in management is the choicest career opportunity available. The only option that is more exciting is starting your own business. Even in this instance you are right back in management, but the difference is you are totally in charge of everything.

If a poll of 100 top executives were taken to find the number one problem in American organizations, I think the majority would say the shortage of competent management people. This may be the hi-tech age, the onslaught of the computer, the era of the specialist; but the *continued biggest problem, as it has been for decades, is the shortage of competency in management.*

Turnover in management is astronomical. It happens because managers retire, get transferred, resign, get fired, die, or are promoted upward. Opportunities abound. Where there is turnover, there is a vacancy. And every vacancy is an opportunity for someone.

If the idea of unlimited opportunity appeals to you, a career in management should be attractive. Heed the warning signs of high turnover, lifetime job probation, and total responsibility, though, and get yourself prepared. Management has pitfalls as well as opportunities.

The majority of managers are thrust into their first management position without any preparation. No wonder so many fail!

Why Do So Many Managers Fail?

American managers tend to be intelligent, highly motivated, success-oriented people who are willing to assume additional responsibility and work unlimited hours. Yet, many fail. Why?

As a group, American managers perform professionally at each level in the organization. Certainly we would not have had the success as a nation we have enjoyed for generations without the outstanding executives, administrators, leaders, entrepreneurs, supervisors, etc. which populate American organizations leading the way. The challenge of management in the 1990s, however, is different.

Today, there is increasing organizational complexity, increased competition, voluminous governmental regulations, and a changed attitude among employees about their work and the work environment. *Quite simply, managers cannot get away with what they once could.* The tempo of the modern organization is much faster, and life styles of both managers and employees are vastly different.

The by-product of all this complexity is trouble for managers—both veterans and newcomers. The reasons they fail are different, however, and can be summarized by the two categories.

Veteran managers encounter the following problems:

1. Managerial obsolescence (the demands of the job exceed the skill and talent of the person)
2. Executive stress and burnout
3. Loss of support from higher management (reasons for this vary, but it dooms the affected manager)

A different set of problems face the newcomer.

The most significant reason for failure is that few newly promoted managers have any training in management before assuming their management duties. This means that these new managers simply do not know what to do once they are in management positions. Many of them are promoted from within their organizations because of technical competence or outstanding performance in a nonmanagement job. There is no direct correlation between being a good worker and becoming an effective practicing manager.

These newcomers need knowledge of the subject of management plus some technical know-how in operations, good human or personal skills, and the ability and background to evaluate and learn from each experience. The latter is not to be confused with On the Job Training, which often is nothing more than trial and error management and is a poor method of management training.

Beyond the lack of preparation for management positions, some of the more common reasons for the failure among newly appointed managers are the following:

1. They have failed to get the objectives clearly established by higher management.
2. They are not given enough authority to get the job done.
3. They are not accepted by their support personnel.
4. They are working against unrealistic goals and objectives.
5. They are working with impossible time standards for the completion of assignments.
6. They have personality conflicts with other managers (especially upper management).
7. They do not have the flexibility and adaptability to adjust to changing conditions.

How Should New Managers Be Prepared?

How can an aspiring manager prepare to succeed in that first management job? The answer is the company can provide the training or the manager-to-be can begin a self-development course to program himself or herself for success when that opportunity knocks.

No organization employs typists, programmers, accountants, welders, or any other person for a skilled job without first testing for competency. *For some reason, however, American organizations promote or hire people for first level management positions without a firm knowledge of whether the employee can manage.*

Management at any level is the key to an organization's future. It is also difficult and challenging. Therefore, sending prepared managers into the ranks is the only way to gain an edge toward success.

Preparing employees for promotion into management should be a priority of all organizations. A program should include the following steps:

1. Supervisory management training conducted by a professional in the field of management training prior to starting the job;
2. An in-depth management orientation program before assuming management duties;
3. Follow-up supervisory management training and evaluation six months after the manager has had experience on the job; and
4. A directed program of reading and study in management.

If this type of training program is not available in your company (or is not yet available to you) and you still want to be ready for an opening in management, what can you do? *You can develop your own management training program.*

Caution must be raised at this point, however, because it is important for you to recognize that regardless of your preparation and knowledge, you may not become an effective practicing manager. Not every prepared person does, but you will increase your odds of success by being prepared.

Knowing a subject well and applying that knowledge effectively are two different things. But you must begin with the knowledge. Otherwise you will go into your first management position without the tools necessary to face the problems.

Begin your own self-development program by doing the following:

1. Go to a local library, a college library is best, and check out a basic management textbook. The year of publication is not important; just read it cover to cover.
2. Pick out two or three successful managers from different organizations and request an hour's time of each. Interview them with such questions as these:
   a. How did you learn to be a good manager?
   b. What tips and suggestions can you give me for getting prepared for a first level management position?
   c. What should I be most concerned about during my early days in management?
   d. What are some of the pitfalls you think I should watch for?
   e. Do you have any suggestions about how I can be a success in management?
   f. Which subject or activity do you think is most important in management?
   g. Do you have any philosophical tidbits or lessons learned in management which you can share with me?
   h. What has been your most troublesome area or your biggest weakness as a manager?
   i. What is your greatest strength as a manager?
3. Review the answers given to you in your interviews and develop a list of the most important points made. Go back to your basic textbook and review the material on these subjects. You may find extra, specialized management books on the topics considered most crucial by your interviewees which will add depth to your knowledge and preparation.

4. *Write down your own ideas and mold them into a personal philosophy of management.* This is what will be a major influence on your behavior and actions when you become a manager.

5. Finally, while on your current job, evaluate everything around you and learn from all of it. Watch other managers as well as your own boss to see how they operate. A keen observer can learn from the very personal style of other managers. You will acquire a background of knowledge to help you learn and grow with each experience.

How Does Training in Management Give You an Edge?

True Training in management is invaluable to the new manager or management candidate.

Training in management will include such subjects as the following:

1. How the American economic system works
2. The basic concepts of management
3. The fundamental functions of a manager
4. Organizational behavior and communication
5. Problem-solving and decision-making
6. Personal growth and career development
7. Motivation skills and human relations techniques.

These are the most significant topics. Each of these subjects includes dozens of subtopics, concepts, and principles. Chapter 3 of this book lists and describes practical points in management to help you get prepared.

How does this kind of training in management give you an edge?

Simply, if you receive professional management training, you acquire the following:

1. Familiarity with management jargon
2. A body of knowledge that allows you to learn from your daily management experiences
3. Greater confidence in your actions as a manager
4. Stimulation of your thinking about your job
5. New ideas and techniques which you can consider, adapt to your needs and apply.

Consider the topics carefully. Imagine going into your first management job without any of this knowledge or any ideas on these subjects. *Almost 98 percent of new managers take the plunge into management without first receiving management training.*

Don't you think you will have an "edge" if you learn something about the subject of management first?

Ideally, your employer should provide additional management training after you have been on the job about six months. The second phase of training allows you to pursue subjects in much greater depth. You can stress the importance of problem-solving and decision-making. This second phase also allows you to step back and reflect on your experiences as a manager during the initial six months. Then, you can evaluate your strengths and weaknesses and dedicate yourself to being a complete professional for the remainder of your career.

If your employer does not offer any of this management training, you should seek it for yourself. Local colleges, trade associations, industrial management clubs, and many other groups or organizations offer management training programs. Costs vary from nominal to very high, lengths of programs range from a few days to several weeks, and all of the programs have some merit.

Your investment in your future will pay off in big dividends in your career advancement. *Without question trained managers have an "edge," but there are still no guarantees that they will stay on top without continuing growth and development as a way of life.*

Should You Have Your Own Personal Philosophy of Management?

Every new manager feels somewhat lost when first starting that management job. After all, you are in a new world with different kinds of problems and drastically changed responsibilities. Furthermore, expectations are great, and you have no background of experience on which to rely. You can see that such emotions as inadequacy, insecurity, and worry (perhaps even fear) would not be unusual. As time goes by and you weather some management storms, your confidence gradually builds. Eventually, you will learn what you can and cannot do, what works and what doesn't, and what your managerial strengths and weaknesses are. From that point on, you begin to manage with more assurance.

A personal philosophy of management on which you can rely helps you and veteran managers most when dealing with daily problems and making decisions. Managers who behave inconsistently in their dealings with people or who appear to be running scared when confronted with problems undoubtedly do not have a personal philosophy of management.

A personal philosophy of management consists of your fundamental beliefs, basic concepts, convictions, and firm ideas about management. Since management involves achieving objectives working through others, many of your beliefs about management will concern people (your employees). Your managerial philosophy also could include values relating to the organization, to yourself, to customers, stockholders, your bosses, and any other factor which influences your management decision-making process.

The importance of having a personal philosophy of management is that it influences every action you take and all decisions you make leading to consistency in your behavior as a manager.

Part of your managerial philosophy might be the following:

1. Every decision I make will be in the best interest of the organization.
2. I will strive to be totally fair-minded and objective when handling employee problems.
3. I will base every action I take on all of the available facts.
4. I will take full responsibility for the work of any of my employees.

Fundamental beliefs and ideals like these provide much strength and confidence to a manager when dealing with hundreds of problems and decisions.

New managers should begin early to write down those ideas, beliefs and concepts which he or she believes are most important in the daily practice of management. Not having a managerial philosophy is like managing with your eyes closed and your ears plugged!

What Is the "Charge" to Managers?

If you decide that a career in management is for you, remember that the *great managers are only a little bit better than the average ones.* There is not a whole lot of difference between excellence and mediocrity, but that slight variance makes the big difference over time.

Strive to develop yourself to the fullest by acquiring all of the knowledge you can in the field of management. Mix this knowledge with experience on the job, and then evaluate your experiences to learn from doing. *Great employees like professional managers tend to be developed over time on the job.*

You can expect to make many mistakes no matter how prepared you are for a career in management. Do your best to space your mistakes and grow and learn between them. Concentrate on improving your managerial techniques in all areas of management. Accept criticism positively and keep your attitude positive.

Take full responsibility and look for more. If you have ambition to "go to the top," do not balk at promotional opportunities. If you have employees who are not motivated, not excited about their jobs, or who make costly mistakes, guess what? The blame lies with you!

If you like excitement, risks, and organizational adventure, you are going to find it as a manager. But, *even if you fail in one organization, you may succeed in another.* It has happened often, *but you must have the fundamental ability and skill as a manager mastered so that you did not fail because you were unprepared or lacked management know-how.*

If you do well in management, you will be doing a great service to your employees, bosses, and to yourself. Indirectly, you will also benefit consumers, owners, and society in general.

There is a shortage of competent professional managers in every type of organization at every management level. Managers, men and women, who really know the subject of management and know how to use resources effectively and produce timely and efficient results in a quality-oriented way are always at a premium. Professional managers pride themselves on the results they achieve and on the full development of the personnel they manage. Professional managers accept total responsibility for outcomes, good and bad, and look forward to the challenge of each new day. Do you think all managers have this attitude?

The Management Movement

Management as a practice has existed since the creation of formal organizations. Thousands of years ago man decided that more could be accomplished through organized group efforts than through individual effort. People in charge of group effort, no matter what the title given to them, were managers. They had the power to direct and control human activity. While the evolution of management as a formal discipline spans centuries, the emergence of general theories of management is relatively recent.

Management did not emerge as a recognized discipline until the Twentieth Century, and it was not taught as an academic subject in American colleges until the 1920s. In the beginning, the stress was on industrial management rather than on general management This is understandable since America's growth as a world power was based on its newly realized industrial might.

By the 1940s collegiate schools of business were in vogue and management became a major field of study. By the 1950s colleges offered courses in general management and stressed that management is a basic process. In effect, this means that **managers in any type of organization, located anywhere, will engage in the basic process of management (planning, organizing, implementing and controlling) as they work through people toward the achievement of objectives.**

Pioneers in Management

The modern management movement began over 100 years ago. Between 1880 and 1920 about twenty individuals, who pioneered management theories and techniques routinely practiced today, started their work. Prior to that time, all the way back to the beginning or recorded history, groups and individuals made contributions to the development of management. Figure 1-1 is entitled "The Continuum of Management." This shows the evolution of management history through the major contributions by ethnic groups and individuals from about 5000 B.C. to the mid-1980s.

From this listing of pioneers the most important individuals, in a modern sense, are Frederick W. Taylor, Frank Gilbreth, Lillian Gilbreth, Henri Fayol, Henry L. Gantt and Elton Mayo. These management pioneers were well known in their own time and made a lasting impact on the practice of management today.

Frederick W. Taylor. Taylor is considered the "Father of Scientific Management." He pioneered time studies, methods analysis, job costing and incentive plans. Taylor was thorough in applying the scientific method when determining how to improve various operational activities. He died in 1915, and the epitaph on his gravestone in Philadelphia reads "Frederick W. Taylor, Father of Scientific Management." As a side point, Taylor won the United States Amateur Doubles Tennis Championship in 1881.

Frank Gilbreth. Gilbreth's pioneering work in the field of motion study laid the foundation for efforts to simplify jobs, develop accurate work standards, and create incentive plans. He should be called the "Father of Work Simplification," and it was his theory that there was always a better way to perform any task. Gilbreth was the first to study work activity on film (micro-motion analysis). He developed principles of motion economy which on application eliminated wasted motion and lessened fatigue. Gilbreth and his wife originated the process chart and flow diagram. Frank Gilbreth died in 1924.

Lillian Gilbreth. Wife and work partner of Frank, Mrs. Gilbreth is rightfully called the First Lady of Management." She lived 94 active, productive years (1878 - 1972). She gained fame not only because of her twelve children and her partnership with her husband, but also because she outlived Frank Gilbreth by forty-eight years during which she made many significant contributions to the advancement of management. Mrs. Gilbreth did pioneering research on the psychology of the workplace and carried on the work of Gilbreth, Inc., after her husband's death. She did extensive work on improving life for handicapped and disabled people, especially whose injured in war. Lillian Gilbreth was the first woman in the United States to receive a doctorate in psychology (University of California). Upon her retirement from Purdue University in the 1950s, Mrs. Gilbreth was a Professor of Industrial Engineering and Psychology. Five presidents appointed her to special committees, and she was well-known throughout the world in management and engineering circles. The Gilbreth family was immortalized in the successful book *Cheaper by the Dozen*, which became a famous movie in 1950.

Henri Fayol. A French management pioneer and administrator, Fayol originated the process school of management. This approach in the study and practice of management stresses the main functions or jobs of managers and the universal application of these functions to all management jobs in any type of organization located anywhere. He published the first complete general theory of management. In 1916 Fayol's *Administration Industrielle et General* included fourteen principles of management which still are valid today. Unfortunately, Fayol's book was not readily available in English until 1949 when it was translated and published as *General and Industrial Management*. Fayol was interested in general management, not management at the operational level (which was the focus of Taylor and others). He strongly advocated that any credible theory of management could not be limited to business, but must be equally applicable to all types of human endeavor. He identified the major functions of all managers as planning, organizing, commanding, coordinating and controlling. These functions are similar to the management functions taught and practiced today. Fayol was a major contributor to management thought, but he also applied his theories and ideas effectively as head of a French coal mining company from 1860 until 1918.

Summary of the Development of Management Thought

Approx. Time	Individual or Group	Significant Management Contribution(s)
500 B.C.	Sumerians	Script; record keeping
4000	Egyptians	Recognized need for planning, organizing and controlling
2700	Egyptians	Recognized need for honesty or fair play in management; therapy interview
2600	Egyptians	Decentralization in organization
2000	Egyptians	Recognized need for written word in requests; use of staff advice
1800	Hammurabi	Use of witnesses and writing for control; establishment of minimum wage; recognition that responsibility cannot be shifted
1600	Egyptians	Centralization in organization
1491	Hebrews (Moses)	Concepts of organization, delegation, scalar principle, exception principle
1100	Chinese	Recognized need for organization, planning, directing and controlling; job descriptions for civil servants
600	Nebuchadnezzar	Production control and wage incentives
500	Mencius	Recognized need for systems and humane standards
	Chinese	Principle of specialization recognized
	Sun Tzu	Recognized need for planning, directing and organizing
400	Socrates	Enunciation of universality of management
	Xenophon	Recognized management as a separate art
	Cyrus	Recognized need for human relations. Use of motion study, layout and materials handling
350	Greeks (Aristotle)	Scientific method applied. Use of work methods and tempo
	Plato	Principle of specialization
325	Alexander the Great	Use of staff
175	Cato	Use of job descriptions
120	Chinese	Civil service exam system
50	Varro	Use of job specifications
20 A.D.	Jesus Christ	Unity of command; Golden Rule; human relations

FIGURE 1-1.1: THE CONTINUUM OF MANAGEMENT (continued)

Approx. Time	Individual or Group	Significant Management Contribution(s)
284	Diocletian	Delegation of authority
900	al-Farabi	Listed traits of a leader
1100	Ghazali	Listed traits of a manager
1340	Genoese	Double entry bookkeeping
1395	Francisco Di Marco	Cost accounting practiced
1410	Soranzo Brothers	Use of journal entries and ledger
1418	Barbarigo	Forms of business organization; work in process accounts used
1436	Venetians Arsenal of Venice	Cost accounting; checks and balances for control; numbering of inventoried parts; interchangeability of parts; use of assembly line techniques; use of personnel management; standardization of parts; inventory and cost control
1500	Sir Thomas More	Called for specialization; decried sins of poor management and leadership
1525	Niccolo Machiavelli	Reliance on mass consent principles; recognized need for cohesiveness in organizations; enunciated leadership qualities
1760	Richard Arkwright	Efficient management principles applied to large-scale industry
1767	Sir James Steuart	Source of authority theory; impact of automation
1776	Adam Smith	Application of principle of specialization to manufacturing workers; control concepts; payback (depreciation) computations
1785	Thomas Jefferson	Called attention to concept of interchangeable parts
1799	Eli Whitney	Scientific method; use of cost accounting and quality control; applied interchangeable parts concept; recognized span of management
1800	James Watt and Matthew Boulton Soho, England	Standard operating procedures; specifications; work methods; planning; incentive wages; standard times; standard date; employee bonuses and Christmas parties; mutual employee's insurance society; use of audits

FIGURE 1-1.2: THE CONTINUUM OF MANAGEMENT (continued)

Approx. Time	Individual or Group	Significant Management Contribution(s)
1810	Robert Owen New Lanark, Scotland	Need for personnel practices recognized and applied; assumed responsibility for training workers; built clean row homes for workers
1820	James Mill	Analyzing and synthesizing human motions
1832	Charles Babbage	Scientific approach emphasized; specialization emphasized; division of labor; motion and time study; cost accounting; effect of various colors on employees
1835	Marshall, Laughlin, et al	Recognition and discussion of the relative importance of the functions of management
1850	Mill, et al	Span of control; unity of command; control of labor and materials; specialization/division of labor; wage incentives
1855	Henry Poor	Principles of organization, communication and information applied to railways
1856	Daniel McCallum	Use of organization chart to show management structure. Application of systematic management to railways
1871	W. S. Jevons	Made motion study of spade use; studied effect of different tools on worker; fatigue study
1881	Joseph Wharton	Endowed first college course in business management (U. of PA)
1886	Henry C. Metcalfe	Management based on system and control
1891	Frederick Halsey	Premium plan of wage payment
1900	Frederick W. Taylor	Scientific management; systems applications; personnel management; need for cooperation between labor and management; high wages; equal division of work between labor and management; functional organization; exception principle applied to the shop; cost system; methods study; time study; definition of scientific management; emphasis on management's job; emphasis on research, standards, planning control and cooperation
	Frank B. and Lillian M. Gilbreth	Science of motion study; therbligs; Human relations; psychology; reducing fatigue; retraining handicapped for new jobs

FIGURE 1-1.3: THE CONTINUUM OF MANAGEMENT (continued)

Approx. Time	Individual or Group	Significant Management Contribution(s)
1901	Henry L. Gantt	Task and bonus system; humanistic approach to labor; Gantt chart; management's responsibility for training workers
1910	Hugo Munsterberg	Application of psychology to management and workers
	Harrington Emerson	Efficiency engineering; twelve principles of efficiency
1911	Harlow S. Person	Initiated first scientific management conference in U.S.; gave academic recognition to scientific management
	J. C. Duncan	First college text in management
1915	H. B. Drury	Criticism of scientific management reaffirmed initial ideas
	R. F. Hoxie	Criticism of scientific management reaffirmed initial ideas
	F. W. Harris	Economic lot size model
	Thomas A. Edison	Devised war game to evade and destroy submarines
1916	Henri Fayol	First complete theory of management; functions of management; principles of management; universality of management concept; basic process school of management thought; recognized need for management to be taught in schools
	Alexander H. Church	Functional concept of management; first American to explain the totality of managerial concepts and relate each component to the whole
	A. K. Erlang	Anticipated waiting-line theory
1917	W. H. Leffingwell	Applied scientific management to office
1918	C. C. Parsons	Recognized need for applying scientific management to offices
	Ordway Tead	Application of psychology to industry
1919	Morris L. Cooke	Diverse application of scientific management
1921	Walter D. Scott	Brought psychology to advertising and personnel management
1923	Oliver Sheldon	Developed a philosophy of management; principles of management

FIGURE 1-1.4: THE CONTINUUM OF MANAGEMENT (continued)

Approx. Time	Individual or Group	Significant Management Contribution(s)
1924	H. F. Dodge H. G. Romig W. A. Shewhart	Use of statistical inference and probability theory in sampling inspection and in quality control by statistical means
1925	Ronald A. Fisher	Various modern statistical methods including Chi-square test, Bayesian statistics, sampling theory, and design of experiments
1927	G. Elton Mayo	Sociological concept of group behavior; Hawthorne Effect; concept of morale
1928	T. C. Fry	Statistical foundations of queuing theory
1930	Mary P. Follett	Managerial philosophy based on individual motivations. Group process approach to solving managerial problems
1931	James D. Mooney	Principles of organization recognized as universal; named scalar principle
1938	Chester Barnard	Theory of organization; emphasis on systems; sociological aspects of management; need for communication
	P. M. S. Blackett, et al/British	Operations research
1943	Lyndall Urwick	Collection, consolidation and correlation of principles of management
	Abraham Maslow	Hierarchy of needs motivation theory
1947	Max Weber	Organizational theory called bureaucracy
1951	Ralph C. Davis	Three categories of objectives; primary objective is service
1954	Peter F. Drucker	Management is a practice and should focus on results; humans are greatest resource, technology just a tool
1950s	Frederick Herzberg	Motivation theory based on hygiene and motivator factors; job enrichment
1957	Northcotte Parkinson	Humorous look at administration; Parkinson's Law: Work expands to fill the time allowed for it.
1960	Douglas McGregor	Theory X and Theory Y views of workers and managers
1961	Rensis Likert	Participative management
1962	Chris Argyris	Sensitivity training for managers

FIGURE 1-1.5: THE CONTINUUM OF MANAGEMENT (continued)

Approx. Time	Individual or Group	Significant Management Contribution(s)
1964	Victor H. Vroom	Expectancy theory of motivation
1969	Laurence Peter	Peter Principle of promotion to level of incompetency; expressed dangers of preoccupation with growth; need for conservation
1971	Ernest Dale	Empirical school of management theory
1981	William Ouchi	Theory Z system of management
1985	Gifford Pinchot, III	Coined term "intrapreneurs" for new type of corporate manager who runs own business within framework of large corporation

FIGURE 1-1.6: THE CONTINUUM OF MANAGEMENT (continued)

Henry L. Gantt. Gantt is noteworthy because he added a humanistic approach to management. As a protege of Taylor, he learned much working with Taylor for fourteen years; however, Gantt developed his own philosophy of management. He concluded that the human element was the most important resource of management. Gantt designed a wage incentive plan that provided a bonus to employees if they produced above the daily standard. He understood the importance of employee morale and attitude, and the impact of morale on job satisfaction and employee performance. In 1913 Gantt created the visual control chart used in measuring output against expectations along a time axis. One of Gantt's most important contributions was to suggest that organizations have a social responsibility. It was Gantt who first introduced the idea that the service objective should be the primary objective of organizations.

Elton Mayo. This Harvard professor introduced managers to the importance of good human relations in the workplace. Mayo did his major work between 1927 and 1947. He worked in the Department of Industrial Research at Harvard, and his work was experimental rather than theoretical. His greatest fame was gained through the Hawthorne Studies conducted over several years at Western Electric's Hawthorne Works near Chicago. This project, funded by the Rockefeller Foundation, was initiated to determine the effect of lighting on worker output. As chief researcher, Mayo conducted many experiments but in spite of improved or worsened lighting conditions, the female employees in the control group and in the experimental group both increased output. Over five years from 1927 until 1932 hundreds of experiments were conducted involving hundreds of employees. Researchers found that despite altering such factors as the work day, rest periods, wages or offering soup and coffee at breaks, employee performance increased. Mayo concluded that psychological and social conditions at work related more to productivity than physical factors. The research team's conclusion was that something other than working conditions affected employee output, and they named this "something else" morale.

The findings of the highly scientific and thoroughly documented Hawthorne Studies stirred academicians and managers alike about the importance of elevating and maintaining high employee morale on the job to achieve top productivity. Interest in the subject of employee morale has never waned since this information was made public.

This brief glance at some of the forerunners of modern management should help managers appreciate techniques and practices still used today.

Nature of This Book

By reviewing the Contents, you will get an idea of the major subjects presented in this book. All these subjects pertain to the management of people in any kind of organization whether profit-seeking or not.

The primary jobs of managers are discussed in depth as well as the continuous activity of problem-solving and decision-making. A special chapter is included on The Practical Side of Management. Every effort has been made to present to you the most important topics in management

Keep in mind that management as an activity is universal in nature. The basic jobs of managers are the same whether one manages in social or government agencies, General Motors or a corner grocery store; whether the locale is Russia, The United States or Japan. All managers must plan, organize, implement and control as they work through people to attain objectives. All managers confront problems and make decisions. All managers tend to be judged on performance and must take full responsibility for the results of their actions. As already stated, being a manager is not a job for everyone.

The approach in this book is general, not specialized. You can learn valuable insight and information from studying the material in this book. The greatest value of this information will apply when you become a supervisor of other people, and the techniques and tools you gain will assist you in any area or level of management. The information covered in this book will help you focus on your responsibilities as a manager.

Management, because it deals with people, is not an exact science. There are no rules, laws or one-to-one relationships in management. There are principles, concepts and research findings to influence a manager's actions. But any manager acts alone and often will not know if today's action is good or bad until some time has passed. The more you know about the subject of management itself, the more confident you should be when you must take management action.

No manager is perfect, however; all managers make mistakes dealing with people, planning, controlling activities, making decisions, analyzing problems and implementing solutions. The great managers simply perform their management duties more effectively and make fewer mistakes than the average ones. Remember "average" means best of the worst or worst of the best, and it is not a standard to strive to achieve.

Studying this text should add to your knowledge about management and give you the opportunity to become one of the great managers of the future.

Summary

The greatest game in the world today is not soccer or baseball. It is being a manager! That is, if you like thrills and risks, success and failure, action and desire visibility.

Of the more than 125 million people employed in the United States civilian labor force today, approximately thirteen million are managers. Many workers in the labor force are not qualified for management. Being a manager is not for everyone.

If you get the opportunity to go into management and desire the benefits of being in management, then you must *get prepared!* Not being prepared for management spells doom.

Management is the most demanding of professional careers. Managers work long hours, are judged on performance, are highly visible, must accept full responsibility for results and operate usually in a stressful environment. On top of this, they are on lifetime probation!

The majority of new managers are promoted from within the organization from the ranks of nonmanagement employees. They tend to be the best at doing their jobs and have exhibited steady and dependable work habits. Few are prepared, however, to be successful new managers.

The number one problem in American organizations is the shortage of competency in management. This continues to be a significant concern of government and industry because management, at any level, is the key to an organization's future.

True training in management is invaluable to the new or prospective manager. Training in management includes subjects such as these: the economic system, basic concepts of management, fundamental functions (jobs) of managers, organizational behavior and communication, problem-solving and decision-making, motivation techniques and human relations skills.

Managers should have a personal philosophy of management. This includes your fundamental beliefs, basic concepts, convictions and firm ideas about management. The importance of having a personal philosophy of management is that it influences every action you take and each decision you make as a manager leading to consistency in your behavior and performance as a manager.

Management as a practice has existed since the creation of formal organizations thousands of years ago. The subject of management did not emerge as a recognized discipline, however, until the Twentieth Century. The modern management movement began about one hundred years ago when certain individuals pioneered their theories and techniques about management. Prior to that time groups and individuals made contributions to the development of management beginning as far back as 5000 B.C. Some of the most famous "pioneers" of modern management were Frederick W. Taylor, Frank Gilbreth, Lillian Gilbreth, Henry L. Gantt, Henri Fayol and Elton Mayo.

Review Questions

1. Why do you think so many men and women desire a career in management?
2. What is the value of studying management prior to or shortly after being promoted to supervision?
3. What is your definition of "Management?"
4. Are there aspects of the role of a manager and the world of management that do not appeal to you? Discuss these in detail.
5. List the major contributions of each modern management pioneer.
6. What is the value of an individual's having a personal philosophy of management?

Assignments for Personal Development

1. Interview a practicing manager with at least five years experience and ask him or her to answer the fifteen questions in "Testing Your Sincerity About Management." If some "no" answers appear, ask the manager to explain these answers.
2. Review some of the major contributions of the pioneers in management. Trace some specific activity or practice used today in your organization back to one of these contributors and follow its changes and refinements over the years.

Incident

PERFORMANCE VERSUS APTITUDE

Lloyd Lacey, the Director of Development of Electronic Equipment Company, faced a problem now that often had perplexed him in the past. As the person in charge of working intimately with new management trainees in their first year with the company, Lacey was directly responsible for evaluating each one and making recommendations to top management for permanent assignment.

Each spring the company recruited approximately fifty college graduates from the finest institutions in the nation. The cream of the applicant crop was carefully selected; each possessed an excellent academic background and scored in the top brackets on psychological tests given by the company. Furthermore, they were individuals, men and women, who displayed good social skills and attractive personalities.

During the one-year training program, the management trainees received formal classroom study, were rotated through all major functional areas of the business, and for the last three months of the year, were allowed to remain in the work area that most appealed to them. For example, some recruits went into sales, or manufacturing, or finance for some practical experience. In each case, their immediate supervisors evaluated their three-month work experience and reported to the Director of Development. As Director of Development, Lacey would then proceed to evaluate all the information available to him. On the basis of his findings, he submitted recommendations to top management as to whether a trainee should be retained, whether the individual possessed top management potential, and where a trainee should begin his or her permanent career within the organization structure.

What really bothered Mr. Lacey was that so many of the trainees who scored highest on psychological tests, including aptitude tests for managerial careers, I.Q. tests, and emotional maturity tests, did not receive the highest evaluations from functional supervisors who worked with them during the last three months of their training program. It was also clear that those trainees possessing the highest academic averages in college did not necessarily perform the best during their one-year training program.

Questions:

1. What is the best way for Lloyd Lacey to evaluate the management potential of these trainees?

2. Is it possible that high quality, new management trainees could come from sources other than college campuses? Explain your answer.

Suggested Readings

Abernathy, William J., Kim B. Clark, and Alan M. Kantrow. "The New Industiral Competition," *Harvard Business Review* (September/October 1981): 68-81.

Boddeqyn, J. "Frederick Winslow Taylor Revisited." *Academy of Management Journal* 4 (1961): 100-107.

Carey, A. "The Hawthrone Studies: A Radical Criticism." *American Sociological Review* 32 (1967): 403-16.

Chang, Y. N. "Early Chinese Management Thought." *California Management Review,* Winter 1976, pp. 71-76.

Gilbreth, Lillian M. *The Psychology of Management.* New York: Sturgis and Walton, 1914.

Gilbreth, Lillian M., Orphae Mae Thomah, and E. Clymer. *Management in the Home.* New York: Dodd, Mead, 1954.

Kolb, David A. "Management and the Learning Process." *California Management Review,* Spring 1976, pp. 21-31.

Merrill, H. F., ed. *Classics in Management.* New York: American Management Association, 1960.

CHAPTER 2

THE MANAGEMENT PROCESS

After studying this chapter, **you will know:**
- The importance of having managers
- The **real** meaning of management
- General skills needed by managers at various levels
- What managers do
- That management is a basic process
- The functions of management
- Some fundamental concepts in management

Introduction

From Chapter 1 you have learned that management is a people-oriented activity. Job titles will vary, but all managers have authority over other people who report to them. This chapter stresses the real meaning of management and describes some general skills needed by all managers. In this chapter you learn what managers do. This chapter describes the main jobs of all managers, whether in the business world or non-profit organizations. Lastly, some of the most important fundamental concepts in management are listed and explained. All these concepts are valid when applied to the many directors, administrators and managers in the world of organizations.

As you read this information, try to relate the points to some individual you know who holds an important job in management.

The World Without Management

Have you ever thought about the world without management? There would be total chaos! Nothing would be organized; there would be no formal associations of people; governments, churches or companies would not exist. It would be a period of survival by instinct. Each person would be on his or her own to sink or survive.

Fortunately, over the centuries, mankind has developed formal organizations for the benefit of society. These formal organizations are administered by individuals called managers. Managers are the people in charge who make decisions, provide leadership, give direction, and handle problems for the benefit of the entire organization.

Without competent managers an organization gradually stagnates; with competent managers an organization can grow, become more effective in achieving its objectives, and provide great satisfaction to its members and to the public it serves.

Requirements for Management

In order for management as a function to exist, these three conditions must be met:

1. There must be a **formal** organization.
2. The organization must have a clearly defined goal or purpose for existing.
3. The organization must have a hierarchical structure in which some people are in charge of others.

Clearly, **managers** are those people who are in charge of others in a formal organization. To be a manager, one is either appointed or elected to the position, or one starts an organization and decides to be the owner-manager.

Management Defined

Management is defined in many different ways by scholars and practitioners. Five of the nation's leading management experts offer the following five different definitions of management:

Management is the process of integrating resources and tasks toward the achievement of stated organizational goals.[1]

It is the process of setting objectives, organizing resources to attain these predetermined goals, and then evaluating the results for the purpose of determining future action.[2]

Management is a process that involves guiding or directing a group or people toward organizational goals or objectives.[3]

Management is the process of planning, organizing, motivating, and controlling in order to formulate and attain organizational objectives.[4]

Management is the process of planning, organizing, leading, and controlling the efforts of organizational members and of using all other organizational resources to achieve stated organizational goals.[5]

While these definitions have similarities, they also have significant differences. One similarity is that each refers to management as a **process**. The traditional definition of a **process** is that it is a logical sequence of steps or jobs arranged in a particular manner to achieve the desired result. Students should not expect management to fit this description of a **process**. Management is not an activity that can be programmed in a

---

[1] Andres D. Szilagyi, Jr., *Management and Performance*, 2nd ed. (Glenview, IL: Scott, Foresman and Company, 1984), p.7.

[2] Richard M. Hodgetts, *Management*, 4th ed. (Orlando, FL: Academic Press, College Division, 1986), p.3.

[3] Leslie W. Rue and Lloyd L. Byars, *Management: Theory and Application*, 5th ed. (Homewood, IL: Richard D. Irwin, Inc., 1989), p.10.

[4] Michael H. Mescon, Michael Albert, and Franklin Khedouri, *Management*, 2nd ed. (New York: Harper and Row, Publishers, 1985), p.17.

[5] James A. F. Stoner, *Management*, 2nd ed. (Englewood Cliffs, NJ: Prentice-Hall, Inc., 1982), p.8.

logical, sequential way. There is no chronology of steps arranged in a one, two, three, four order leading to the ultimate end result. The **process** of management refers to the major duties and areas of responsibility that managers face which may or may not occur in a logical, sequential pattern on a daily basis.

The majority of practicing managers think of their jobs as working through people (their employees) to achieve a desired objective. This definition is less formal than the previous ones, but it is correct. The definition of management which this book uses stresses that the only thing a manager actually manages is people.

Management is the optimal utilization of human resources to achieve predetermined goals and objectives. Chart 2-1 illustrates this definition of management, showing that a manager's true job is to work with and through his or her employees (subordinates) to accomplish the predetermined goals and objectives.

Managers Manage People

In the United States there are approximately 125 million people in the lobar force.[6] Of this number, 10.8 percent (about 13 million of the gainfully employed) are classified as mangers. What do these people manage? They manage people. The titles which these managers have for their jobs, however, may lead to some confusion about just what they manage. For example, there are Office Managers, Sales Managers, Operations Managers, Inventory Managers, Payroll Supervisors and many other misnomers. To clarify, managers have responsibility for and control over many resources, such as money, equipment, inventory, supplies, facilities and such as well as people, but the only thing they manage is people. True management is achieving predetermined goals and objectives working through others while effectively and efficiently using all resources necessary to reach the desired end result.

Management Titles

Management job titles may be confusing to a new manager. Chart 2-2 shows some of the more common job titles in the military, in business, in government and in education.

Regardless of classification, all of these titles and many more show that the individuals holding these job titles are in management positions. They hold positions of authority (power), they are responsible for results, and their job is to achieve predetermined goals and objectives working through others.

Levels of Management

Managers are generally classified as either part of top management, middle management, or first level management as shown in Chart 2-3. At each level, the managers need general management skills to function effectively.

Top Management. The top management of any organization generally includes the organizational executives: the Chief Executive Officer (CEO), President, Executive Vice

---

[6] Bureau of Labor Statistics, "Employment and Earnings," January 1992.

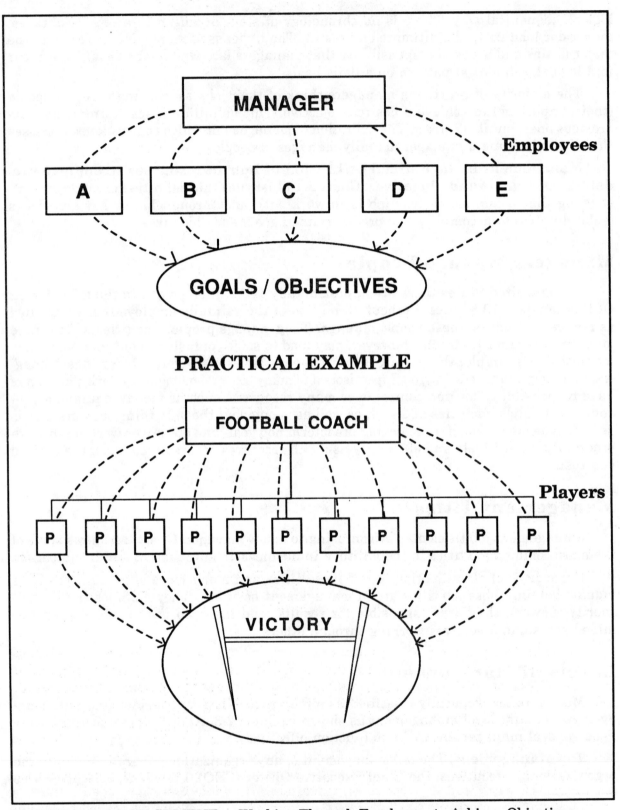

FIGURE 2-1: MANAGEMENT — Working Through Employees to Achieve Objectives

```
MILITARY TITLES:              General
                              Major
                              Lieutenant
                              Sergeant
                              Chief Petty Officer


BUSINESS TITLES:              Chief Executive Officer
                              Owner
                              Superintendent
                              Department Head
                              Supervisor
                              Foreman


GOVERNMENT TITLES:            President
                              Governor
                              Director
                              Commissioner
                              Mayor
                              Chief of Police


EDUCATION TITLES:             Academic Dean
                              Director of Athletics
                              Department Chair
                              Head Coach
                              Provost
                              Chancellor
```

FIGURE 2-2: SELECTED MANAGEMENT TITLES

President and Vice Presidents. Other comparable titles such as Treasurer may exist and be included in this group. These positions provide overall direction to the entire organization. They formulate objectives and policies; plan for the long term; and make decisions that affect every facet of the organization. Top managers need conceptual skill often regarded as the rarest of the three general management skills.

Middle Management. Middle managers such as department heads, superintendents, human resource managers and others are identified as managing through other managers. The middle manager's primary job is to implement programs of action within the framework of the policies set by top management. They do this by working through first level managers who are their immediate employees (subordinates). Normally this task requires good leadership ability, effectiveness as a communicator, control skills, and some comprehension of the technical aspects of the work that is to be implemented. The amount of technical skill needed by middle managers varies widely depending on the nature of the work and the type of organization. All middle managers need human or personal skills to perform their jobs well. In summary, the main skills needed by middle managers are human or personal and technical.

First Level Management. First level managers are often called first line managers. Their job titles are usually supervisor or department head, and these managers deal directly with nonmanagement or operating employees. These people represent the organization to their employees, and these first level managers are vital to the success and survival of any organization. No organization is as effective and efficient as it might be without highly competent first level managers. The main skills needed by first level managers are human or personal and technical. First level managers have the task of delegating work to nonmanagement personnel, instructing them in proper work methods, correcting them, and controlling activity. The manager must know what is to be done, how it is to be done, when it is to be done, and must make certain that it is done.

The general skills needed by each level of management are shown integrated with the management pyramid in Chart 2-4.[7]

What Do Managers Do?

During 1990-91, over 500 managers from several different areas of the United States were asked to list their most important daily jobs, duties, functions or responsibilities as a manager. Chart 2-5 shows the variety of responses received.[8]

From the list of 30 different responses received, several appear to overlap, but 22 of them represent unique job responsibilities that managers should be skilled at performing.

When does a manager find time to get involved in performing all of these duties? A manager rarely blocks a certain period of time just for planning or creating or for any of the listed duties. Normally these duties and responsibilities are performed routinely without much thought about identifying any particular activity or the time taken to perform it. Usually the transition from one activity to another is not clear, such as going from instructing to motivating or from correcting to disciplining. This is especially true at the first level of management. At the top management level, it would be more common to block a period of time exclusively for budgeting or for planning. All managers at any level, however, should be highly skilled at performing all their particular duties.

The Management Process

Rather than state that all managers have twenty or more distinct, major jobs or duties to perform daily, it is more logical to suggest that the main jobs of managers can be categorized into just a few principal functions. Historically, from the time of management pioneer Frederick W. Taylor in the late 19th Century to today, management experts have identified what they believe to be the main jobs or functions of managers. Taylor, called the "Father of Scientific Management,": said the main job of managers is "planning" and that of the workers is "doing."[9] Henri Fayol, a noted French management

---

[7] Ideas taken from article by Robert L. Katz, "Skills of an Effective Administrator," *Harvard Business Review*, 52, no. 5 (September-October, 1974), 90-102.

[8] Personal survey conducted by the author, Francis J. Bridges. Respondents were managers in Michigan, Washington, New Jersey, New York, Georgia, Texas, Tennessee, Arizona, and Florida.

[9] Frederick W. Taylor, *Principles of Scientific Management* (New York: Harper and Brothers, 1911).

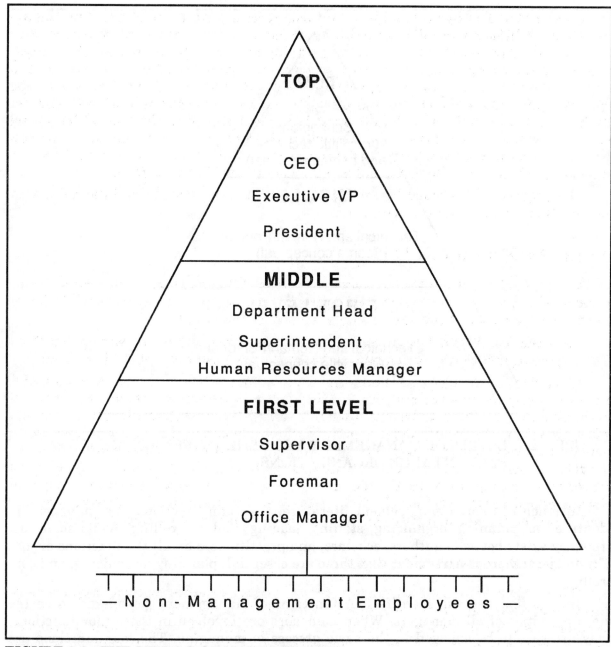

FIGURE 2-3: THE LEVELS OF MANAGEMENT

pioneer and executive, stated in his book, *Industrial and General Administration*, that the five functions of management are planning, organizing, commanding, coordinating, and controlling.[10]

---

[10] Henri Fayol, *Industrial and General Administration*, trans. J. A. Coubrough (Geneva: International Management Institute, 1930).

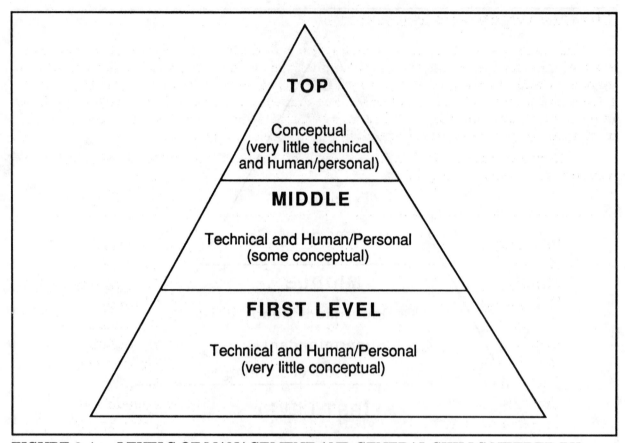

FIGURE 2-4:   LEVELS OF MANAGEMENT AND GENERAL SKILLS NEEDED BY
EACH IN LARGE ORGANIZATIONS

In much of today's management literature, the main functions of a manager are identified as planning, organizing, staffing, leading, and controlling. While some discrepancy exists between authors, scholars, and practitioners on all the functions or jobs of managers, there is agreement that three are essential: planning, organizing, and controlling.

In this text, we will identify four functions of management considered to be the main activities of all managers. When managers are involved in these four functions, they are said to be engaged in the basic process of managing. The four functions are planning, organizing, implementing and controlling. Decision making could be a fifth function of management, but because it is so important an activity and it is part of the other four, we will consider it separately. It is the single most important daily activity of every manager.

If you check the list of duties in Chart 2-5, all 30 identified jobs of managers can be grouped under one of these functions. For example, coordination is part of the organizing function as are staffing, hiring and firing; scheduling is part of the planning responsibility; appraising is part of controlling; and leading is part of implementing. Also note that problem-solving, deciding and execution relate to decision making which pervades all four functions.

The Management Functions

The main jobs or functions of managers, called the basic process of management, are not performed in a logical, sequential manner. By identifying the major activities of managers and studying each one separately, however, one is able to put them all together and understand more clearly the management process of planning, organizing, implementing and controlling. It becomes evident how managers use this process as they work through people to achieve predetermined goals and objectives.

In future chapters, we study each function in depth. For now, we will define and describe each function in general.

Planning	Timing	Organizing
Hiring	Relaying	Interpreting
Firing	Implementing	Disciplining
Evaluating	Executing	Staffing
Controlling	Budgeting	Appraising
Deciding	Repairing	Promoting
Coordinating	Communicating	Originating
Reviewing	Motivating	Leading
Creating	Instructing	Scheduling
Problem Solving	Correcting	Prioritizing

FIGURE 2-5: RESPONSES TO SURVEY OF DAILY JOBS OF MANAGERS

Planning. Planning, as a management activity, **is setting goals and objectives and then developing a detailed method of achieving them within a specified time period, with a minimum of problems, in the most efficient and effective way possible.**

Planning may cover a long-run or short-run time period, may be for an entire organization or for a department, group or individual. The significant point to remember about planning is that all planning activities are futuristic. While top management executives of a large organization are planning five to twenty years ahead, a first level supervisor may be planning a two-week or a quarterly activity schedule. Regardless of the time period or the management level involved, the planning activity deals with the future.

Good planning is designed to minimize problems in the effort of getting from point A to point Z. Good planning leads to a more efficient effort and a more effective end result. Efficiency and effectiveness translate into greater productivity. Good planning becomes the standard which can be reviewed as the plan proceeds to help guide and control performance.

Poor planning, on the other hand, is generally considered to be the number one reason why individuals and organizations fail to achieve their desired end results. Poor managerial planning is the leading cause of business failure in the United States. Planning is a precedent activity to decision-making and implementing programs.

Organizing. Managers have a responsibility to organize the efforts of employees to reach the objectives successfully. This means putting the right employee with the correct job skills into the right job. The sole purpose of sound organization is to create an efficiency of effort. This requires a manager to coordinate effectively the use of employees and all other resources.

Various organizational structures are used to provide a sound framework for the activities of any organization. The type of organizational structure will depend on the nature of the work activities being performed.

A formal organization is a group of people working together toward common objectives with clearly established lines of authority, responsibility, accountability and communication.

The manager's job is to make certain that employees do work together harmoniously and that common goals and objectives are achieved working within the established hierarchy.

Implementing. Implementing is putting the plans and programs of management into action working through the employees. Implementing can be called **executing, actuating** or **directing**. Any standard dictionary defines the verb implement literally as "to put into practice."

Without question sound planning and organizing are essential to successful management; but without effective implementation, the planning and organizing efforts are wasted.

Implementing involves working directly with employees to achieve the objectives effectively and efficiently. Achieving objectives **effectively** means the desired end result is reached. Achieving objectives **efficiently** means you reach the desired result within the optimal time frame and with the least cost or wasted effort.

Managers who are effective implementers understand people. They tend to be good leaders and knowledgeable managers who understand and appreciate the subjects of motivation, incentives, job satisfaction and many other people-oriented skills.

Successful implementers strive to work through people to achieve the desired end result and, simultaneously, bring positive benefits to the employee, the organization, and the immediate manager.

Controlling. The control function is designed primarily **to insure that performance is on schedule according to a plan.** Sound planners include control techniques so that once plans are implemented; there are automatic ways to measure performance against the plan. If discrepancies between the plan and actual progress appear, then corrective action is taken.

All control programs have these three essential steps:

1. Establish a standard (plan);
2. Appraise conformance to the standard (inspection);
3. Take corrective or remedial action when the standard is exceeded (i.e., not met or not high enough).

Theoretically, if planning, organizing and implementing are done perfectly, the control function is not needed. Since people are not perfect managers and cannot perfectly regulate **all** conditions around them, we need the control function.

The need for control programs varies greatly depending on such things as the precision necessary in the work, the type of activity, and the skill and ability of the personnel; but all control programs should be introduced carefully to do a particular job and disbanded when the need is satisfied. Control programs must pay for themselves in saved costs, fewer problems in the future, better quality results and so forth. Introducing control programs can be expensive and the benefits must outweigh these costs for the control program to be efficient and effective.

Decision making is not normally listed as a separate management function because it permeates every other management function. A manager makes decisions throughout the planning, organizing, implementing and controlling functions. But, the importance of decision-making cannot be stressed too much.

Decision-making stands alone as the single most important activity of a manager. Every manager in the world deals with problems, issues and people. Every manager must gather information and facts, assess consequences and make decisions. The majority of these managers are judged on the results of these decisions. If decisions did not have to be made and all the input factors weighed and judged in this process, there would be no need for managers!

Summary of the Management Process

Planning, organizing, implementing and controlling are the functions which form the cornerstone of managerial activity in any type of organization. These functions interrelate and overlap. Rarely does a manager just plan or just organize. Several activities within each function may be occurring at the same time. A manager can review and isolate what he or she is doing at any particular point in time, however, and can readily classify the activity into one of the four functions of the basic process of management.

This approach to the study of management is called the process approach. Other approaches to the study of management stress quantitative methods or human behavior or one of the other factors involved in managing people and making decisions.

Students will gain a better perspective about management as a discipline through studying various schools of thought and the theorists who have contributed to modern management philosophy (as was presented in Chapter 1). Regardless of the importance of quantitative and behavioral approaches in management, all managers have to plan, organize, implement, control and make decisions. The management process is the foundation of any interdisciplinary approach to the study and practice of management whether it is in business, government or education.

Management as a Career

One of the most exciting career options is management. The study of management does not guarantee one a job nor does it mean success as a manager once a job is found. Being a manager does guarantee excitement, risks, and a sense of power and responsibility. The opportunity for advancement in management is unlimited if one demonstrates competency in that first management position.

Should everyone study management and make it a career? The answer is, "No." The best employee in the office, worker in the factory or salesperson in the field is not necessarily suited for a management career.

The factors that make people good managers are diverse and numerous, but one fact remains constant: If you wish to make management a career, you should get prepared. Preparation will not guarantee successful job performance, but the lack of proper preparation is a major cause of management failure. Studying management and learning the time-tested principles that have been developed over the years are the best ways to prepare for a career in management. In addition, a manager must realize there are conditions peculiar to the field of management which make a management career a challenge. The exercise in Chapter 1 testing your sincerity about a career in management describes the real world of management.

Some Fundamental Concepts in Management

Reviewing some of the fundamental concepts in management can provide a better picture of the real world of management. These concepts tend to be valid although there are exceptions to everything in management. The ten concepts that follow have been assimilated over time from observation, consulting, research and conversations with hundreds of practicing managers.

Concept One: Management Is People Oriented

The activity of managing is one involving people. In a formal organization these people are the employees who report directly to you, the manager. Whether you have one, two, ten or forty people reporting directly to you, your job as a manager is to achieve predetermined objectives working through them.

Managers have many resources under their responsibility, authority and control, including people. But the only resource one manages is the people!

You do not manage sales, facilities, budgets, promotions, information and so forth. You manage people!

Thus, many job titles such as marketing and promotions manager, office manager, facilities manager and others are misnomers in organizations today.

These job titles will not change, but you should understand the real meaning of management.

Concept Two: The Synergistic Management Concept

Here is the true **mission** of managers.

Every new manager especially should know and understand the management mission prior to entering the management ranks.

The word **synergy** means the end result is greater than the sum of the parts. In simple arithmetic lingo, 2 + 2 = more than 4.

Applied to the job of a manager, the real mission becomes one of directing the use of resources in such a way that, over a period of time, the manager creates an end result which is far greater in value than the starting values of the resources combined. If managers cannot do this, they will eventually be replaced or the organization will fail to operate efficiently.

Concept Three: Managers Are Judged on Results

Managers are judged on results (performance). If not, managers would be judged on years of service, personality, how hard they try, how many hours they spend in the office, how well liked they are, and on and on. None of these mean anything unless combined with the successful completion of the assigned objectives.

Although there are exceptions to all concepts, the majority of organizations do attempt to judge managers on performance. This is sound and fair as long as

1. All managers know clearly what their objectives are, and
2. Higher managers making the judgments are fair-minded and objective in their evaluations.

Many decisions made today cannot be judged fairly until enough time has elapsed to know the results.

Concept Four: Management Is by Objectives

For a supervisor to manage as efficiently and effectively as possible, every employee must know what to do, when to do it, and why his or her work is important. This is best achieved when the whole organization manages by objectives.

Management by objectives requires the organization to state clearly and in writing the following:

1. The primary objectives (why the organization exists)
2. The operating objectives (annual or twelve month objectives)
3. Unit objectives (annual objectives for divisions, branches, departments, etc.)
4. Individual managerial objectives
5. Individual nonmanagement employees' objectives

The idea is that if every employee, every manager, and every unit (part) of the organization achieves its objectives in the given time period, the operating or twelve month objectives of the organization as a whole will be reached. Achieving these objectives keeps the organization in line with the pursuit of the primary objectives.

Written objectives not only give direction to the efforts of all parties involved, but also they can become the basis for evaluating performance. Written objectives coupled with time standards form the basis of a sound control program to insure that overall performance is on schedule and that costs are within the budget.

Lack of clear-cut written objectives for each person and part of the organization causes disjointed and uncoordinated effort and leads to waste and inefficiency.

Concept Five: Management Is a Science

There is a small part of management that can be called a science. It is an important part of management, but most aspects of management should be considered an **art**. Management may be studied as a social science, since it involves the interrelationships of people. Much research about the whole subject of management is taking place now, and a large body of literature is available with research findings, valid principles, and concepts. All of this points toward management as a **science**; however, management is not an exact science.

The science of management is the application of the scientific method to general management problems leading to problem-solving and decision-making. Although the use of the scientific method in problem-solving and decision-making does not guarantee a right answer or perfect solution to a problem, it **does** increase the percentage of right answers over time. A general management problem refers to any kind of problem in the organization about any subject as long as people are part of the problem—which only encompasses about ninety percent of all management problems!

The scientific method as used by managers is a practical, uncomplicated approach in seven steps. The first step is the most important because it dictates the direction of your analysis. Your analysis of management problems should be in writing unless there is an urgency for a quick decision.

The steps in the scientific method are the following:

1. Clearly identify the fundamental management problem;
2. List all the facts pertinent to the problem;
3. List alternative courses of action to solve the problem;
4. List advantages and disadvantages of each alternative;
5. Review all of the above;
6. Draw conclusions, make recommendations and/or decisions, and
7. Follow up or check to determine if the decision made has brought about the desired results.

Using this approach does not guarantee your answer or decision will be right. It does force you to consider the facts, review alternatives, and be more logical and objective in your analysis than if you made decisions on hunch, intuition, emotion, tradition, etc. It is a sound approach that is used in government, business, the military, education, and by others when making major decisions. This approach is also called **subjective decision making**, and/or **rational decision making**.

The use of the scientific method by managers, even in a limited way, is what makes part of the activity of managing a science.

Concept Six: Management Is an Art

Most of the activity of managing is an **art**. The artistic part of management is how one uses his or her acquired knowledge of the subject and job experience. It is the application of the sum total of all this knowledge and experience to a given situation to bring about the desired results. The emphasis is on "how" or the "way" you do something.

Management styles and techniques are as varied as the number of managers. Given the same decision to implement, ten different managers will cause ten different results. This is because of the "way" managers do things—the **art.**

Every practicing manager is an artist who performs every day in front of employees, bosses, peers, vendors, customers, etc. Yet, every manager is so different in background, experience, education, perception, training, and knowledge that each will manage differently. This adds to the need for managers to be judged on results. Any individual manager should be free to perform in his or her own way as long as there is no violation of organizational policies and the philosophy of higher management is maintained. The bottom line is results not the method!

Concept Seven: Managers Are Totally Responsible

Of all the points a new manager should become familiar with, the Total Responsibility Concept is the most vital. The concept states that a manager is absolutely, totally responsible for everything that happens, good or bad, from his or her position in the organization downward. This responsibility begins the first day you are in the job.

A manager is employed to work on behalf of another manager above him or her (the boss). In the manager's area of supervision, often referred to as the scope of responsibility, no matter what problems occur, no matter how much success is achieved, and no matter the nature of the activity, that immediate manager is responsible.

The Total Responsibility Concept wipes out excuses. If you are the person in charge, the manager, then you are the one responsible for everything from your position downward. You cannot shift the blame nor fault those below you for the failure to attain results. Some management prospects shrink from this kind of responsibility, and they refuse to be promoted into management positions because of it.

Being a manager is not for everyone. Not all employees, no matter how good an employee they are, want the additional responsibility that accompanies supervising people and directing the use of organizational resources.

Concept Eight: Management Is a Basic Process

All managers have the same main functions, duties, or responsibilities. Although the identification of these may vary in number depending on your source, the following are generally accepted as essential responsibilities:

> To Plan
> To Organize
> To Implement
> To Control

Every manager may not be a sound planner, organizer, implementer, or controller, but the requirements of the manager's job dictate these fundamental responsibilities.

A new manager should learn everything possible about each of these functions and realize that each consists of many sub-activities.

When you are involved in planning, organizing, implementing, and controlling, you are engaged in the basic process of management. **And the process goes on continuously forever.**

Concept Nine: Management Is Decision-Making

The most common activity in management is decision-making. Every manager makes decisions, good or bad, and stands on the results. Decision-making is an unavoidable responsibility that leads to action. This action, multiplied by every decision made, brings about the results which are the goal of the manager's job.

Most decisions in management are subjective in nature and involve problems that include people. These are called **general management problems**. Nonpeople problems or technical problems can be difficult, but they represent only about ten percent of a manager's total problems.

Decision-making is not very scientific and many factors affect how a manager acts under certain circumstances. Mathematical decision-making is used in some organizations if the variables in the problem can be quantified. But this is not always the case and such precise decision-making is therefore limited in use.

A general notion is that the best management planners tend to be the best decision makers who in turn tend to be the best managers.

Concept Ten: Management Is the Significant Difference

Every organization has competition. If you are part of a business firm or even an education institution, you have much head-on competition. Even the United States Postal Service has competition. There are few monopolies left.

When you review successful organizations in a highly competitive field, you wonder why some are more profitable or successful than others. If they provide about the same services or similar product lines and the prices do not vary much, you invariably wonder what makes the difference. You wonder because inevitably one organization is better than the others.

The significant difference between competing organizations originates in the hundreds of decisions managers make over a period of time. Decisions in any organization flow downward and create action which results in change. Changes affecting pricing, styling, merchandising, programs, advertising, location, efficiency, product lines, customer services, personnel selection and hundreds of other things over time make the significant difference between competing organizations. All these change-initiating decisions have one common factor: the managers who made and implemented them. It is the quality of those managers' decisions that makes the critical difference.

Summary

Organizations exist to provide goods and services for consumers and to satisfy the needs of their members. Managers direct the organizations' efforts and are given authority and responsibility over resources.

Managers manage people. Management is defined as the optimal utilization of human resources to achieve predetermined objectives. Simply stated, management is an activity of working through others (employees) to achieve organization objectives.

Managers tend to be categorized as either first level, middle or top level managers. Management job titles are plentiful and they vary from "Foreperson" to "Chief Executive Officer."

Managers at all levels tend to need three general skills but to varying degrees. These skills are technical, human or personal, and conceptual. Top level managers need conceptual skill to a greater degree than any other level, especially first level. But first level managers need much more detailed technical knowledge that those managers at the top. Middle level managers, who work primarily through other managers, need a great degree of human or personal skill with their need for technical skills varying directly with the nature of the work, the type of industry, and expertise of their employees.

Managers are responsible for performing many tasks and duties, but all of them can be consolidated into one of four main jobs—called functions of management. These functions are planning, organizing, implementing and controlling. When managers are performing these functions, they are said to be engaged in the basic process of management.

Fundamental concepts in management are basic ideas about the practice of management. They have much validity, but they are not laws or absolutes. Fundamental concepts help one acquire an early perception of the real world of management.

Review Questions

1. What conditions must exist in an organization in order to justify having managers?
2. Are there risks in being a manager? If so, explain them.
3. Name five of six management job titles in nonprofit organizations.
4. Should managers at the three different levels of management have the same skills? If not, why not?
5. The fundamental functions of management are also the main jobs of all managers. Name and briefly describe them.
6. Ten fundamental concepts are listed in this chapter and are explained briefly. Which two do you think are the most important for a new manager to remember? Justify your answers.

Assignments for Personal Development

1. Interview two different managers. Ask them to list or tell you their most difficult management problem(s). Then, have each of them list the factors about being a manager which they enjoy the most. Exchange these responses with others in your class discussion so that you will begin to get a more realistic perspective of the job of a manager.

2. Executive managers are often referred to as "uncommon" or "non-normal" people. This means they are unique, one of a kind individuals, or they might be called "originals." There was only one Napoleon, one Vince Lombardi, one Margaret Thatcher and one Ronald Reagan. Locate or research two outstanding executives, in any field, who by their record are considered great! Identify five or six personality traits of each of your choices and explain to your colleagues why these people are unique.

Incident

PROMOTION OF A PEER

Majorie Atkins was one of the more experienced women in the old stenographic pool, now renamed the Communications Center. The new name was accompanied by a new location, new equipment and a new supervisor—Majorie!

Majorie had not asked for the management job nor had she denied any interest in it. She knew she was as qualified as any of the other twenty women working in the "pool," and she knew she had more seniority than most. The prospect of being the boss, however, had bothered her a bit. The main problem, as she saw it, was that about half of the women were doing about seventy percent of the work, and the other half were floating—out sick a lot, constantly complaining, and not doing a full share of the work. If a person appointed to the supervisor's job were to take the work seriously, that person had to correct the situation. Correcting it could mean firing friends.

One week after Majorie took over the supervision of the Communications Center, she noted that overall performance was slipping, complaints from other company departments were mounting, and several women per day were out sick.

She decided it was time to call her first meeting and get a few things straightened out.

Questions:

1. Put yourself in Majorie's place and conduct that meeting using management techniques and principles covered in Chapter 2.

2. What special problems face new managers who are promoted from the ranks of nonmanagement employees to supervise their former peers?

Suggested Readings

Boettinger, Henry M. "Is Management Really an Art?" *Harvard Business Review*, January-February, 1975, pp. 54.64.

Culbert, Samuel A. "The Real World and the Management Classroom." *California Management Review*, Summer 1977, pp. 65-78.

Drucker, Peter F. *Management: Tasks, Practices, Responsibilities* New York: Harper & Row, 1974.

Franklin, William H., Jr. "What Japanese managers Know That American Managers Don't." *Administrative Management* 42 (September 1981): 36-39, 51-54, 56.

Katz, Robert L. "Skills of an Effective Administrator." *Harvard Business Review*, September-October 1974, pp. 90-102.

Miles, Raymond E. *Theories of Management: Implications for Organizational Behavior and Development.* New York: McGraw-Hill, 1975.

Mintzberg, Henry. "The Manager's Job: Folklore and Fact." *Harvard Business Review*, July-August 1974, pp. 49-61.

Wetzler, Robert T. "Management Theory Can Product a Continuing Bottom Line Impact." *MSU Business Topics*, Winter 1976, pp. 5-10.

CHAPTER 3

THE PRACTICAL SIDE OF MANAGEMENT

After studying this chapter, **you will know**:

- The value of practicality in management
- That managing is mostly an art
- That great managers are only a little bit better than average ones
- That managers cannot be taught what to do, how to do it and when
- Many practical concepts about management generally
- Many useful concepts about managers specifically
- Many concepts that managers can apply to their employees

Introduction

Many important subjects will be presented in the chapters of this book. Theories are presented and explained which apply to the practice of management. Theories are valuable for stimulating debate and encouraging further research. Theory, however, is of no value to a practicing manager unless it can be applied to achieve effective and efficient end results.

This chapter focuses on the practical side of management. To be specific, it uses the ideas and knowledge gained from performing the management functions rather than from theorizing about management.

Managers are called "practical" if their actions are levelheaded, efficient and sensible. Managers who use good judgment have common sense. A manager cannot hope to succeed if he or she does not use good judgment and operate in a consistent and prudent way. **What to do, how and when to do it** are often judgment calls managers must make without much factual information. Results from what you do, how you do it, and when generally determine whether a manager is viewed as successful or not.

It is important to remember that the activity of managing is mostly as art, not a science. The art of managing is **how** and **the way** managers make decisions, deal with people, implement action, and perform their many other tasks. Managers cannot be taught **what to do, how to do it**, and **when**. A person cannot be taught to be an effective performer (artist), but the subject can be discussed and studied so that every manager can develop his or her own style of managing.

This chapter presents many points and concepts drawn from the real world of practicing managers. Suggestions are given which can influence managerial behavior, but the final determination of what to do, how to do it, and when rests with the individual who stands alone in the world of management. By studying the theories and principles of management, a supervisor can develop a philosophy of practical application of management to guide his or her daily job performance.

Materials in this chapter are based on *So You Want To Be A Manager?* by Francis J. Bridges and are reprinted with the permission of the publisher.

PRACTICAL CONCEPTS

In Chapter 2 some fundamental concepts or principles of management were introduced. Familiarity with these concepts is considered necessary if one wants to understand the practical world of management. Beyond those ten concepts are many points and suggestions of a **practical** nature that may help a new manager.

These ideas or concepts have validity and provide a new manager with more insight about the field of management in three specific categories: **About Management Generally, About Managers Specifically, and About Employees You Manage.** These practical points have been gathered and refined over many years of experience, from observations, and from sharing ideas with thousands of American managers. The suggestions in these concepts can give an inexperienced manager insights and knowledge that usually take many years of on-the-job experience to gain. Some of the concepts overlap with subjects discussed in the previous chapters, but many are unique and can be of great value to a practicing manager.

ABOUT MANAGEMENT GENERALLY

The Universality of Management Concept

Henri Fayol, a Frenchman, pioneered study and research in the field of general administration in the 1920s. He originated the universality of management concept. The theory is that any manager in any kind of organization, located anywhere, will engage in the basic process of management (planning, organizing, implementing, and controlling) as he or she works through people to achieve objectives.

The fundamental concepts of management do have universal application. Managers around the world do have the same major responsibilities. The difference in management, one company to another or one nation to another, rests in the styles and techniques used by individual managers as they plan, organize, implement, and control; and in the different attitudes, cultural disparities, values about work, etc. that employees bring to the workplace.

Managers Need Three General Skills

Practicing managers need many special skills. By category, however, the most general skills needed are the following:

1. Technical,
2. Human or personal, and
3. Conceptual.

Technical skill means that you understand the details of the job. You know procedures, operations, methods of doing the work, and the many specifics that are part of a supervisor's responsibility. If you are overseeing the work of operative employees, you need to know their jobs, be able to train and correct them, plan work schedules, and understand the relationship of work in your area to other work performed in the organization. An essential skill for first-line supervisors and most middle managers is this type of technical knowhow.

Human or personal skill refers to a manager's ability to relate effectively with other employees, groups, departments, peers, and bosses so that desired objectives can be attained. Examples of good human skill would be the ability to communicate effectively, provide sound leadership to your employees, and **most importantly**, be able to get along well with others in the organization. This is an absolute requirement for supervisors and all middle managers.

Conceptual skill is considered to be the rarest of all management skills. Much like the general of an army, a manager must plan, lead, decide, and act at all times in terms of what is best for the total organization. Plans and decisions must be made that override individuals and vested interests. The health of the whole organization takes precedence over any individual or any part (department, division, branch) of the organization. Top managers must be able to see this "big picture" and to do that they must have conceptual skill.

Managers Are Uncommon People

Once you go into management, you become different! You are no longer "one of the gang," and you may even lose some of your friends if you have been promoted from within. Becoming a manager requires an adjustment in your behavior and your thinking. Management is full of responsibility, high expectations, and **pressure**.

All your thoughts as a manager must be centered on what's best for the organization. You, the manager, are the "company" to nonmanagement employees. And don't think that every statement you make and every action you take is not being observed by your employees! They won't miss anything!

These changes from nonmanagement to management make you "different." You have new, greater responsibilities; you have authority; your perspective is different; indeed, your **world** is different. This makes you a vastly different type of person from the ordinary employee. You are now part of a group called the "uncommon."

As you move upward in the management ranks, you become even more different, more uncommon, than the nonmanagement employee. You may advance high enough to be considered humorously **abnormal**! This means you have achieved managerial success, but people like you are few in number.

Professional Managers Share Few Traits

Individuals in management are uniquely different, yet there are a few personal traits common to the successful professional managers.

First, research has shown that successful managers are more **opportunistic** than nonmanagers. They take advantage of situations which arise and try to capitalize on them. This is not to imply that they seek personal gain at the expense of others. Rather, they visualize opportunities in company problems, they generate ideas to improve conditions, they plan continuously for the future. These are the kinds of things that an opportunist in management does.

Second, research indicates that successful managers are better at differentiating between facts and opinions and that they draw wiser inferences from observations. All of this suggests that successful managers tend to have better perception and judgment than nonmanagers. Having this ability helps a manager make sounder decisions which is the heart of the manager's job.

Third, successful managers are highly motivated about their work, their organizations, and their future careers. Being highly motivated alone is no guarantee of management success. Motivation added to knowledge of your job and proper direction toward worthwhile goals is required, however, to reach your objectives on time in an effective and efficient way.

Although these traits are found in many successful managers, the "personal trait theory" should not be used to select people for management jobs. This theory, which holds that management selection should be based on the candidate's having a select number of personal traits which are supposedly common to other successful managers, does not cover enough territory. The reason is that many more actions than opportunistic behavior, sound judgment, and high motivation make up a manager's job. Every veteran successful executive has his or her own management technique, which is largely different from any other person's. It does not hurt to develop these traits, because they are common to most successful managers and they are valuable traits to have, but they are not the only ones you will need.

Education, IQ, and Success in Management

Advanced education and having a high IQ are not requirements for success in management. If you possess a college degree and if you have a high IQ, congratulations! But, neither of these things guarantees success in dealing with people, making sound decisions, being creative, planning properly, etc. Most of managing is an "art" which cannot be taught in school. Being bright or having a high native intelligence does not necessarily produce stability, high motivation, or the human skills needed to work with and through people. In fact, the highest IQ in an organization may belong to a secretary or a shop worker, not a top manager.

Management is so complex that it is hard to isolate any single characteristic as a true key to success. You need to be smart enough to get the job done and know enough to minimize mistakes. No one is handicapped in management by lack of an extensive education or an IQ in the genius range. Willingness to learn, hard work, dedication to professional goals, and good common sense are qualities that lead to success in management.

Professional Managers Control Time

Professional managers at any level know the value of controlling "time." Since time is the one resource we cannot recapture, recycle, or reconstruct, it becomes our most important nonhuman resource.

Obviously time passes whether we are productive managers or not. We have the choice about the use of time. We can squander it, or we can control and use it for personal and organizational gain.

Sound planners tend to make better use of time than others. Managers who plan carefully always project time standards along with objectives. Planners attempt to visualize the future, prepare for possible problems, and reach desired goals within a set time frame in the most effective and efficient manner.

You have probably heard people say, "I'd like to do that but I don't have enough time." Usually when such a statement is made, the individual is either a poor planner or badly organized.

Time is too valuable a commodity to waste. It is too valuable a commodity to fill with mediocre effort.

Control your time carefully with check lists, control charts, and time checks. Set time standards for doing something at a "level of excellence." Then, when you have more free time, enjoy it to the fullest, produce even more, and find you can do all those things you did not have time for before.

In management, time equals money. The manager who makes the best use of time normally will be regarded as the efficient manager.

Discriminate Your Way to Competency

The word **discriminate** has taken a beating over the past thirty years. Laws tell us what discrimination can lead to in society, and the punishment for breaking antidiscrimination laws has much of the business community on edge all the time. There is, however, a positive side to this word, and every professional manager must know it.

If you are a manager, it is good to discriminate between good employees and bad, between sound decisions and risky ones, and between what actions are good for the organization and those that are wrong. All managers should be discriminating. What's bad about discrimination, and what gets you into trouble, is when you let biases prejudice the decisions. This can occur when the subject pertains to employment, promotion, or reward of employees on the basis of sex, age, race, religion, or national origin. This is really not a problem if you adopt competency as the standard for making these kinds of decisions.

The most qualified applicant should be employed and the most productive employee should be promoted and rewarded. Forget the questions of sex, race, religion, and national origin. Go with the employees who are overall the most highly qualified to do a particular job and who, by their performance, deserve promotion and recognition.

Remember, your decisions should be made in view of what's best for the organization. This should override individual prejudices and biases at all times.

The Reflective Phenomenon

In management circles, the reflective phenomenon occurs when the supervising manager has a strong or dominant personality. This figure may be the president of the organization or a first level supervisor or both. The phenomenon is that individuals surrounding these strong personalities, managers and nonmanagers alike, will tend to adopt that person's mannerisms, personal habits, and even the style of management.

Every new manager should learn from experienced managers; but you want to be individuals, not mimics, in management style.

Be objective in your evaluation of other managers and borrow only the best points, discarding the rest. Every manager should be different, and all management styles are different. Use what you pick up, but make it yours. Don't be too influenced by the dominant boss or strong personalities of managers around you, no matter how successful they are. Their ways won't necessarily work for you.

Managers Can Sink or Swim

Approximately 98 percent of all new managers are promoted into their jobs without any management training. This is the unconscious "sink or swim" approach taken by higher managers who control promotions.

Why this is the way it is no one knows! This has been the practice of most American organizations since their beginning. Without question, the job of the manager is the most complex and demanding job in the entire organization. No other specialized position would be filled in the organization without some test of competency or extensive preparation being given the candidate.

If you are given the opportunity to go into management, request management training first. If training is not offered or available, then develop your own management training program (review Chapter 1 for details).

Get prepared to be a manager or plan to "sink." If you don't sink, you will probably end up "dogpaddling" (barely staying afloat) in management most of your career.

Number One Economic Waste

When you get into management, be careful not to fall into one of the major traps that characterize average (synonym of mediocre) managers. The trap is doing part of the work your employees should perform. When fifteen dollar per hour managers do the work of six dollar per hour employees, there is a waste of nine dollars per hour. Multiply that by real wages and you can see the scope of the economic waste.

Your job, by definition, is to achieve the objectives of the organization by working **through** others, not **for** others. Your job is to see that the work is done properly and on schedule, not to do the work yourself.

Emergency situations and crises will occur occasionally which demand everyone's efforts to complete a job or accomplish the desired results. This sort of involvement by a manager should be an exception and not a rule. And proper planning should all but eliminate these situations.

Think about the purest management situation: the football coach. He will incur a strong penalty if he loses control and runs out on the field to make a tackle. Instead, he develops eleven others (players) who can and will execute the plays while he stands on the sidelines. This is the real job of the manager.

Professional Management Orientation Is Essential

Have you heard the expression, "Give me a break!" That should become the war cry of new managers who are promoted into management without professional management orientation.

Professional management orientation refers to the provision of a highly organized, well-conceived orientation program that lasts for several days, includes all new managers, and stresses subjects such as the following:

1. The new manager's mission
2. The total responsibility concept
3. The importance of the job
4. A history of the company
5. The philosophy of the organization's management
6. Why you were selected—your importance
7. The Company's organization structure

All of these topics and more (review Chapter 1) should be part of the formal management orientation. If a new manager is not properly conditioned when he or she enters management in the organization, then all of his or her ideas are likely to be acquired from others whose attitudes and information may be poor.

Developing a professional management team requires planning, time, and attention on the part of any organization. If a company wants a positive spirit of professionalism among its management team, it must have a program of professional management orientation. The program should begin for you, the new manager, prior to the first full day on the management job. This is the way to achieve a unified effort among all management team members, and leads to mutual respect for each other.

Managers Tend to Be Underpaid

Normally when you get promoted to management, you get an increase in pay. This is one of the incentives that attracts people to the field. The increase in pay is exciting, but it alone is hardly reason enough to accept a manager's job.

When you review the demands on managers, the risks, the total responsibility, being judged on results, the long hours, the pressure, the deadlines, and the problems with employees, then pay (and increases in pay) fades as a reason for a career in management.

Many top level managers earn spectacular salaries on the surface, but the risks of their jobs are so great and the longevity in the position so brief on average that annual income may not be as high as it appears.

The point to keep in mind is that management is a performance oriented world. Adequate compensation for a job done well **follows performance**. Don't expect to be overcompensated in advance of your contribution to the organization. For this reason, managers tend to run behind others on pay schedules.

Be careful of managers who have the attitude that "when they pay me more, I'll do more." These people are "losers" and are likely only temporary employees in management.

Management Training Is a Three-Step Process

Once you settle into your management job, you should consider picking one of your employees to become your replacement in the future. Sound peculiar? It is not. Over time you can share your knowledge and experience with this person and give him or her added responsibility so that, when an opening in management comes, this person will be ready to step into it. It could be your position when you move up, or it might be another position in the organization. One-to-one tutoring of this type may be the best of all management training if the tutor is a real professional!

While you are training a replacement, you should be receiving instruction and guidance from a manager above you so that, when the opportunity arises, you'll be ready to assume a higher management job.

The objective of this three-tier approach is to have highly competent managers at every level in the organization and to have someone prepared, trained, and **ready** to move up whenever a need arises. If the new manager can do the job as well as or better than the predecessor (you), it reflects even more positively on you than your own performance in that position alone.

Always Do a Benefit/Cost Analysis

The objective of every decision a manager makes is to do what is best for the organization. This means that the return or **benefit** from your decisions or actions must be greater than the **cost**. This concept implies that return and cost be measured in more ways than just money.

The cost of something may be in the employees' feelings, your loss of face, a decrease in morale, the lack of assurance provided to customers, and so on. This is in addition to monetary concerns. The benefit of something may be measured by improved employee attitudes, higher morale, less turnover and absenteeism, more satisfied customers, and content stockholders, etc., in addition to a greater monetary return above costs.

Much of your actions/decisions as a manager are based on subjective analyses. In these cases you don't have all the facts, but you must act anyway. You cannot always measure the effectiveness of a decision in dollars and cents, especially immediately.

Regardless of the circumstances, the manager should never forget that the objective of his or her decisions is to try to effect a result far greater in value than the cost.

"Average" Is an Unacceptable Standard

The term "average" is a totally undesirable word when used as a standard of performance in American organizations. It is a condemnation when applied to an employee. No one wants to work for an average company, be considered an average employee, or receive average pay.

As a new manager, you want to supervise work that is considered the **best**; you want to work for a **leading** company; you want your employees to be **excellent** workers; you want to be on the **number one** team; you want to set goals that **are outstanding**.

This attitude depicts a great manager, not an average or mediocre one.

Professionals in management set high standards and goals and work doubly hard to achieve them.

This is what sets them apart. They never settle for **average** performance as the standard of expectation—in themselves or in others.

Management's Mistakes Are Fodder for Unions

Most American managers would prefer not to deal with unions if they had a choice. The reasons are simple: Unions force management to adjust to an agreed upon union-management contract with all of the provisions and rules regarding employees' wages, promotions, grievances, working conditions, etc. Stated explicitly, unions cost management much of its flexibility and part of its control over operations.

The first union in the United States began in 1792. After nearly 200 years of existence, the union is not likely to vanish. Both unions and American business management, however, must abide by the provisions of the Taft-Hartley Act, the major legislation controlling union and management activity in the United States.

Why does the union continue to exist and in some industries grow? *Because of management's mistakes!*

Managers often mishandle employees, make poor decisions regarding wages, changes, standards, work methods, etc. without proper planning and careful consideration of employees' interests before implementing a decision. Management may act arbitrarily with one group of employees or even an individual, and the result is a demand for representation by a union so that the rights of employees may be outlined and protected. Since unions may be "voted-in" by a majority of the certified employees, they may also be "voted-out" by a majority of the certified employees. Elections are authorized and supervised by the National Labor Relations Board (NLRB).

It is unfortunate that some employees receive needed recognition, status, and a sense of belonging from the local union rather than from the company that employs them. The needs of the employees should be provided by the company via the supervisor on a daily basis. Once again, remember that unions thrive on management's mistakes!

Get Ready for Stewed Supervision

As a new manager, you should be aware of the number one game played in America. It is called "grandstand quarterbacking," and to play you merely have to criticize anyone who does anything. It can be your superior managers in the organization, officials in government, the Pope, or even the coaches and players on a sports team. It is a healthy game to play when kept in proper perspective, but it is played regularly whether healthy or not!

To the new supervisors, here is a word of caution about playing this game. You are going to be discussed! Your employees will observe every move you make, every reaction you have, and hear every word you speak. They may criticize all of it. When something occurs that affects them significantly and you have been part of the action, you will most likely be **roasted**! You will be on the table that evening (and perhaps for many evenings) as the main dish—stewed supervision!:

Be prepared for this kind of criticism and don't let it get the better of you. Listen to it, and turn positive and negative criticism into constructive suggestions for improving your job performance. Above all, recognize the game and your natural role in it, and don't overreact.

Learn to Avoid Managerial Obsolescence

There is much turnover in management. This creates a wide world of opportunity for the new manager. Managers retire; they get promoted, transferred, fired, sick, and some die while employed. Something else happens to managers, too, which you must be aware of. It is *managerial obsolescence.* Beware of becoming obsolete in your management job.

Managerial obsolescence occurs when the demands of the job become greater than the skill and/or talent of the individual who holds the position. You do not have to be promoted to become obsolete.

Obsolescence can set in when a manager fails to stay in touch with advanced technology; when he or she cannot adjust to a new type of employee; when reorganization has changed the way the manager must operate; or it can happen when new top management has different, perhaps greater, expectations and demands. There are other ways to become obsolete, but the idea is that you must not rest on past performance.

No matter how effective you were as a manager in the past, don't rest on your "laurels!" Management is a dynamic environment; and you can become obsolete anytime conditions change and you do not adjust.

ABOUT MANAGERS SPECIFICALLY

Managers Make Things Happen

When you observe the real professionals in management, you note immediately that they are action oriented. They are self-starters. They make things happen. These managers know where they are going, what needs to be done to get there, and when to do things. These managers are enthusiastic about their work. They are creative and motivated to achieve. Anticipating results generates enthusiasm.

Remember the three types of people in the world:

1. Those who make things happen;
2. Those who watch things happen, and
3. Those—the **overwhelming majority**—who have no idea what has happened!

Without question, professional managers are among those who make things happen.

Managers Must Be Aware

When you go into management for the first time, you are likely to be awed by the fact that the experienced managers seem relaxed, confident, and positive enough to enjoy their work. On the other hand, you, as a novice, may be swamped by the responsibility of your job, the complexity of decision-making, the people problems, and the constant time pressure facing you.

The underlying factor which makes these experienced managers seem relaxed and confident in the same world you find stress-filled is **awareness**.

Developing awareness is a conscious activity. You plan a program to determine the answers to questions about the organization, about activities, about personalities, about future projects, etc. Externally, you seek answers to questions about your industry, general economic conditions, political actions and the resultant impact, world affairs, etc.

Gaining this information in a systematic, deliberate fashion averts the panic of being suddenly uninformed when you need to have all the information available. Being more informed allows you to view your job and your work more objectively. You have a better perspective.

Awareness is not the same as having all the answers. Awareness is identifying activities, people, events, and statistics, and then making your value judgments in an unfrenzied state. All of which leads to improving your odds of making a sounder decision. An informed, more aware manager should develop better plans, make sounder decisions, and feel more comfortable about the future.

There is no excuse for being uninformed—not knowing what's happening inside and outside the organization. Spend at least ten minutes each day staying current on everything, asking questions, reviewing the economic and political news. It is a great investment of time in your future.

Managers Can Be Turtles or Hares

One of the great lessons to be learned in management is that steady performance on the job will be much more impressive than occasional bursts of brilliance.

Organizations and departments that are outstanding have managers who are productive on a daily basis not once in a while or just when a major project deadline is approaching. Steady attention to the problems at hand and consistent progress toward achieving objectives are characteristics of professional managers.

Organizations like managers they can depend on day in and day out. They like managers who are reliable, productive, and positive every day.

New managers should strive to develop this kind of stamina and consistency in their job performance.

Managers Are on Lifetime Probation

Most new managers don't realize they are on lifetime probation. Usually it is not mentioned in any interview; it is not in the employee handbook; it is not covered in orientation, nor is it posted on the bulletin board. It is a well-guarded secret that should be made public.

Most organizations have probationary periods for new nonmanagement employees that range from thirty days to six months. This probationary period is well-publicized and strictly enforced in most cases.

New managers are not on probation for a certain number of days, months, or years. Managers are on probation from the first day onward. They never get off probation! They may retire after forty years or be fired or quit after one week. They were on probation their last day on the job just as they were on their first.

Regardless of the seniority, a manager has no guarantee of employment except that assurance which may be gained from repeatedly demonstrating competency on the job.

Managers Must Wear the Management Hat

Whether you begin your career with a position in management or are promoted into management from a nonmanagement job, you will have to adjust your attitude. You will have to think and act like a **manager**.

You, as a manager, are the 'company' to your employees. What you say, do, don't say is the company. One of your major responsibilities is to act and speak in the best interest of the organization. For this reason, you should associate with managers, think like a manager, act like a manager, and in every way be a manager.

This does not imply that you can have no friends among nonmanagement employees. It simply means that they should know and you should know that every decision you make as a manager is going to be in the best interest of the organization. Sometimes these decisions may override friendships.

Maintain your friendships at all levels, but be sure you wear your management hat twenty-four hours a day.

Managers Are Physically Healthier

Managers are physically healthier than nonmanagers, based on days absent from work each year due to sickness. Nonmanagement employees are absent, on the average, six times more per year for illness than managers.

Why is this true? The answer is simple. When managers get up in the morning, every morning, they know that other people are depending on them at work. They know that decisions are in process that they are a part of. They know that excuses are unacceptable. They know total responsibility is theirs, and they know they will be judged on results. They know they cannot afford to be absent from work for routine reasons or minor illnesses.

Furthermore, managers tend to be much more excited about their jobs and more interested in their work than nonmanagers. They **want to go to work**. Everyone should feel this way, but unfortunately not all employees do.

Managers Should Be Surrounded by the Finest People

One of the real secrets of being a great manager is that you are only as good as your employees. Have highly trained, highly motivated, dedicated and loyal employees, and you have a great manager!

There is no greatness or real professionalism in management if the employees are average or mediocre.

Since everything employees do reflects on managers, it behooves a manager to develop every employee to his or her full potential. Doing this benefits the employee, the manager, and the company. Only after you adopt this standard of excellence as part of your management work do you have a chance to become a real professional in management.

Every Manager Has an M.O.

Whether admitted or not, every manager like every courtroom attorney, every professional criminal, and every concert musician has his or her own M.O. (modus operandi) or method of operation. A manager's M.O. is a description of the manager in action. It portrays the manager's predictable patterns of behavior as he or she works with and through people to achieve objectives. The M.O. would include expected reactions to problem situations and the individual techniques and habits observed in daily supervision.

Ideally a manager's M.O. should match his or her personal philosophy of management.

The best way to obtain a manager's M.O. is through employees. Request the employees of the manager to write a description of their boss—in complete confidence and anonymity. Have the employees include all the noticeable strengths and weaknesses of the manager and omit nothing. From these individual accounts, develop a composite profile of the manager. This is that manager's M.O.

The only value in developing a manager's M.O. is for improving managerial effectiveness. The M.O. should be compared with the manager's personal philosophy which details how he or she **thinks** he or she is performing as a **manager. If the comparison** shows variances, changes will need to be made to improve **managerial performance.**

Just what changes to make and how much variance to accept are questions that each manager must explore in the ongoing attempt to improve his or her managerial effectiveness.

Managers Set the Tone and Example

An often overlooked responsibility of new managers is that of setting the tone and example for the employees you manage. Setting the tone refers to the "spirit" of the work group. Establishing a positive attitude toward work, generating an air of enthusiasm, and creating a sense of importance about the work being done are examples of positive "spirit."

Setting the example for other employees to follow relates to absenteeism, work habits, being on time, having a positive attitude toward higher management and the company, and actions that demonstrate company loyalty.

It is unlikely that your employees will be the ideal types of workers in attitude and behavior unless you set the example and lead the way.

Management Is One on One

One of the best tips for a new manager to remember is that although you may be in charge of eight, ten, or twenty or more employees, you manage each one at a time.

Managers have group meetings, departmental discussions, and make decisions that affect whole groups of employees; but the activity of managing effectively is best done one on one.

The reason for this is that every employee is different. The job needs, responses to stimuli, and perception both of you as a manager and the work situation vary greatly from one employee to another. You can see that managing everyone in the same way when each employee is so different would lead to frustration on your part and theirs, and ultimately lack of effectiveness as a manager.

Managers Need a Personal Style of Management

Although much has been written about styles and types of managers, there is no one best way to manage. Benevolent, autocratic, democratic, participatory, Theory X, Y, and Z are only a few of the "styles" of management. What every manager needs is his or her own **personal style of management.**

You can and should study and observe successful managers. You will find that they are different in virtually every respect: personality, technique, background, experience, manner in handling people. Yet, if you judge these managers on results, all are successful.

You can watch and listen to managers and read on the subject of management. You can discuss philosophies and styles of management with others. In the final analysis, however, you will succeed or fail on what you do as an individual. So develop your own style!

Imitation may be the greatest form of flattery, but it is no shortcut to management success. Concentrate on maximizing your personal assets and minimizing your shortcomings as you evolve a style of management that suits you.

Your style of management will be uniquely yours. It will also be subject to change when circumstances and situations dictate. Underlying your personal style, however, should be a consistency that your employees can count on. Employees need the sense of security you provide as a manager when you deal with them in a consistent manner regardless of the changing problems and situations you face.

Be a Non-Conformist Who Knows When to Conform

Most progressive organizations like managers who are alive with ideas, who challenge the old ways of doing things, who produce many viable suggestions and proposals, and who seek added responsibility. This type of manager is also a trouble maker to other organizations. It is precisely this type of nonconformist manager who has paved the way for progress in American business, but not every organization wants one. It depends on the attitude and philosophy of the organization.

If your organization encourages the above action, then enjoy the opportunity to be different and develop your skills at innovation and creativity. But never forget the cardinal rule that says, *know when to conform!* There will always be guidelines or limits of acceptable behavior for managers in every organization. Exceeding these limits is foolish and dangerous for your career in management.

When you get into management, find out immediately what the rules of the game are. Determine what your limits will be and what the boundaries are. Especially, find out what higher management encourages lower managers to do. You may not like what you uncover and subsequently change organizations, but you may also map yourself a road to higher management by steering well within the borders while fulfilling your maximum potential.

Management's Most Embarrassing Moment

When problems in a manager's area of supervision attract the attention of higher management and higher management investigates, that manager had best know all about the problem. If not, he or she has just suffered the most embarrassing thing in management—being caught unaware.

This would never happen if every employee were educated, conditioned, and programmed to keep his or her immediate boss informed of any unusual action taking place.

Managers must control their work group, know what's happening at all times, and accept the responsibility for all of the action, good or bad. There is no excuse or defense for not being on top of everything going on in your own area of supervision.

Management's Most Difficult Situation

The most difficult thing in management happens when decisions are handed down by higher management to be implemented by lower management. When these decisions are made at the top for the purpose of benefiting the organization, but they conflict with what lower management would like to do personally or thinks is best for the organization, then the lower manager has his or her most difficult assignment.

The job of the manager is to do what is best for the organization. Often what one manager thinks is contrary to the thoughts of another; however, your job also is to respond to the direction and orders of managers above you whether you totally agree with the decisions or not.

Examples of these kinds of situations include the following:

1. Being instructed to cut the size of the labor force;
2. Reducing operating budgets;
3. Skipping or postponing an expected wage hike, and
4. Scrapping a project that has a lot of potential.

It is a true test of a manager's mettle to handle these situations; but if professionalism is your goal, you must learn how to put these decisions into effect with the least amount of disruption to your employees.

Leadership Is Badly Needed in Management

Not every manager is an effective leader and not all effective leaders are in management. Ideally an organization would like every manager to be competent in the knowledge and practice of management **and** also possess and demonstrate effective leadership.

Being a leader in a management job is different from being a competent, knowledgeable manager. A competent manager with good leadership skills generates the "extras" that make some departments outstanding in performance while others are good or average (remember average is undesirable).

Effective leadership creates employee loyalty, pride in work, an *esprit de corps*, a willingness to volunteer for overtime work, a positive attitude toward the company and fellow employees, and job satisfaction.

There is a shortage of effective leaders in every kind of organization. When you go into management try hard to develop soundness in management and also become an effective leader. Read and study about people and leadership, and glean ideas you can use in practice to enhance your professionalism in management.

Little Things Make a Big Difference

Remember this statement when you go into management. Nothing is more true than the fact that managers who are the best do things a little bit better than the average. This small difference separates the "excellent" from the "mediocre."

Becoming a real "pro" in management requires improvement in all of your areas of supervision over time. But improvement tends to be gradual, **almost subtle**, not sudden or startling. You may not observe much difference in other managers on a daily basis, but you'll see a big difference in end results.

Your objective should be to strive to improve your planning skills, decision making techniques, your ability to communicate effectively, your leadership ability, etc. a little as you gain experience. Work hard to improve slightly in the dozens of areas of management, and you'll be amazed how that small improvement multiplies in the end results.

One or two seconds separates first place and second in a 500 mile speedway race. One stroke can be the difference between first place and second in a major golf tournament. A baseball player who hits .300 gets only one more hit every ten times at bat than a .200 hitter. Yet, the difference between the end result is as if one wins by hours, dozens of golf strokes, or ten hits out of ten at-bats. That same disparity holds true in management. Little improvements make a **big** difference.

Gaining the Personal Edge

As important as management training is to your career, it requires time to digest and time to learn to apply the wide variety of information you acquire. In the short run, what can you do to gain the personal edge toward making you stand out as a new manager?

The answer is simple and yet overlooked by many. There are three things you can do which will enhance your image as an employee and a manager in any organization.

First, when you are given an assignment, *begin to do it immediately!* The fact that you don't delay, procrastinate, don't question the assignment, and act immediately is always impressive to bosses.

Next, perform the assignment *on time!* Nothing makes a better impression than to do a job on schedule (or ahead if possible) without grumbling, and with enthusiasm.

Finally, make certain you *do the assignment well!* Strive for exceptional quality in every task you perform. After all this is what you expect of your employees as a professional manager, and you should deliver no less to your managers.

In summary, when any employee performs an assignment immediately, on time, and does it well, in time that employee stands out as a true professional. This kind of performance on a consistent basis gives you the personal edge.

ABOUT THE EMPLOYEES YOU MANAGE

Develop Employees to Their Fullest

Of all the factors of production only "people" can grow and develop into something more valuable than they were originally.

Managers have a major responsibility to develop employees to their fullest. This is a twenty-four hour a day job.

Since people are the number one resource of any organization, a number one priority of every manager is to guide, direct, educate, train, inspire, stimulate, and encourage all employees to grow and develop to their maximum potential.

The benefits of this are obvious. The employee becomes more valuable and will either gain more job security, a promotion, or both. The manager benefits because all employee efforts reflect on him or her. Finally, the organization benefits from having a more productive and valuable employee.

It is economically and socially sound to develop employees to their fullest. You do this through practicing positive leadership techniques and professional management.

Make Perfectionism a Disease

The definition of management includes working "through others" to achieve objectives. It is a totally people-oriented activity. Management is also a largely inexact science full of risks, uncertainty, and the unpredictable behavior of people.

Any manager at any level who expects or demands perfection from employees is living in an unrealistic world. It is professional to aim high, to encourage the perfect job, to strive to maximize profits and minimize costs, but mistakes and errors are bound to occur. There are too many variables which managers cannot control and cannot foresee with pinpoint precision to expect perfection.

Perfectionism is a disease that destroys people. Keep standards high, but as a manager learn to adjust to the imperfections of your employees, peers, and bosses. And learn to adjust to the imperfections in you.

Know Your Personnel

If you ask managers the question: Do you really know and understand your employees? Most will say, "Yes." If a third party talks confidentially with the employees about how they think about their jobs, the company, what they want, need, and desire from the job and company, then often you get a different set of answers from those given be managers.

When this is the case, and it too often is, there exists a conflict area between management's thinking and that of the employees. The employees and the managers are on different wave lengths. What results is management bases its employee relations efforts on what it **perceives** not what employees truly think and feel.

Do you think this could cause problems? You better believe it does!

When managers take action based on their concept of employees' needs, interests, and desires and the expected results are disappointing, then management has proved they really do not know their employees as well as they think. Every manager should work hard to understand each individual employee.

Know your personnel! Talk to them, seek their thoughts, try to draw out their needs, wants, and desires as employees under you. This will help you minimize internal problems in the future.

Settle for Nothing But the Best

There should be two types of employees, excellent and "ex." Unfortunately nearly every organization has many ordinary, average employees. These employees are performing in a manner no better than minimally acceptable. Organizations also have marginal employees—the ones barely holding their jobs. Then, organizations have a few employees they can call excellent. These employees are the "pros." They are dedicated, motivated, productive, and loyal to the organization.

Since every organization has a few excellent employees, why do you think every job is not filled with excellent employees? Why should any organization settle for less than the best when it comes to employees?

The excuses you hear go like this: Those excellent employees are hard to find and keep. They just are not available. Things are different today, people don't feel the same about work as they used to. The unions and the government encourage mediocrity.

The truth is the "great" or "excellent" employees have never been "out there." The unions and the government do not condemn excellence. Managers have to take the responsibility themselves for average or marginal employees, just as they must take the credit for creating "excellent" employees.

The source of the vast majority of excellent employees is right there in the ranks of current employees. Ordinary employees can become *extraordinary* under the direction, training, education, leadership, and inspiration of a professional manager. If some employees resist growth, don't want to become extraordinary, and wish to remain mediocre; then, when conditions are right, replace them with people who do want to grow.

Managers as well as organizations are judged by the performance of their employees. Learn to recognize the factors of excellence in your employees, and strive to instill the desire for excellence in them all.

Don't Confuse Seniority with Competence

Seniority refers to the length of employment a person has had with the present organization. Length of employment or seniority is used widely in American organizations as a basis for job promotion considerations and salary increases, and, when necessary, layoffs of nonmanagement employees.

Seniority has little place in management. Years of service is important as an indicator of loyalty, but it should never be confused with competency in the individual. People can work for twenty years and simply repeat the first year of experience nineteen times, or twenty years seniority can be the sum of twenty years of solid experience. Time is not the differentiating factor, competency is.

In management, the person considered most qualified to perform a job is usually promoted or transferred, etc. The action is taken to benefit the organization, but it is rarely made on the basis of seniority.

Union-management contracts nearly always require that seniority be considered in most decisions about employees (such things as promotions, layoffs, raises, vacations, etc.). Union members believe in using seniority because it is objective, can be easily understood, and is simple to apply. Managers, however, are not subject to this kind of seniority protection. Competency is the rule for survival and promotion in management.

Seniority does not exclude competency, but you must learn to make the distinction. You must make that distinction, when allowed to do so by work agreements, upper management, etc., in your decision about employees' promotions, salaries, work assignments, transfers, and dozens of other cases.

Employees Have Job Needs, Wants and Desires

When you first go into management, you will meet all of your employees. These people consider you their "boss." To you these people are "support" personnel. Over time, they will try to figure you out. You should be doing the same with each of them.

To help you solve the mystery of stimulating your support personnel consider these facts: Every employee has basic job needs, wants, and desires; and when these basic job needs, wants, and desires are not satisfied to a reasonable degree, the employee becomes a problem or quits (and make no mistake an employee can quit and leave the company or quit and still be on the job!).

Every manager has the challenge of understanding each employee. Since each employee is different from the next, then every employee should be managed differently, To do this, you need to know what the basic job needs, wants, and desires of each employee are. You do this by listening, asking questions, engaging in discussions, exchanging ideas and thoughts with your employees over time.

Some of the more common job needs, wants, and desires of employees are job security, higher pay, opportunity for advancement, better working conditions, recognition, better supervision, etc. When an employee's job needs, wants, and desires are not satisfied to a reasonable degree, you as the manager have a disgruntled employee. The individual employee determines what is reasonable, not you the manager. You can watch for signs of dissatisfaction such as absenteeism or tardiness, more mistakes or sloppy work performance, frequent complaints about most everything, perhaps some diffidence or even belligerence toward you and other managers, and the ultimate signal—resignation from employment.

Every manager will do a better job of working through people if he or she really makes a conscientious effort to understand each individual employee and reasonably satisfy the basic job needs, wants and desires.

Learn the Value of Empathy

Empathy is defined as putting yourself in the other person's place. Having empathy is a positive characteristic of managers who really care about communicating effectively. Psychologically the manager who can consider the feelings and attitudes of employees before he or she talks or writes to them will do a better job of getting a particular message across. Trying to understand how people feel and think before praising, criticizing, or delegating work to them allows a manager an opportunity to select a method of communication and a form of communication that should be more effective.

Putting yourself in the employee's place tells him or her that you place a high value on employees' needs and feelings. It tells your employees you are concerned with doing whatever is necessary to communicate more effectively and get along more smoothly with them. It gains their support for all you try to accomplish when you begin your tenure with them in this manner. You find your employees more cooperative, supportive, and productive when they believe you genuinely take their feelings into consideration in your day to day management decisions.

The Three Kinds of Job Income

Every employee receives three different kinds of income on the job.

First, the employee receives *monetary* income. This is the total dollars and cents per payday we enjoy talking or even bragging (or complaining) about.

Second, the employee receives *real* income. This is what can be bought in goods and services with the monetary income. This kind of income really measures an employee's standard of living. It doesn't matter how much monetary income you receive, it is what you can do with it that counts.

Finally, the employee receives *psychic* income. This is the psychological satisfaction from a job. This kind of income is just as important as monetary or real income in terms of creating job satisfaction, preventing employee turnover, and boosting employee morale. Psychic income can be given or received from a pat on the back, a nice raise, verbal praise, special responsibility assigned, a promotion, a new title, a bigger office, etc. The important point to remember is that whenever any employee receives less than enough of any of the three incomes, he or she is likely to leave the organization or at least be looking and waiting for a chance to leave.

You as a manager can make sure that a satisfactory level of all three incomes is maintained. Lack of psychic income can cause as much turnover as lack of monetary income.

Learn to judge when to give psychic income for maximum benefit and don't deflate its value by overdoing it.

The Correlation Between Morale and Productivity

Morale is the outlook an employee has at any given moment about his or her work environment. The work environment includes the working conditions, the supervision, the opportunities, the job security, the wages, the recognition given, and so forth.

Most managers believe there is a strong positive correlation between morale and productivity, i.e., the higher the morale, the better the performance of the employee. With a few exceptions, this tends to be true.

The exceptions occur largely when recession, business failures, and layoffs cause large scale unemployment. Those remaining employed in the hardest hit industries tend to have low morale, but they produce more, work harder, and strive to remain employed. Here morale is low, but productivity is high.

In general, American managers invest considerable time and money trying to improve the morale of their employees so that they will be more satisfied with their jobs and, in turn, achieve and maintain high job performance.

How Pay and Performance Correlate

One of the myths in management is that higher employee pay results in higher employee performance. In about ninety percent of the cases, this is not true.

Wages and salaries have little to do with individual performance, once the pay is above the subsistence level. The primary reason for this is that pay received is not related directly to performance. About ninety percent of all employed people are paid according to time standards, not performance standards. Employees are paid by the hour, day, week, month, year, etc. rather than by what they do. It is implied that if an employee doesn't do enough satisfactory work, the employee is discharged; but the pay is not directly related to performance—especially in the minds of the workers.

About ten percent of the jobs in America are held by people paid according to what they produce. Examples are sales people working on direct commission only **and** employees working on a one hundred percent piece rate plan. Here employees are paid directly according to what they produce. No performance—no pay!

The most highly motivated employees are those who are rewarded according to performance. One of the important rewards is money (pay).

As a new manager you can capitalize on this correlation by basing promotions and pay increases on **merit**.

How Do You Motivate?

New managers are interested in their employees' becoming highly motivated. Employees who are highly motivated are excited about their jobs, the objectives, the assignment, their responsibilities, the mission, etc.

People who are highly motivated tend to like what they're doing and have confidence they can do their jobs well. If employees are not highly motivated, the manager has a responsibility to stimulate them.

Since motivation comes from within a person, a manager cannot motivate someone else. What a manager does is inspire, stimulate, and enthuse employees to become more highly motivated.

The best technique to use to achieve this is to inspire someone positively about the importance of his or her job. Stress that the work is essential; emphasize the value of what each is doing and its importance to the department, the organization, and other employees; and generously recognize outstanding performance after the fact. Encourage outstanding performance to continue. Don't engage in negative stimuli such as coercion or threats of doom to get people motivated, even if it might work in the short run. Employees motivated by fear or from threats will leave an organization when they get a chance, and the effect on performance is short-lived at best. You are after permanent change and long-lasting results.

Motivation tends to be the highest when morale is high. Employees who have a good feeling about the importance of their work, their place in the organization, and their future normally will be highly motivated and satisfied.

The Rotten Apple Concept

Anyone who has ever seen a rotten apple in the middle of a barrel of good fresh apples knows that, in due time, the rotten apple will spoil the other apples unless removed.

The same holds true for employees who are dissatisfied, complain a lot, and are problem employees in general. If they are not removed, they will infect the employees around them.

Employees should not be dismissed to cover management's weaknesses. They should be dismissed only after their manager has tried sincerely every approach to correct, change, and improve their attitude and work performance. Some employees are in the wrong job and in the wrong company. Some employees bring outside problems to work, and these affect both performance and attitude. If problem employees do not respond after a reasonable period of time and effort, however, they should be dismissed.

You may have to don your gloves and become an "industrial surgeon" early in your management career, or your may never have to dismiss a problem employee. You cannot leave such an employee in the ranks without correcting the problem. To do so would be a disservice to the organization and to all of the productive employees.

The Danger of the Headless Chicken

Have you ever seen employees who run around and act like chickens with their heads cut off? They are the highly motivated employees who seem to have no direction, no visible goals, and yet are constantly in motion. A majority of these employees may be managers or staff personnel.

Somehow this type of employee is willing but not able. They may have ambition but no talent; they may have inspiration but no purpose. Some have ideas but no backing, or they have objectives but no plans. These employees are "dangerous"—much like a bull in a china shop.

Employees like the headless chicken type need direction, specifics, guidelines, and goals to become productive employees. Remember behavior of employees below you reflects on you as a manager.

Practice Personnel Preventive Maintenance

About ninety percent of all management problems involve people in some way. These may be employees, other managers, customers, suppliers, or others. Problems involving people are called general management problems.

A lot of time and effort is spent by managers on people problems. The practical approach is to try to prevent these problems before they occur. Anticipating many of these problems in advance requires a program of personnel preventive maintenance.

Companies budget millions of dollars annually for physical plant maintenance. Why not budget monies for personnel maintenance and avoid some of the human problems before they occur and cost even more? Such an expenditure should bring about a large return on investment.

A personnel preventive maintenance program requires management to organize a department or group for the sole purpose of continuously reviewing employee job needs, wants, and desires. Its objective would be to bring about complete job satisfaction among employees while insuring good employee performance, efficient operations, and increased loyalty to the company. It is a very good concept.

You as a manager can perform much the same function individually, in the absence of such an organized effort, by knowing your personnel and practicing effective leadership and communication techniques.

Above all, don't wait for a problem to develop; try to prevent it.

The Critical Factor in Personnel Selection

Every manager is involved in the personnel selection process. Even if your company has a personnel department to recruit, interview, process, test, and recommend personnel for employment, you as the manager should make the final decision regarding new employees.

Employees may be new to the organization, or they may be new to the department after transferring from within the company. In either case, there are always questions about new employees and their future job performance.

The process of selecting individuals for jobs in organizations is not scientific. You cannot guarantee successful work performance in advance of employment or promotion regardless of interviews, testing, references, etc. What you can do in the personnel selection process is weed out the applicants not highly qualified for a job. From the applications left, the manager must make a judgment based on information available and a personal interview.

One point stands out. New managers should remember that the **best** indicator of future job performance is the record of performance in the past. This applies to everyone.

The difficulty is gathering accurate data about past performance. This is hard since information is not always readily available. Furthermore, a good record of past performance is still no **guarantee** of good future performance. But it is the best predictor available to the manager making the selection decision.

Keep the Objectives in Harmony

One of the important guiding concepts for new managers is the harmony of objectives concept. The idea is that a manager should so well know his or her individual employees that every day, as you work with these employees, you try to align their employee job needs, wants, and desires with the objectives of the organization.

The purpose of doing this is to create harmonious effort toward organizational objectives while satisfying individual employee's needs, wants, and desires on the job. Bringing this about on a daily basis requires much skill and insight on the part of the manager. The manager must know the values and aspirations of each employee and keep these in mind when delegating responsibility, controlling activity, and planning future work. Doing this successfully benefits the total organization.

The Overlooked Income

Most organizations proudly advertise their job openings and the accompanying wages or salaries. Advertising "fringe benefits" is not as common.

Fringe benefits go with the job and have now become approximately one third of the total wage bill. Most of the benefits provided an employee are paid for by the organization. Benefits may include health insurance, life insurance, worker's compensation, some form of retirement or pension plan, social security, etc. Additionally, the organization may subsidize the food services provided to employees, may provide free parking, recreational facilities and equipment, reduced-cost vacation opportunities, pay part or all of the cost of advanced education, and many more things.

These benefits are expensive to provide; yet, most organizations do a poor job of selling these benefits to their employees as part of their income. The typical employee takes these things for granted and doesn't put into dollars and cents the value of receiving them. The company doesn't get any extra credit with employees for providing them with such benefits. This is why fringe benefits are often called the "overlooked" income.

You can sell these benefits to the employees and make them aware of the value they receive. Doing so becomes a real asset to the organization, and you will find the employees have a better attitude when they realize fully the changes in life style and standards of living these benefits make possible.

Put It In Writing

One of the true pearls of wisdom in management today says, "Put things of importance in writing."

In this world of legal relief for virtually everything it is essential to document in writing every event, reprimand, commendation, accident, etc. because organizations have many laws and legal regulations with which they must abide in the conduct of business. Nowhere is this more true than in the area of personnel—dealing with your employees.

As a manager, you will conduct performance appraisals, issue commendations and reprimands, counsel employees, hold departmental meetings, investigate problems and accusations, assign work, allocate any overtime necessary, receive instruction from your supervisors, and on and on. In all of these cases, you should record in writing the significant points that involve people, objectives, time standards, rule violations and any other subject of importance.

It is essential to document in writing the performance records of your employees and their responses to your discussion of the evaluations. Whether the subject recorded reflects positively or negatively on an employee does not matter. Write it up and have the employee read the written statement and sign the document. The signature verifies that the report has been read and discussed and a copy given to the employee. File a copy and forward a copy to your supervisor, in addition to giving a copy to the employee.

Beyond the legal requirement to maintain documentation, it is simply good management practice to make written records of anything of importance that occurs in your domain.

Job Enrichment

Job enrichment is exactly what it implies. Managers have a chance, actually an opportunity, to enrich the jobs of employees if they are interested in increased employee job satisfaction. To enrich a job requires some creative thinking on the manager's part and from the employee as well.

Enriching a job does not mean changing performance expectations! It means changing the work environment, the flow of work, perhaps the job title, maybe introducing flex-hours, adding new and improved equipment, or a combination of things which will cause the employee to be more satisfied with his or her job. There is no formula to follow to bring about job enrichment. It is an individual effort to bring about better performance through more job satisfaction.

There is a strong tendency for employee performance to improve when job satisfaction is increased. Think about how to enrich the jobs of your employees. Be empathetic as you plan methods of increasing employees' satisfaction though job enrichment.

The P and I Concept

The P and I Concept is the basis for the practice of participative management, which is the philosophy of management practiced in many American organizations today.

"P" stands for participation, and "I" stands for identification. The theory is that if you allow employees to participate in the actions or decisions affecting them, then they will identify with what takes place and be much more supportive of it and less resistant to it.

Possible additional benefits include increased organization loyalty, an improvement in employee self-esteem, more pride in work, a feeling of increased importance, and an overall improvement in morale. There is much merit to the P and I Concept, and many benefits can accrue to the manager who applies it properly. It can, however, backfire!

For example, if input from employees is requested on a proposal and the employees reject in advance what management wishes to do, management has created a major problem. To override employees' opinions will ruin the use of the P and I approach in the future. If management backs off on the proposed action because of employee rejection in advance, there is a question of who's running the organization!

Using the P and I approach carefully and properly can produce benefits. Perhaps the best way to increase employee participation and get positive results from P and I is through excellent one-on-one supervision. In this case, the manager—you—gets the employee directly involved in changes, decisions, proposals, and suggestions; and in this way you can provide immediate positive praise and recognition for the employee's contribution.

The Job Dictates the Pay

In the vast majority of jobs in America (where people are employed by the hour, day, week, month, or year), the *job dictates the pay—not the person who holds the position.*

You will make a major management mistake if you allow employee pressure to influence the value of a job. Having a person perform a certain task every day or do a specific amount of work every day is worth just so much to the organization. It doesn't matter about the employee's sex, marital status, race, personal needs, problems, or ambitions. As long as the employee is doing the particular job, the pay is what the **job** is worth.

If the employee wishes to be paid more than he or she receives, then a promotion or transfer to a higher level job is necessary.

Pay rates need to be fair and equitable. Job evaluation is one approach to achieving this. Regardless of individual qualifications (experience and education), however, the job is worth only so much to the organization relative to the worth of other jobs being performed. That worth becomes the base pay.

Beyond this most organizations have merit increases, cost of living increases, and adjustments for seniority over and above base pay. A point of maximization is eventually reached in each job.

In managing, you must be sure that the employee fits both the work involved in the job and that the pay scale is appropriate. Don't waste your valuable time with an employee who expects the salary to be altered because of him or her. And remember an overqualified employee will most likely eventually become a troublesome employee.

The challenge is to match the right person to the right job.

Summary

Once again the question of whether you should go into management is raised. Not everyone should be a manager! If you believe the field of management is attractive, however, you should understand the universal "charge" to managers and the importance of developing a personal philosophy of management. The importance of having a personal philosophy of management is that it influences every action you take and all decisions you make leading to consistency in your behavior as a manager.

Fifty-six concepts of management are presented in this chapter. These ideas, points and suggestions have validity and can be helpful to a new manager. The concepts are about **management generally, about managers specifically, and about employees you manage.**

Much about managing is "common sense" although many of the ideas about how to do things originate from theory. Often managers have to decide **what to do, how to do it, and when** with little or no factual information to guide them. Experience and acquired knowledge provide the sources of information upon which many managers base their decisions and actions. Managers are performing artists on the job every day, and much of their success as managers is determined by the way they do things or their style of management.

Review Questions

1. Discuss the value of "theory" versus "common sense" in management.
2. Why do you think opportunity is unlimited in management?
3. Explain the value of having a personal philosophy of management.
4. Which ten concepts do you think have the greatest practical value to a new manager?

Assignments for Personal Development

1. Now that you have studied the first three chapters and have reviewed the concepts in this chapter, develop and write your own personal philosophy of management, i.e., your current beliefs, convictions, etc. about management that will make up your personal style as a manager.
2. After auditing your own personal strengths and weaknesses, prepare a statement that justifies your entry into the world of management.

Incident

AT THE END OF HER ROPE!

Mary Perkins and Debbie Jones were close friends socially as well as at work. They entered the company a few months apart, worked in the same department, and often had lunch together. When Mary was promoted to the supervisor's job, Debbie was the first to congratulate her. She was thrilled that her good friend was becoming the new boss. After a few weeks in the job, however, Mary began to change.

Often she was irritable, made negative comments to her employees, demonstrated inconsistent behavior, overreacted to problem situations, and was very unpopular with the employees she supervised in her department. She also never had time to go to lunch with Debbie anymore; instead, she usually ate by herself.

A few weeks later Debbie got a call from Mary after she got home from work. Mary said that she wanted to visit with her that evening and discuss the situation at work. She said that she was at the end of her rope with the supervisor's job. It was ruining her health, and she dreaded going to work every day. She wanted Debbie to give her some friendly advice about keeping the job, going back to her old job, or quitting the organization.

Questions:

1. If you were Debbie, what advice would you give Mary?
2. Which of the concepts in this chapter might be of value to Mary in her new supervisory job?

Management Journals and Related Periodicals for Future Reference

Academy of Management Journal
Academy of Management Review
Administrative Management
Administrative Science Quarterly
Business Horizons
California Management Review
Canadian Business Review
Columbia Journal of World Business
Decision Sciences
Forbes
Fortune
Journal of Small Business Management
Harvard Business Review
Human Resource Management
Industrial and Labor Relations Review
Journal of Applied Behavioral Science
Journal of Applied Psychology
Journal of Business
Journal of Human Resources
Journal of Management Studies
Journal of Systems Management
Long-Range Planning

Management Accounting
Management International Review
Management of Personnel Quarterly
Management Review
Management Science
Managerial Planning
Michigan Business Review
Monthly Labor Review
Organizational Behavior and Human Performance
Organizational Dynamics
Personnel
Personnel Administrator
Personnel Management
Personnel Psychology
Public Administration Review
S.A.M. Advanced Management Journal
Sloan Management Review
Strategic Management Journal
Supervisory Management
Training and Development Journal
The Wall Street Journal (newspaper)

CHAPTER 4

THE MANAGEMENT ENVIRONMENT AND MANAGEMENT'S ETHICAL AND SOCIAL RESPONSIBILITIES

After studying this chapter, **you will know**:

- The definition of the term "environment"
- The internal and external constraints that affect management
- The main contemporary trends that affect management
- The meaning of "social responsibility" and what society expects of management
- The meaning of "ethics" and what constitutes ethical management behavior
- The economic responsibilities of managers
- Critical problems facing management as the year 2000 looms ahead
- How management can adapt to changes in the environment

Introduction

Chapter 4 provides an **overall** view of the social and economic environment in the United States as we approach the turn of the century. Major legislation, trends and movements are discussed. Managers must be aware of the total environment and not narrow their focus to the trends and problems in their unique organizational world. Issues in society in general affect the actions and concerns of managers in every industry.

The purpose of this chapter is to give individual managers an opportunity to learn the components of the environment in general and to see those segments of the environment that affect their jobs in particular. It is important that managers in every industry relate events and contemporary issues to their own situations.

THE MANAGEMENT ENVIRONMENT

The **environment of management** in any industry *is the sum of all the social, cultural, economic and physical factors that influence the life-style of an individual, organization or community*. No person or organization can function separately from these surroundings which always present constraints on behavior. Managers may exercise power or authority, but they must adjust to their environment. Management's authority is limited by the internal and external constraints imposed by the environment.

Internal and External Constraints

Among the large number of environmental constraints that affect managers are those that originate within the organization. These are called internal constraints, of which the following are principle examples:

Constraints imposed by organizational documents. Many corporations, government agencies, and nonprofit organizations have organizational documents which specify what that organization can and cannot do. These documents may be constitutions, corporate charters, bylaws and their amendments. Other internal constraints that affect management include employment contracts, job descriptions, and the regulations in the employer's personnel handbook. The purpose of each of these is to define what the organization is, tell how it is expected to function, and set the limits on its actions. Management's actions in these organizations is restricted by the language of such documents.

Constraints imposed by limited resources. An organization has capital resources, personnel and physical facilities. None of these, even capital, is unlimited. Once an organization has reached the limit of any of these resources, its actions are restricted. Eastern Airlines, for instance, had lost money for several years; and finally faced bankruptcy unless it could be bought by another organization. This forced the management of Eastern into the action that led to its being acquired by Texas Air Corporation which led to its demise. Both operative and management personnel can place limits on management's actions, also. If the expansion of production cannot be supported by employees in the right numbers and with the right skills, such expansion may have to be postponed. If the current management team is stretched already and new management talent is not readily available, a new product line or new area of market expansion may have to wait. Physical plant facilities can also limit production or expansion. Management's decisions must consider all limited resources.

Constraints imposed by organizational guidelines. Organizational guidelines are anything that management introduces to influence employee behavior (discussed in more detail in Chapter 5). Organizational guidelines include policies, procedures, rules and many other specific plans. All organizational guidelines place limits on what the organization and its managers may do. For example, a policy that the company will not be undersold places pricing limits on managers. If the company has a rule against family members working in the same department, personnel hiring is affected. And if there is a set procedure or series of steps to take in purchasing new equipment, that restricts a manager from bypassing the system. Organizational guidelines are developed by top level management. Top level managers also set the broad, long-range plans called strategies (see Chapter 5) to achieve goals and objectives. Within these strategies are guidelines that also restrict the actions of lower-level managers. For example, if the long-range objective is to reduce the work force by two percent per year, a first level manager may be restricted in replacing retiring employees.

Constraints imposed by custom or long-established practice. A custom is a practice which has been carried on for so long with mutual consent that is becomes unwritten law. Customs are often associated with employees in a particular area. It is the custom in some areas of the U.S. to observe Columbus Day as a holiday; in other areas, the Friday before Easter is traditionally a work holiday. If management tries to change these customs, it could cause morale problems and would be difficult to effect. If it has been the custom in an organization to be lenient with sick leave or not to expect a doctor's excuse for absence due to illness, the manager who attempts to reinstate the requirement for a doctor's note will face limits and may be unable to make the change. Custom can be a strong limiting force on management's action, especially concerning management-employee relations and management-community relations.

External constraints are those environmental constraints imposed on an organization from the outside. External constraints are generally beyond the direct control of an organization. Some major external constraints that can restrict management action are the following:

Constraints imposed by legal and political consideration. Legal-political constraints include laws and regulations, taxes and political stability. Laws originate usually from some type of management abuse of power. When the best interests of society are served by restricting the power of an organization or its management to act, laws are passed. For example, when air pollution became a national tragedy, laws were passed to force businesses to end their pollution practices. The Wall Street scandal of 1986-87 involving violations of insider-trading rules will undoubtedly lead to harsher rules and stricter enforcement. Managers face laws that limit their power to act in such areas as fair hiring practices, minimum wages, working conditions and the safety of workers, competitive practices, pricing, product safety, the sale of stock, the acquisition of other companies or mergers with other companies, business locations, and many other factors.

The location of a business is particularly influenced by legal and political constraints. Within the U.S., local zoning laws, freeport exemption laws, state tax laws, and right-to-work laws (laws that say a person may not be required to join a union in order to keep a job and which vary by state) concern management in making location decisions and limit management's action. Internationally, political stability may be the most important factor in restricting management's action.

An organization has no control over the action of a foreign government. Organizations which operate abroad are subject to special taxes, requirements that they employ a certain percent of native workers, and even nationalization of property. The stability of the government is of utmost concern to management of multinational organizations. The ability to continue operating in some foreign countries is affected by political decisions, not action taken by the organization's management. For example, when the U.S. escalated its hostility with Libya, several oil companies were required to cease operations there by the U.S. government. And multinational organizations always have management action restricted by the foreign nation's customs and mores (moral attitudes and habits).

Management does have avenues to affect government action in the U.S. at the local, state and national levels. Managers often testify before governmental committees and commissions, present evidence, or lobby to influence the action of government. An organization cannot usually control what any government body does, however, and its efforts to do so may bring it more unfavorable publicity and cause more harm than the ultimate governmental action. This is especially the case if tampering or illegal activity is involved, such as excessive contributions to a friendly official's campaign fund or entertaining members of a commission which has the power to rule favorably or unfavorably on a particular issue. This brings up the question of ethical and social responsibility which restrict a manager's actions (discussed in detail later in this chapter).

Constraints imposed by the public. As consumers, the public holds tremendous power over the practices of any organization. The production decisions of any organization's managers depend on public acceptance of their products. If the public cannot be convinced to buy a particular product, this is a constraint imposed by the consuming public. If a company gains bad publicity or is exposed as practicing poor quality control, the public can place a constraint on management action through boycotts or by seeking greater publicity for its point of view. For example, when several hundred consumers had problems with the Audi 5000 automobile and got no positive action from the manufacturer, they took their case to the public (CBS' *60 Minutes*) and were successful finally in forcing Audi to recall the cars and make an effort to correct the problem. A classic example of how a public event—the tampering with capsules—affected management decisions is found in Tylenol. The makers of Tylenol, after suffering and recovering from one episode of product-tampering, experienced a second wave of its capsules' being poisoned. The second episode led them to discontinue manufacturing all their products in capsule form and to develop a new form, the coated caplet which is tamper-proof. Management's action was constrained by public demand for a safe product, and management's action was constrained by a public problem (random product tampering) which forced them to delete their bestselling form of Tylenol from their product line.

Constraints imposed by the actions of competitors. To continue the Tylenol example, other producers of over-the-counter painkillers were forced to follow Tylenol's example and eliminate capsule-form products from their product lines. This represents a constraint imposed by the competition in this case because these other manufacturers were trying not to appear careless in the wake of Tylenol's consumer-oriented action. The so-called air fare war that began with airline industry deregulation in the 1980s is another example of a constraint imposed on management action by competition. Airlines must match competitors' prices in common markets in order not to be beaten. This shows how competition can affect (and impose a constraint on) management's action in pricing and marketing. If a firm holds an important patent, the action of its competition may be restricted. We have seen this in the case of Polaroid and Kodak, where Kodak was forced to leave the instant camera market due to Polaroid's exclusive patent on the camera and process. Few organizations can act without being restricted by the actions of their competitors.

Constraints imposed by labor unions. Management action is limited by the contracts it negotiates with labor unions. These contracts limit management decisions about wages, vacation policy, retirement plans, working conditions, grievance procedures, and employment (including termination) policies. Although labor unions represent only about 17 percent of American employees (in 1986) and they no longer appear to wield the power they once did in negotiating contracts for their members, unions remain a strong force in those industries in which they do exist. The manufacturing industry, especially automobile, textile and steel; the transportation industry; coal mining; all professional sports leagues, and many communications and media industries (such as telephone companies, newspapers, and the television and motion picture industries) remain union strongholds. In these industries, unions have a significant influence on management practices and affect the actions of managers.

Constraints imposed by society. Through its elected officials, society ultimately sets the legal and social climate in which organizations operate. If any segment of society is concerned with product safety, pollution, protection of the environment and natural resources, energy conservation, unfair employment practices, etc., that concern will eventually appear in the form of laws and regulations restricting management's actions.

If an organization or an industry needs particular skills in its work force, it must look to society for the education and skills it needs. If these skills are not available, the decisions of management are affected.

One of the most significant ways that society in general affects management is through the sociological attitudes toward work, profit seeking, and change. Management's actions are restricted by these attitudes and are constrained by how eager people are to work and be supervised.

Constraints imposed by the economy. Economic factors that affect management's actions include the availability of capital, the interest rate, the inflation rate, and other monetary and fiscal policies within government. The Federal Reserve System holds virtual control over interest rates and the money supply. Action by the Fed restricts management's ability to get the amount of money it wants, when it wants it, and at a favorable rate of interest. This can mean management decisions regarding expansion, research and development of new products and techniques, and pricing are affected. The timing of management's decisions and implementation of those decisions can also be affected by the ready source of attractively-priced capital. Management can be forced to fund projects through internal financing if the economic environment is not right for borrowing; and this can be an expensive way to meet financial needs. The price that any organization must pay for needed capital is not in its control, and this lack of control over the cost of capital influences and restricts management's actions.

Significant Contemporary Trends that Affect Management

One of the few constants in society today is change. Managers must remain flexible and be able to adapt to changing attitudes about work and authority, about increasing government intervention with business, about the expansion of markets internationally, about the demands of better-educated and more aware consumers, and about changes in the population that impact the labor force. In addition, managers must cope with the movement of American business away from manufacturing toward a service-oriented economy.

One of the reasons that management is such a challenging career is that managers must be prepared to deal with a constantly changing environment. This means that the success or failure of a service-oriented organization is directly related to the satisfaction of its customers. To satisfy customers, who are the users or purchasers of a product or service, requires managers to stay abreast of changes in society as well as changes in technology which affect their operations. Well designed programs in administration should prepare students to follow contemporary trends in society and adapt to them. For example, the average age of the American population by the year 2010 will be significantly higher than it is today. By 2010 over 65 million citizens will be over age 65. Will managers be prepared to offer the services and products needed and desired by such a large segment of the population? The following sections detail some of the pertinent trends affecting management in all types of organizations.

Statistics on the New Breed Work Force

- Women: 45% of the labor force in 1988; expected to be 47% by 2005.

- African-Americans: 11% of the labor force in 1990; expected to be 12% by 2005.

- Hispanics: 8% of the labor force in 1990; expected to be 11% by 2005.

- Asian and other: 3% of the labor force in 1990; expected to be 4% by 2005.

- White, non-Hispanic: 79% of the labor force in 1990; expected to be 73% by 2005.

- Age: Median age = 36.6 years in 1990; expected to be 40.6 years by 2005.

- Education: Those with 1-3 years of college up from 15% in 1975 to 21% in 1990; 4 or more years of college, up from 18% in 1975 to 25% in 1990; 4 years of high school or less, down from 67% in 1975 to 53% in 1990.

- Jobs Profile: Service-producing jobs are up from 70% in 1975 to 77.1% in 1990 and are expected to be 81% by 2005. Goods-producing jobs are down from 29.5% (1975) to 22.9% (1990) and projected to be 19% by 2005.

- More Affluent: Median family incomes are up from $20,800 in 1980 to $34,788 in 1991 with half of all families depending on two or more wage earners.

- Cost to Employers: The Employment Cost Index (ECI) for civilian workers is up from 100 in June, 1989 to 112.2 in 1991.

- Employed Fewer Hours Per Week: 39 in 1991 vs. 39.3 in 1989 with more paid benefits and more paid holidays.

FIGURE 4-1: CHANGES IN THE WORK FORCE

Sources: Bureau of Labor Statistics, *Occupational Outlook Handbook,* 1992-93 edition, pp. 9-10 and *Statistical Abstract of the United States 1992,* pp. 389, 413-414.

Changing ideas about work and authority. No one has defined work as fun, but today's generation takes such a dim view of work that new terms have been coined to describe it. The old puritan work ethic that work is good and necessary for moral well-being has been replaced by the "new work ethic" and the "new breed" workers, as described in figure 4-1.

The social revolution among young people in the 1960s and 1970s has generated a whole new set of values for American society. Alfred L. Seelye has described the aims of this generation as follows: "Advocates express desire for 'a better quality of life,' defined as a cleaner environment, consumerism, rights of minority groups including women, egalitarianism with emphasis on redressing all economic and social inequities, and more participatory decision making."[1] This can also be described as a revised American dream.

The revision of the American dream may be an outgrowth of the "me generation." It replaces working hard to achieve greater material success with emphasis on mental and physical well-being, balance between work and leisure, greater personal satisfaction, and dissatisfaction with dull, unchallenging jobs.[2] The obvious emphasis is on self-fulfillment and achieving personal happiness.

Some observers attribute the decline in the work ethic to the turn toward a welfare society. Because of welfare programs, food stamps, unemployment insurance, social security and similar programs, it is now possible to survive economically without working. This makes people less willing to work at any job they dislike. A second reason for the decline in the work ethic may be that the advances in technology which have produced such strides have made many jobs boring for workers, particularly people who are better educated. It is a fact that the labor force as a whole is better educated now than it was 20 years ago (see figure 4-1). Further, younger workers do not value pride in work and craftsmanship as highly as older workers; they do not wish to become as involved in company and community affairs; and they are less loyal to a single organization.[3] Couple these factors with an increasing challenge to authority in general, and it is apparent that managers face tremendous challenges in dealing with employees.

The challenges to authority have evolved since the 1960s when draftees challenged the authority of the federal government and refused to serve in the armed forces. The challenge extended to business where the authority to discharge employees has been questioned in various court actions. The old-time manager who was a virtual dictator is being replaced by one who must gain acceptance of his authority before exercising it.

The reasons that authority has been challenged are many. Abuse of power by managers is the most important one. When managers abuse their authority and extend it beyond common sense, such as imposing unreasonable conditions on employees, the power will be challenged. Permissiveness in society in general is a second reason that employees challenge authority. Many people who have authority now decline to use it, and authority not backed with action soon becomes weaker. Finally, scandals in business and government, such as Watergate in the 1970s and the insider-trading scandal of the 1980s, have left people disillusioned with those in power. Followers want their leaders and authority figures to set a proper example and to lead by action not words.

These changes in the attitudes of American workers have brought management many problems. Excessive absenteeism, poor workmanship, high personnel turnover, working at minimal capacity, and other symptoms present distinct problems for management. The overall result of these changes has been the decline of American productivity and America's loss of status in world markets. The challenge to managers today is what can they do to reverse the effects of the new work ethic and how can they restore respect for authority among American workers.

----

[1] Alfred L. Seelye, "Societal Change and Business-Government Relationships," *MSU Business Topics* 23 (Autumn, 1975): 7.

[2] Daniel Yankelovich and Bernard Lefkowitz, "The New American Dream," The Futurist 14 (August, 1980): 14-15 and Daniel Yankelovich, "New Rules in American Life: Searching for Self-fulfillment in a World Turned Upside Down," *Psychology Today* 15 (April, 1981): 35-91.

[3] David Cherrington, "The Values of Younger Workers," *Business Horizons* 20 (December, 1977): 18-30.

Competent professional managers who are people-oriented can overcome all of the negative trends and attitudes in society. Managers have a challenge to become as professional as managers as there are in any other field of endeavor.

Those who follow the new work ethic want challenging and meaningful work in addition to good monetary pay and generous fringe benefits. They also need nonmonetary rewards such as recognition and respect from their peers. One measure which managers can take to make work more interesting it to use job rotation (moving a worker from one task to another). Another device management can use is job enlargement (the worker performs a greater variety of tasks). Both of these can help with the boredom of routine jobs.

Managers must remember that they manage individuals, not groups of people; and they must know their personnel so well that they can align personal goals with organizational goals. This will aid in motivating workers, which is one of management's biggest challenges.

The demand for a different quality of work life leads organizations to offer employees more flexibility in work schedules and to attempt to change the work place to increase worker productivity and satisfaction. The broad concept of quality of work life refers to the way in which work "provides an opportunity for an individual to satisfy a wide variety of personal needs—from the need to survive with some security to the need to interact with others, to have a sense of personal usefulness, to be recognized for achievement, and to have an opportunity to improve one's skills and knowledge."[4]

In addition to placing emphasis on the factors stressed in the quality of work life concept, managers must face other challenges in dealing with the new breed of workers to achieve greater acceptance of managerial authority and to increase worker productivity. Specifically, the new breed of worker expects management to address the social philosophy of **egalitarianism** with direct action. Egalitarianism advocates social, political, and economic equality. Women will enter the work force in increasing numbers, and the gap between the earnings of men and women as well as that between whites and minorities must be addressed and narrowed. More women in the work force (see Figure 4-2) will also spur management to erase the inequalities in status and increase both the number of women in management in general as well as the number of women in higher-level management jobs. Equal Employment Opportunity laws which already exist will be more closely obeyed by management because of the continual efforts of women and African-Americans, and other minorities.

Intervention in business by government. Equal Employment Opportunity laws are just one of the many current laws affecting business. Despite an attempt in the late 1970s and early 1980s to deregulate the transportation, banking, petroleum, and other industries, the overall effect of government regulation of business increased. And the signs are that it will continue to increase as society grows more complex and the rights of individuals need protection.

---

[4] G. Lippitt and J. Rumley, "Living with Work—The Search for Quality in Work Life," *Optimum* 8 (January, 1977): 38.

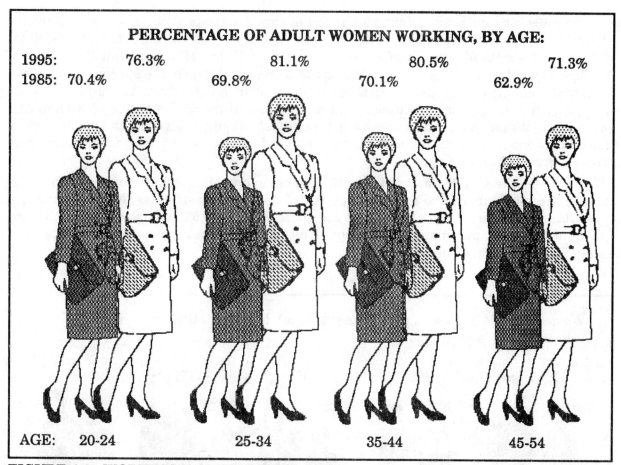

PERCENTAGE OF ADULT WOMEN WORKING, BY AGE:

1995:	76.3%	81.1%	80.5%	71.3%
1985: 70.4%	69.8%	70.1%	62.9%

| AGE: | 20-24 | 25-34 | 35-44 | 45-54 |

FIGURE 4-2: WORKING WOMEN ON THE RISE
Estimates for 1995 predict 59% of all women will be working, compared with 55.4% in 1986

Source: U.S. Bureau of Labor Statistics

In 1991-92 there are more women and minorities in key managerial roles. While the numbers are not large, the trend has been established. Numerous colleges in the U.S. have women as the top administrator, and more African-Americans have been named as managers and executives than ever before. Other minorities are seeing more opportunity in management positions as well although the numbers are small. Being properly prepared for job openings in management is the best way for anyone to gain an advantage in the job market. Preparation begins with education and knowledge of the field of administration.

Forty years ago an employer could advertise a job opening and specify what race, sex and age range the applicant must be. The employer could also pay one worker less than another doing the same job for no certifiable reason. Promotion into management positions for women and minorities was rare. Today, it is illegal to discriminate in hiring on any of the above bases and workers doing the same job are entitled to equal pay. Government regulations, in response to such social movements as the Civil Rights Movement of the 1960s, has on paper eliminated much of this discrimination. The Equal Employment Opportunity Commission, which reports directly to the president, enforces equal employment rights for women and minorities. Under Title VII of the Civil Rights Act of 1964, organizations are required to take **affirmative action** (make special effort, often by establishing special programs, to increase the proportion of women and minority-group members in management positions) to eliminate inequities in the status of women and minorities. While these programs have brought about much change and much paperwork for businesses to comply with them, progress is slow in correcting all the inequities (see Figures 4-3 and 4-4).

By 1992, the U.S. Bureau of Labor Statistics reports that women comprise 45.4 percent of the total labor force and 40.6 percent of the jobs classified as "Managers/Executives/Administrators (*Employment and Earnings,* January 1992). The most reliable estimates of women in pure management positions by 1992 is that approximately 28 percent of all managers are women.

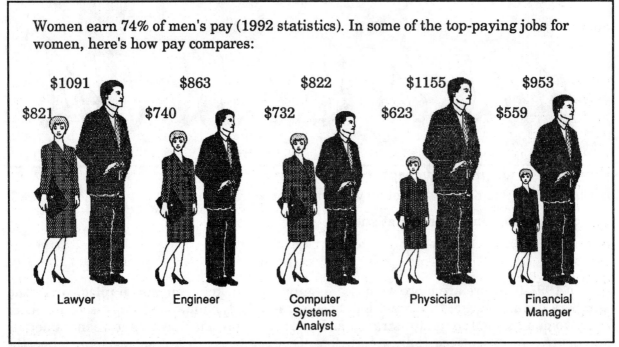

FIGURE 4-3: INEQUALITIES IN PAY AND STATUS (Weekly Salary)

Source: U.S. Bureau of Labor Statistics, *"Employment and Earnings." Jan., 1992,*
          Table 56, p.223.

All businesses are influenced by federal, state, and local governments. Reporting requirements for such activities as payroll (federal, state and local income taxes withheld; social security taxes withheld, and other deductions from paychecks); sales taxes; specifications for safety of work environments; and even starting and ending a business place demands on all American organizations. For an employer, the federal government requires a quarterly report of income and social security taxes withheld from employees'

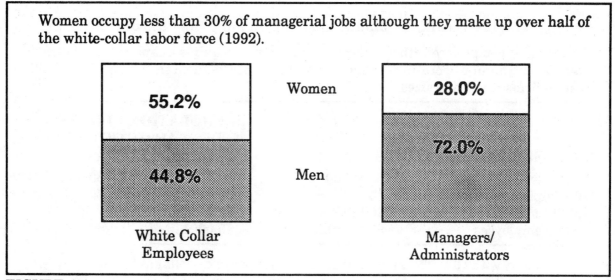

Women occupy less than 30% of managerial jobs although they make up over half of the white-collar labor force (1992).

FIGURE 4-4

Source: Bureau of Labor Statistics, *"Employment and Earnings," Jan., 1992,* pp. 223-225.

salaries—even if the business is small and has only one (perhaps even part-time) employee. As long as a taxable income is paid, the organization (profit-seeking and nonprofit as well) must file this report. And this does not include reports to the state and/or local government, the state labor department for unemployment tax which every employer must report and pay, and possibly reports to the EEOC on changes in employees' status. Figure 4-5 shows how the reporting requirements of government regulation affect different size organizations.

Other government regulatory agencies which have had a major influence on American management's actions in the last 15-20 years are the Occupational Safety and Health Administration (OSHA) and the Environmental Protection Agency (EPS). OSHA was established in 1970 to ensure that a safe and comfortable work environment could be guaranteed every worker. While managers agree that the purpose is sound, not all believe the regulations and requirements themselves are good. OSHA's section in the Code of Federal Regulations is almost 1,500 pages, and managers must be constantly aware of the requirements these regulations place on them and the work environment. The EPA, established in 1970, is supposed to guard the environment against contamination and pollution. It has not been popular when a plant shut down and jobs were lost because the company could not meet the EPA specifications for pollution; but the problem the EPA addresses is a serious one which American managers will have to continue working to correct in partnership with the government.

How does the continued involvement of government in business affect today's managers? Management action is restricted by some government regulations, but primarily it makes the job of a manager more complex and involves the manager in keeping detailed records on hiring, firing and promotions; safety of the workplace and accidents; quotas of women and minorities in various levels of management, and many other facets of day-to-day work.

Identical Compliance Costs Hit Small Firms Harder

Assume that compliance with a government regulation requires a capital expenditure of $50,000 and annual operating expenditures of $5,000. The table shows the effect of this cost on firms of varying sizes.

FIRM SIZE	SALES	REGULATION COST PER DOLLAR OF OUTPUT	
		YEAR 1	YEAR 2
10 employees	$500,000	$0.11	$0.01
100 employees	$5 million	$0.011	$0.0011
1,000 employees	$50 million	$0.0011	$0.00011
10,000 employees	$500 million	$0.00011	$0.000011

The company with 10 workers pays 10 times as much per sales dollar as the company with 100 workers. If you assume that employee productivity rises with company size, which is generally the case, the burden of a fixed cost of compliance on a smaller company is still more disproportionate.

FIGURE 4-5:   HOW GOVERNMENT REPORTING REQUIREMENTS AFFECT DIFFERENT SIZE ORGANIZATIONS

Source: *Inc.*, June, 1980, p. 54.

No one suggests that the government intervention is not necessary, but many managers will agree that compliance with increasing government regulation is an added burden.

Expansion of markets internationally. International competition is not a thing of the future, it is a fact of today's economy. American productivity diminished and the quality of American output slipped so much that many consumers turned to goods produced in foreign countries for satisfaction. An example is the highly popular videocassette recorder (VCR). It is believed that between 75% and 90% of all homes will own at least one VCR in the near future, and none is manufactured in America. American consumers have bought foreign-made products in record amounts in the last ten years, and America's trade deficit has grown dramatically as a result.

The effect of increased international competition on American managers is to force them to become more productive, more efficient, and more creative. America's strength in the international market lies in high technology industries and services.

Factors which have opened international markets include better and faster communication and easier travel to all parts of the earth. Many higher-level American managers will have their jobs complicated by international trade. They must know different languages, the laws of trading nations, customs and traditions of other countries, what the foreign political climate is and other facets of each country with which their organizations trade. In addition, they must remain current on any American tariffs and/or trade agreements affecting each of these countries. Further, many managers will be travelling abroad as part of their duties. Perhaps a middle-level manager in a textile firm has production contracts with foreign manufacturers. He or she will be travelling there to confirm deals, sign formal agreements, and to monitor compliance with the contract specifications. As recent news events have shown us, travel to some areas is not always safe for Americans. This adds a further complication to the manager's job which some "new breed" workers (who are also in management) may decline to accept. So, management can be affected by having difficulty filling jobs for personnel who must communicate and travel internationally.

The rise of consumerism. Today's American consumer is better educated and less willing to accept defective and inferior products than in years past. Since Ralph Nader inaugurated the current trend toward consumer protection in the 1960s, American consumers have demanded better and safer products and have gained a consumer "bill of rights," as published by the Consumer Advisory Council established by President John F. Kennedy in 1962.

Among the rights now advocated by consumers are the following:

The right to safety. Consumers have the right to be protected from dangerous products or those which could become dangerous if misused. Laws require warnings and explicit use instructions.

The right to be informed. Information directed at consumers must not be fraudulent, deceitful, or misleading. The Federal Trade Commission polices advertising to protect consumers from false information. And, the Truth-in-Lending Act of 1969 requires that consumers are clearly informed about the interest rates and terms of loans they make. Care labeling laws give consumers information on the proper care (washing, dry cleaning, etc.) of garments to protect them and maintain any properties of the fabric (such as fire-retardant children's clothes).

The right to choose. Consumers are guaranteed through several trade and antitrust laws that competition will not be unlawfully restrained.

The right to be heard. The Consumer Protection Act of 1975 and the Agency for Consumer Advocacy that it established work to provide consumers a voice in legislative matters affecting them.

Management must clearly take the interest and concerns of consumers seriously when manufacturing products and providing services. Managers will have to focus on increasing product quality to meet the demand of consumers and on providing goods and services desired by consumers. Service-producing industries are not exempt from consumer scrutiny.

A reader poll conducted by *The Atlanta Journal and Constitution* and published on March 1, 1987, shows that 90 percent of the 610 respondents believe service has deteriorated in the last 20 years. This is another consumer alert to which American management must respond or the same factors which have hit the manufacturing industry will also appear and doom the service sector: inattention to quality, emphasis on economies of size rather than on customer satisfaction, and short-term profit orientation.

Figure 4-6 shows how various service industries fared in the reader poll. Management action in the near future must be focused on repairing this careless image with consumers if they wish to survive.

Industry	Good	Bad	No Response
Airlines	55.7%	16.2%	28.0%
Auto dealers	15.6	52.1	32.3
Auto service	8.7	71.5	19.8
Banks	44.6	36.4	19.0
Brokerage firms	20.3	13.8	65.9
Car rental	27.2	16.2	56.4
Department stores	29.3	46.2	24.4
Discount brokers	18.0	50.5	31.3
Doctor/Dentist	47.9	26.6	25.6
Dry cleaning	47.9	26.6	25.6
Electric hookup	23.9	12.6	63.4
Fast food	35.1	36.1	28.9
Grocery stores	45.4	25.6	29.0
Hospitals	27.1	34.4	38.5
Insurance companies	19.8	44.3	35.9
Local governments	9.0	59.3	31.5
Motels/Hotels	44.4	16.7	38.9
Newspapers	49.7	20.0	30.3
Restauranta	35.9	27.2	36.9
Small appliance repair	9.2	29.7	61.2
Telephone hookup	26.1	30.0	43.9

FIGURE 4-6: HOW READERS RATE SERVICE IN THE U.S.

Of 610 respondents, 555 (91% way the quality of service has declined in the past 20 years; 37 (6%) feel it has improved; 18 (3%) believe it has remained the same. Readers blamed poor service on greediness, a lack of pride in one's work, poor pay, a lack of training, and the trend toward automation.

Source: Thomas Oliver, "Studies: Both Workers, Management are at fault," *The Atlanta Journal and Constitution*, March 1, 1987, pp. 1E, 4E.

Changes in population and demographics. Changes in the growth of the population are important to an economy, but of even more importance to management in the future is the demographic makeup of that population. **Demography** is the statistical study of human populations with emphasis on size and density, distribution, and vital statistics. A demographic fact about the U.S. population is that it is growing at record **slow** rates. This, coupled with lower death rates in the U.S., changes the composition of the population: fewer young people, more older ones. Some have dubbed this change in the population the "graying of America," and it has significant implications for management.

These changes in the composition of the U.S. labor force will produce interesting results. Because the baby boom generation will reach middle age in the 1990s, there will be more competition for middle-level management jobs. The low birth rate will shrink the supply of entry-level workers, which could cause labor shortages and raise pay rates in an effort to compete effectively for the best available workers. The retirement age has already been raised from 65 to 70, so managers must be prepared to have older employees who will work longer than ever before. Each of these factors will have to be met with management adjustments.

These population changes also affect the demand for goods and services which management will have to project. It is estimated that the median age in the U.S. will reach 35 by the year 2000,[5] and this means a shift in consumer goods from those aimed at the under-25 generation to the larger middle-age group. Older Americans, both those working and those retired, will comprise a larger market than in previous history, giving rise to new products designed for senior citizens and putting emphasis on products used by them. Gerber Products Company of Freemont, Michigan, a leading producer of baby foods, has seen enough of a trend to diversify into insurance, apparel and trucking. It is also interested in marketing food for seniors, according to spokesman Leonard Griehs.[6] The political clout of the older segment of the population will also grow and have more influence on laws and government.

Figure 4-7 shows the anticipated changes in the population through 1990 for people of working age.

Shift to a service economy. According to the Bureau of Labor Statistics, the service field will lead all others in job growth into the 1990s. Specifically, jobs in the medical services and business services areas will expand. Many service industries are dominated by small, private companies. This limits the need for many levels of management but opens the door to whole industries which provide management services.[7]

Such a trend can lead to more entrepreneurs among the managers of tomorrow. It may be the right match for the personality of the new breed of worker: great satisfaction and no one to blame or answer to except oneself; set one's own work/leisure mix; achieve just as much material success as one desires, etc. It is also a fact that more inventions per firm are produced by small businesses, emphasizing the innovative quality of management and employees.

In the May, 1987 issue of *Inc.*, a list of the 100 fastest growing small public companies was published. It is dominated by service firms, with the leaders long-distance phone companies, broadcasters, medical research firms, and computers. Of the 100 fastest growing small public companies, 55 are service companies.[8]

Managing in the service industry involves the same functions as managing in the manufacturing sector, but there are differences. Managers of service organizations will work more closely with the consumers. There will be fewer middle-level management jobs, since many of these service organizations are small firms; therefore, more empha-

---

[5] "The Graying of America," *Newsweek* 89, February 28, 1977, p. 50.
[6] William Dunn, "New age for the aged," *USA Today*, August 20, 1986, p. 1A, 8A.
[7] Charley Blaine, "Services field leads job growth," *USA Today*, February 24, 1986, p. 1E
[8] Harriet C. Johnson, "Future belongs to services, 'Inc.' says," *USA Today*, April 30, 1987, p. 1B.

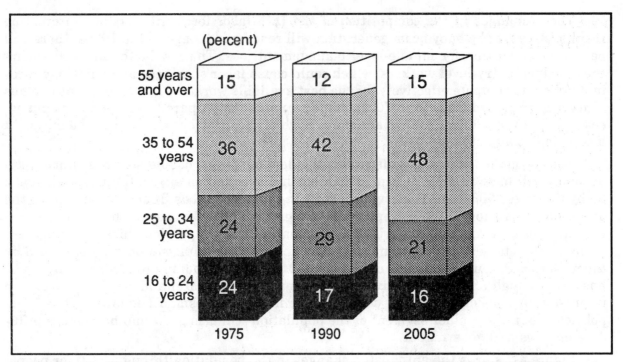

FIGURE 4-7: THE AGE DISTRIBUTION OF THE LABOR FORCE IS CHANGING.

Source: Bureau of Labor Statistics, *Occupational Outlook Handbook, 1992-93 Edition*, p. 9.

sis will be placed on first level managers. In some service industries, it is common for employees to work outside a central office, at home for instance. This makes these employees more difficult to monitor and increases the complexity of the manager's job.

The continued importance of technology. Technology has been the dominant factor in the workplace for many years, and the future shows no sign of its diminishing. Managers do not manage technological forces such as machines, but technology has a significant effect on management. Those managers who work in high technology industries are concerned with research and development and innovation of new machines, new features for existing machines, and other devices. They must also market their inventions. Those managers in industries not directly involved with creating technological advances must be concerned with whether to use and how to use the new technology. People will be affected in either case, as managers will have to determine how much to invest in machinery that replaces people.

Manufacturing managers may soon find their "employees" include robots. Robots themselves will not pose difficult management challenges, but integrating them with people and retraining people who are displaced by them will be challenges for management.

The implications for management involved in technological change are to create and maintain an atmosphere which encourages innovation so that technological advances can be developed. Management must also hone human relations skills to deal with the problems people will encounter when high technology becomes a part of their work environment or displaces them, specifically how to prepare them to accept change and how to retrain employees displaced by machines.

MANAGEMENT'S ETHICAL AND SOCIAL RESPONSIBILITIES

Ethics

Ethical behavior is the focus of much attention today in all types of industry. Government has been caught in illegal and unethical behavior at every level, and such actions have left the people in the United States suspicious and dubious of any controversial government action. There have been scandals in business, such as the insider trading and product manipulation reports widely publicized, that have left consumers wary of nearly all business practices. Religion has suffered its own scandals involving everything from fraud in fund-raising to sexual indiscretions.

Colleges and universities have responded to the challenge by revamping curricula to include courses on ethics, social responsibility and social issues affecting modern people. It behooves managers at any level of any type of industry to become familiar with ethical considerations and develop a code of ethical behavior. If managers do not behave ethically, some governance authority will develop and enforce its own ethical behavior system over them eventually. The demand for ethical action has never been greater.

Ethics is generally considered to be a set of moral values or principles. It deals with what is good or bad and with the moral duty and obligations of individuals or societies. A professional organization may have a "Code of Ethics" to govern the conduct of its members or subscribers. Often ethical and legal conduct are confused. Ethical behavior goes beyond what is legally correct and adds to the behavior a degree of social acceptability. Ethics change with the fluctuating attitudes of society. An example of this is the change in participation in the Olympics. For many years, the United States would not allow any Olympic athlete to be defined as a "professional" in his or her sport. Now, professional athletes can participate.

The difference between morality and ethics is often one of semantics. Morality defines a value structure that limits behavior. Ethics concerns the justification and application of moral standards. Most dictionaries indicate these two words as synonyms.

Making Ethical Decisions

The most widely known and practiced theories of ethics are either based on deontology (the theory of moral obligation) or teleology (the doctrine that ends or results are the true reality in nature). The focus on deontology is on the basic moral good of the action; while teleological ethical theories, primarily utilitarianism, focus on end results or consequences—"maximizing the best effect for the greatest number."

When an administrator in any industry makes a decision, he or she must weigh the ethical implications of both the end results of the decision and the process. Laws, governance organizations and the demands of the general, consuming public may even add the dimension of intention of the decision to these factors.

A model that can be followed in making decisions based on these considerations is shown in Figure 4.8. In this model, four criteria are used to evaluate the ethical quality of a decision. If there is some confusion or conflict among these four criteria, more in-

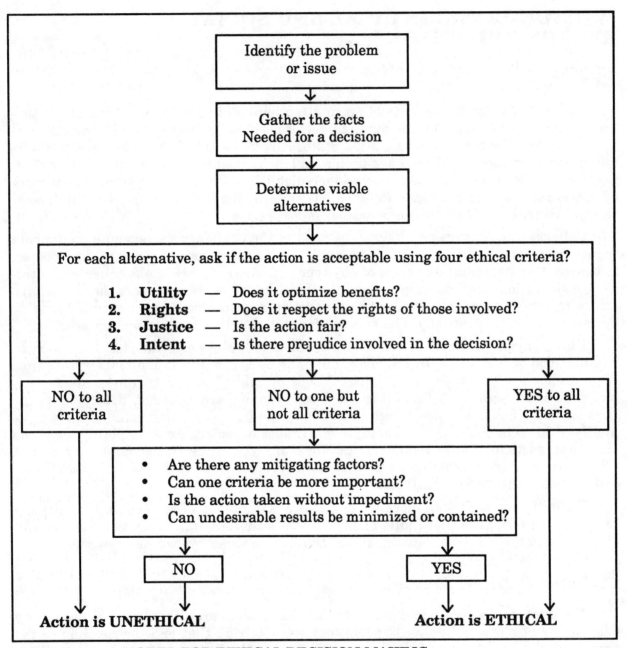

FIGURE 4-8: A MODEL FOR ETHICAL DECISION-MAKING

Based on Cavanaugh, G., *American Business Values*, 2nd Ed.,
Englewood Cliffs, N.J.: Prentice Hall, 1984.

depth analysis must be made on the weighted importance of each factor, the freedom
with which the action is taken, and the prospect of undesirable results. In each instance
of judgment, the ethics of the decision-maker and his or her personal ethical beliefs are
the basis for any consideration of facts and information. After a decision is reached using this model, the decision-maker should always follow-up to determine how closely the
actual consequences or effects of the decision came to those that were expected.

Professional Ethics

Controversy surrounds the concept of professional organizations who develop a self-regulating Code of Ethics for their members. But most would agree that such a statement of professional conduct and expectation would be a step in the right direction.

Such a creed or code is another step toward professionalism. Many factors that affect segments of industries are controlled by legal regulations, but much behavior and conduct depends on the personal ethics of the practitioners. Individuals must consider how strong their own personal ethical values are; their personal integrity and the courage they have in following their conscience; the degree to which ethical behavior is demanded or encouraged in their work environment; and the various role models and mentors that have influenced their attitude and work environment. The professional ethics of any group is merely the sum total of the individual members or practitioners personal ethics.

Social Responsibility

There is no one clear, widely accepted definition of the social responsibility of management. One authority defines it as: "the moral and ethical content of managerial and corporate decisions over and above the pragmatic requirements imposed by legal principle and the market economy."[9] Another source says that it is simply "the duty of business to promote (or at least not damage) the welfare of society."[10] As people consider the concept of social responsibility and ethical behavior in every industry, they should see the complicated factors and issues that arise. For use in this text, however, we will condense the social responsibility of management into acting in the best interests of society in general.

The concept of social responsibility originated with Henry Gantt (refer to management history in Chapter 1) whose humanistic approach to management included industry's responsibility for training workers. Gantt did more to encourage industrial responsibility than anyone before him. Increasingly in more recent years, the public has demanded accountability from all types of institutions.

Management's failure to perform in the best interests of the public had led to bad publicity that eroded confidence and trust in that organization and in business in general. When the public outrage becomes great, the government usually steps in with some type of regulation or punishment.

The most important social responsibilities of organizations, and thus of the managers who make and carry out decisions, are these:

To provide safe products. As we have seen with the Tylenol and Audi 5000 examples, organization are expected to improve the safety of their products or remove the unsafe ones from the marketplace. The public holds the producer accountable if its product injures consumers.

---

[9] Robert H. Bork, "Modern Values and Social Responsibility," *MSU Business Topics*, Spring, 1980, p. 7.
[10] Ferdinand F. Mauser and David J. Schwartz, *American Business* (San Diego, CA: Harcourt Brace Jovanovich, 1986), p. 94.

To provide a safe and healthy work environment. When accidents and injuries on the job reached high levels, the public demanded action. It came in the form of the government regulations (OSHA). Now, the concern management faces about the workplace involves eyestrain from video terminals and other health effects of high technology. In addition, many companies are responding to the social pressure to provide substance abuse counseling and physical fitness programs as part of a healthy work environment.

To protect the physical environment. Since the early 1960s, great emphasis has been placed on conserving resources and eliminating pollution from our environment. Management decisions have been affected by the public pressure and ultimate government regulation which resulted. Many socially responsible businesses have taken this even farther by landscaping plant sites into parklike facilities and doing more than meet the government requirements for pollution control. These actions cost money and must be allocated in plans for construction of facilities.

To provide equal opportunities for women and minorities. We have discussed this elsewhere in this chapter, but many organizations have responded to the public interest in equal opportunity by deliberately filling management openings with women or minorities. Organizations which have well-developed affirmative action programs make them public to gain the favorable reaction. One effect of going beyond government requirements has been a growing number of lawsuits charging reverse discrimination by predominately white males who were bypassed without any other reason. Management must proceed with care to achieve equal opportunity without encountering legal challenges to its actions.

To obey both the spirit and letter of laws—be ethical. The public is demanding that organizations and their managers not only obey laws but also respect the intent of the regulation. If a company chooses to ignore pollution-control requirements that would be more expensive than paying the fine associated with noncompliance, its critics will not be satisfied. The intent of the regulation is to control pollution, not to collect fines; and public pressure will continue to swell until managers are held personally accountable for such decisions. Organizations have the resources to maneuver within the law, but the public now expects more ethical behavior. Ethical behavior is defined as taking the action that is right and just and that conforms to accepted standards for behavior. Increasingly, the public is demanding not only legally correct behavior of managers, but highly ethical conduct as well.

To provide public-service programs. Society demands that organizations give back to the community some of the profits they take. In Georgia, the electric utility, Georgia Power Company, has increased rates dramatically to pay for a nuclear power plant. Public pressure forced them to initiate a program to aid those who have difficulty paying the higher rates. Many companies recycle waste products; others sponsor scholarship programs for their employees' children; and some donate organizational time and talent to the United Way and other charities. Managers who favor these actions believe it advances the long-term best interests of their organizations as well as provides a social good deed.

Not everyone believes that organizations have social responsibility. Economist Milton Friedman, who has repeatedly advocated that the only responsibility business has is to maximize profits, says this:

The only entities who can have responsibilities are individuals; a business cannot have responsibilities. So the question is, do corporate executives, provided they stay within the law, have responsibilities in their business activities other than to make as much money for their stockholders as possible? My answer to that is, no, they do not. Take the corporate executive who says, "I have responsibilities over and above that of making profits." If he feels he has such responsibilities, he is going to spend money in a way that is not in the interest of the shareholders.[11]

Despite the debate over just what social responsibility is and whether organizations have responsibilities, the general consensus is that managers will have to face greater social responsibilities in the future.

Economic Responsibilities of Managers

Most people agree that the primary responsibilities of management are economic: to provide products and services, to provide employment, and to earn profits. Even in non-profit organizations, managers must provide services, employment, and generate enough capital resources to continue operating. Managers in any kind of organization cannot escape economic responsibilities.

To provide products and services. The first economic responsibility of management is to produce and distribute the goods and services that consumers want. Managers must determine consumer needs and wants and then take the action necessary to satisfy them. Since American consumers have great freedom to choose between alternatives, management decisions about production and providing services are complex. Managers must always be alert to changes in consumer preferences and must take quick action to accommodate such changes.

To provide employment. If the private sector of the American economy did not provide adequate jobs for those who can and want to work, the government would have to intercede. In America, private enterprise provides approximately 85 percent of all jobs, with various levels of government providing most of the rest.

The level of employment is a key economic factor. Most economists concur that the maximum level of employment at any given time is 96 percent. When 96 percent of the work force is employed, the economy is at **full employment**. An economic recession occurs when the employment rate is between 90 percent and 96 percent, with the lower percentage indicating the severity of the recession. If employment falls to 90 percent or below, we are experiencing an economic depression. The **labor force** is defined as those people ready and able to work.

Management has a responsibility to make jobs interesting and challenging as well as available. For most people, time spent at work represents one of life's most important facets; so, society expects management to make work psychologically rewarding. It is a challenge to managers to keep jobs interesting and to create new jobs for people displaced by technology.

To earn profits. Profit-seeking organizations cannot survive for long without earning profits. In addition, profits are necessary in the capitalistic economic system to pay taxes; finance growth and modernization; and to fund research and development that leads to new products and improvements in existing ones. Stockholders and creditors pay close attention to profits earned in deciding whether to invest capital or fund projects. Management's first purpose is always to survive, and earning profits is a necessity to achieve this.

In accomplishing these economic responsibilities, management must contend with the current problem of declining productivity. Inflation and energy resources, which have been problems for management in the recent past, are not as prominent in the 1990s.

---

[11] Quoted in Robert A. Dahl, "A Prelude to Corporate Reform," *Business and Society Review*, Spring, 1972, pp. 17-18.

THE CRITICAL PROBLEMS FACING MANAGEMENT IN THE 1990s

The environment of management in the 1990s has one critical problem that is must overcome: declining productivity. Other crucial issues such as inflation and limited and increasingly expensive energy resources have diminished somewhat.

In 1992 there was an oil glut and energy prices were down, but oil remains a nonrenewable resource. Conservation of all limited resources has become a way of life for managers since the energy crisis of the 1970s and will continue to be a prime concern in the future. As decisions are made about production, pricing, business location, expansion, and many other routine matters, energy management programs and alternatives will have to be considered.

The 1980s have seen the severe economic problem of double-digit inflation disappear. But the American economy is still vulnerable to the same forces that started the spiraling inflation of the 1970s and early 1980s. Too much dependence on imported minerals and an uneven economic growth cannot be overlooked. While coastal areas experience economic growth, the midsection of the country does not. Service industries boom, but manufacturing jobs are lost daily because of foreign competition and other factors. Such uncertainty could trigger another surge of inflation, an economic recession, or stagflation. All these economic woes require managers to plan carefully, have contingencies built into plans, and judge information astutely. Information on a wide variety of topics will be readily available to every manager in the decision making process. The ones who can evaluate the facts and make judgments about the predictions and suppositions will gain the competitive edge.[12]

The remaining critical problem facing management is how to increase productivity. To begin to understand how to improve productivity, we will discuss the factors that have combined to slow productivity.

C. Jackson Grayson, head of the American Productivity Center in Houston, a private, nonprofit research foundation dedicated to improving productivity in the U.S., lists these as the problem areas:

- Lagging capital investment
- Lagging research and development
- Negative influence of government regulations
- Required environmental investments
- Age-sex change mix in the workforce
- An increasing shift from agriculture to other sectors
- Drags from major low productivity areas
- Higher energy prices
- Worker alienation
- Poor management and labor attention to productivity
- A series of accidental shocks to the economy
- Stop-go economic policies that create uncertainty about the future
- Inflation
- Wage-price controls and standards
- Work rule restrictions

---

[12] Roy Amara, "Management in the 1980s," *Technology Review* 83, April, 1981, pp. 78-80.

Grayson goes on to prioritize the factors and lists these as the most important to overcome: government regulation, inadequate capital and research and development investments, inflation and stop-and-go economic policies, and management and labor's inattention to productivity.[13]

The productivity problem appears to be equally the fault of government intervention and economic policy and management decisions. Managers have the power to initiate capital investments and to fund research and development programs. Managers also have the most control over the work environment and over the activities of employees.

We have discussed how managers must accommodate government intervention in business and cooperate to create the proper setting for economic growth. Some stabilization in the economy may lessen the effect of changing economic policy, although recent tax law changes will affect investment by organizations in capital equipment and in research and development programs.

A major share of the responsibility for ending the decline in productivity falls to management. Managers must become more professional in carrying out their duties. They must reach individual employees and stimulate that employee's motivation to do better work because the employee wants to perform better. The effect of management establishing a deliberate program of improving productivity will be a more stable economy and a return to international prominence of American goods and services.

How Management Can Adapt to Changes in the Environment

Managers must be aware of the changes in the environment and remain flexible in responding to them. One key to doing this is to plan effectively and to make contingency plans.

In Chapter 5 we will discuss planning in detail, including when and how to allow for contingencies.

Managers can accommodate changes in the environment by gathering and using information well. Internal sources of information are readily available: absenteeism reports, sales data, equipment repair records, quality-control reports and so forth provide managers with valuable information for making new plans and altering existing ones.

Managers can also read newsletters, professional journals, popular magazines, attend trade shows and meetings, join professional organizations, and use other external sources for information about trends and developments in the economy and their industries. Part of the decision-making process which we will discuss in Chapter 6 involves gathering all available facts about a problem before attempting to solve it.

---

[13] C. Jackson Grayson, "The Need for a 'National Productivity Program,'" *Management World* 10, January, 1981, pp. 1, 7.

Summary

The **environment** of management is the sum of all the social, cultural, economic, and physical factors that influence management action. Management authority is limited by various internal and external constraints in the environment. Some of the primary internal constraints are organizational documents, limited resources, organizational guidelines, and customs. External constraints include those imposed by legal and political considerations, the public competitors, labor unions, society, and the economy.

The practice of management is affected by many current trends. Among the most important trends are changing ideas about work and authority, increased intervention in business by government, the expansion of markets internationally, the rise of consumerism, changes in the size and demographics of the population, the shift away from a manufacturing-based economy to a service-based one, and the continued growth and importance of high technology.

There is some controversy about the social responsibility of management and business, but society is demanding more accountability of organizations and managers. Ethical conduct is expected as well. A manager's social responsibility is defined as acting in the best interests of society in general. Ethical behavior translates into doing what is just and right and obeying the spirit as well as the letter of rules, regulations and laws.

Some of the social responsibilities expected of management and organizations are to provide safe products, to provide a safe and healthy work environment, to protect the physical environment, to provide equal opportunities for women and minorities, to act ethically as well as legally, and to provide public service programs.

Controversy does not exist with regard to the economic responsibilities of management. They are to provide products and services, to provide employment, and to earn profits (or generate the funding required to continue operations if a nonprofit enterprise).

Management's most critical challenge today is to stop the decline in productivity and reverse the downward spiral that has crippled American manufacturing. Other problems are dealing with uncertain economic conditions and inflation and managing nonrenewable resources while finding alternative energy sources.

In order to cope with the rapidly changing environment, managers must remain flexible and must master the function of planning, including allowing for contingencies. Above all, American management must become more professional in carrying out the duties and functions of their jobs.

Review Questions:

1. Define the environment of management.
2. List and discuss the internal constraints to management action.
3. List and discuss the external constraints to management action and explain their significance.
4. Discuss the "new breed" worker and the decline in the work ethic.
5. How has government regulation affected management?
6. What does international marketing mean for American management?
7. What do today's consumers demand?
8. How do changes in the size and composition of the population affect management?
9. Define social responsibility and explain what society expects of management.
10. What are management's economic responsibilities?
11. What is the most critical problem facing management today?
12. How should managers adapt to the changing environment?

Assignments for Personal Development

1. The situation for group discussion:

    A well-liked, longtime employee develops AIDS. What is the organization's social responsibility to other employees? To that worker? To the customers? How can you see problems like AIDS and substance abuse, which involve the protection of an individual's right to privacy and confidentiality, affecting the work environment and the job of management?

2. Management has the best opportunity of anyone to solve the crucial current problem of productivity shortcomings. In outline form, list five or six specific steps your organization could follow to improve employee efficiency and productivity.

Incident

THE ORDINARY OFFICE

After working in various clerical and secretarial positions in the local branch office of Mercury Insurance Company, Ruth Calder has been promoted to Office Manager. She will now supervise a clerical operation which processes claims and new policies. None of the work is unusually difficult, but it is detailed and exacting. Most records and standard accounts are kept on computers, and many of the workers under her supervision work at computer terminals all day. Overtime is rare, but management expects claims and new policies to be processed within 48 hours of receipt in the office.

Ruth's new charges are a mixed group of men and women, white, African-Americans and other minorities, and most are veterans of at least six months on their respective jobs. She has worked well with these people for many years, but two problems show up immediately.

The second day after she is introduced by her manager as the new office manager, Ruth catches employee Wayne Smith smoking a definitely unusual cigarette in the employees' lounge. Wayne has also been less productive than other computer operators and is often late getting to work and in returning to work after lunch and breaks.

While this incident is fresh on Ruth's mind, she overhears claims clerk Myoshi Nguyen talking rudely to a customer.

Questions:

1. Identify and discuss the environmental factors found in this office scenario.

2. How should Ruth Calder approach these two immediate problems? Are these employees' actions symptoms of a larger problem which management should address?

Suggested Readings

Anshen, Melvin, ed. *Managing the Socially Responsible Corporation*. New York: Macmillan, 1974.

Cressey, Donald R., and Charles A. Moore. "Managerial Values and Corporate Codes of Ethics." *California Management Review* 25 (Summer 1983): 53-77.

Davis, Keith, and Robert L. Blomstrom. *Business and Society: Environment and Responsibility*, 3rd ed. New York: McGraw-Hill, 1975.

Diebold, John. *The Role of Business in Society*. New York: Amacom, 1982.

Edwards, Owen. *Upward Nobility: How to Succeed in Business Without Losing Your Soul*. New York: Crown, 1992.

Lodge, George Cabot. "Business and the Changing Society." *Harvard Business Review*, March-April 1974, pp. 59-72.

McGuire, Joseph F. *Business and Society*. New York: McGraw-Hill, 1963.

Steiner, George A., and John F. Steiner. *Business, Government, and Society: A Managerial Perspective*, 5th ed. New York: Random House, 1988.

Walton, Clarence C. *Corporate Social Responsibilities*. Belmont, Calif.: Wadsworth, 1967.

CHAPTER 5

THE FUNCTION OF PLANNING

After studying this chapter, **you will know**:
- The importance of the planning function
- The real purpose of planning
- How sound planning benefits the organization
- Types of plans
- What organizational guidelines are
- The relationship between planning and control
- Steps in planning
- The planning process

Introduction

While every manager will make some planning mistakes, the professional managers will minimize these errors. There is no such thing as perfect planning because of the many risks and uncertainties that can occur when plans are implemented. Planning always deals with the future and managers cannot totally foresee nor perfectly predict what can occur in the future. They cannot always, therefore, be prepared for what can occur. The failure to anticipate and prepare for the unexpected is the major cause of planning mistakes.

The information in this chapter will guide a manager toward better planning skills. Studying this chapter and using the techniques suggested can improve planning performance. You must remember that the great managers make fewer planning errors!

The Importance of Planning

Of all the functions of management, planning is the one which anchors all other managerial responsibilities. Planning is a precedent activity: Planning should occur prior to organizing, implementing, controlling and decision making. Sound planning is the activity necessary to achieve efficient utilization of resources and effective attainment of end results. Poor planning or no planning at all by managers generates inefficiency, ineffectiveness, and often leads to the failure of the organization as a whole. Without question, poor managerial planning is the primary cause of organizational failure in the United States.

There is no mystery to the function of planning. Planning is a common sense activity that is futuristic in nature. Individually, we plan our upcoming weekends and vacations, how to spend our money, what television programs to watch and so forth. Organizationally, managers plan for capital expenditures, manpower needs, cash flow needs, growth of sales and market share, introduction of new products and services and many more factors. All of these planning activities relate to the future. All of today's activity is the result of past planning. Tomorrow's or next year's activity will be the result of today's planning.

The future success of an organization correlates closely to the planning skills of the managers running that organization now. An interesting case study illustrating this point involves the K-Mart Corporation.

Top management of K-Mart deliberately planned to change its image from a variety store chain known as S. S. Kresge Company to a discount operation. K-Mart's great success since the early 1960s can be credited to the vision and planning skills of its managers over twenty years ago.[1] Similar organizations which were originally known as variety stores have not fared as well as K-Mart after expanding into discount operations. In fact, several organizations, such as the F. W. Woolworth Company, have closed their discount operations.[2]

Planning is not the only factor that directly affects the success or failure of an organization in the future, but planning does represent the first and most important step in achieving future organizational success.

The Purpose of Planning

The purpose of planning is to formalize objectives and develop a plan to attain these objectives in the desired period of time with a minimum of problems in the most efficient and effective way possible.

This statement of purpose captures the essence of planning. Whether planning is for the long run, short run, departmental, or company-wide, the purpose of planning is the same. Let's look at each point in this purpose of planning statement.

---

[1] "Finally, Woolworth Wields the Ax," *Business Week*, October 11, 1982, pp. 118-119..

[2] "Woolworth's Big Losses at the Top," *Business Week*, January 24, 1983, pp. 26-27; and "Woolworth Is Still Rummaging for a Retail Strategy," *Business Week*, June 6, 1983, pp. 82-83.

Formalize Objectives. To formalize objectives means first to determine what the goals or objectives are; then to submit the objectives in writing to higher management for review and approval. When written objectives have been approved by higher management, lower level managers have the authority to proceed.

Time Standards and Efficiency. Planning to reach your goals or objectives in the desired period of time refers to setting a **time standard**. Time standards should accompany the pursuit of any objective. A time standard should be set at a **level of excellence,** which is a time standard well within the average amount of time usually needed to complete the task. Everyone involved in the implementation of the plan should know the time standard. The key to efficiency when implementing a plan is to produce quality work in the shortest possible time period. Not only does a tight time standard improve efficiency, it also tends to boost the morale of employees performing the work or carrying out the plan. Meeting a tight time standard usually generates a sense of excitement among employees because it denotes that the work is important.

Minimum of Problems. The most effective managerial planners try to formulate plans that, when implemented properly, will reach the desired objective in the proper period of time with a **minimum of problems.** Sound planning does not eliminate or avoid all problems. There is no such thing as a problem-free plan. But, sound planners try to anticipate major problems in advance. When major problems are anticipated, then steps are taken to prepare for them so that the loss or damage will be offset or minimized if they do occur. One of the most common examples of this kind of anticipation is carrying fire insurance on personal property. Another example is cross-training employees to do more than one job. Managers can anticipate bad weather that may keep part of their work force at home. To offset the potential loss of being idle or short-handed, managers can reassign employees to other jobs to maintain basic operations. Managers have no excuses if they fail to anticipate major problems in advance when planning and fail to be ready to offset the effect.

Effective End Results. Sound planning leads to effective end results. This point simply means that the **desired** end result is achieved. How is this accomplished? Sound planners think in advance and answer the questions of who, when, where, how and why. Then, they put these answers in **writing.** When all parties directly involved in implementing plans understand the answers to the above questions and their individual roles in carrying out the plans, the odds are increased that effective end results will be achieved. These points will be discussed in more detail later in this chapter under the topic The Planning Process.

Overall Benefits from Planning

The function of planning as practiced by managers at all levels generates many benefits to an organization:

1. Sound planning gives direction to the efforts of employees.

Can you imagine floating in a small boat in the middle of the Pacific Ocean with no motor, no sails, oars, charts, compass, rudder or tiller? What are the odds you will reach some desired objective? Slim indeed! That's how an organization would operate without planning. Sound planning does give direction to organizational effort through the establishment of purpose, objectives and goals. Detailed plans provide the blueprint for small group and individual effort which, when put together with efforts of others, makes up total organizational effort toward the pursuit of objectives. Policies, procedures, rules and other planning tools provide the influence on employee behavior which makes certain everyone and every part of the whole effort is moving in the right direction toward achieving desired objectives.

2. Sound planning helps an organization determine its own destiny.

Rather than being overly influenced by competitors actions or trends in an industry, or public opinion, or changing technology, an organization can use sound planning to decide what it wishes to do, when it wants to go, what niche in the marketplace it wishes to fill, what product or service it will provide or delete. Simply, through sound planning, an organization determines its own destiny. Managers decide how much control over the future and subsequent events they wish to have knowing they must accept risks associated with their actions. Then they engage in planning the destiny of the organization rather than letting trends and outside forces, over which they have little or no control, do it for them.

3. Sound planning is a key to effective control.

The primary function of controlling is to measure performance against a plan (standard) and take remedial action if the plan (standard) is exceeded. Sound planning leads to effective control programs which minimize wasted efforts, defective quality, loss of time, loss of money and customer dissatisfaction. Clear cut objectives which become standards of control are the result of sound managerial planning. While control programs can be costly activities, the lack of control may cost even more. Without sound controls based on planning standards organizations would not be capable of adapting to rapid change occurring in today's world. Think of all the changes in the economy, in the political arena, in technology and in the social field that directly affect success and survival of organizations. On-going activities of an enterprise which are a result of yesterday's planning must be monitored carefully; and if change has occurred which threatens the attainment of objectives, adjustments must be made to insure greater probability of success. Good control programs are built into plans so that these adjustments to changing conditions can be made at the proper times.

4. Sound planning is essential to managerial success.

If managers are competent as planners, then the organization will most likely be relatively successful in achieving its desired objectives and goals. The emphasis is that sound planning should precede the manager's efforts to organize, implement, control and make decisions. The managerial function of planning permeates all other management responsibilities. Managers plan what organization structure is best for group effort; they plan how the programs of action will be carried out working through the employees (implementation); they plan the standards against which results are compared (control); and they make all of the decisions in all of these functional areas as need arises.

Since the majority of managers are judged on their performance over time, it is logical to conclude that sound planning is critical to achieving desired end results which in turn reflects well on the managers. When managers perform well, the entire organization benefits.

Types of Plans

Classifying plans varies according to the classifier. The jargon in management is not standardized. Most scholars in management agree, however, that plans can be typed as follows:
>Strategic
>Operational
  •Single use
  •Standing
>Functional
>Short-run and long-run

Strategic plans are those that are developed and designed to achieve the broadest objectives of the organization. They encompass every aspect of activity and are directly related to the primary reason the organization exists. Often these plans are called master plans.

Operational plans are those that are very detailed in content and are used in carrying out the strategic plans. Operational plans can be divided into two main types: Single use plans and standing plans.

Single use operational plans are designed to implement programs of action that likely will not be repeated. Once these plans have achieved a specific objective they are withdrawn from further use. For example, designing a plan to enlarge and renovate executive offices would be a single use plan. The most common single use plans are programs, budgets and projects.

Standing operational plans are those that exist to guide managerial actions when organizational activities repeat. For example, a manufacturer may have a standing plan to follow when production managers order additional raw materials. Standing plans are established to provide managers a standardized and consistent way of handling similar, repetitious occurrences. Standing plans use policies, procedures and rules to guide managerial actions.

Functional plans are plans classified by their use or function. The most common types are marketing plans, manufacturing plans, finance plans and human resource plans. As an example, marketing plans may include how to obtain a larger share of the market; how to advertise more effectively; how to distribute finished goods more efficiently. Functional plans often overlap and interrelate because each major activity is interdependent with every other one. Sales plans, for example, may relate to and affect human resource plans.

Short-run and long-run plans are plans that are classified by periods of time. Although there is no standard period of time which identifies either plan, one-year or less time span is generally considered short-run; longer than one year, long-run.

Short-run plans can have pitfalls. Organizations that pursue short-run objectives intensely may overlook long-run consequences. It is also true, however, that the achievement of short-run goals often is critical to succeeding in the long-run. An organization such as United Way definitely is interested in reaching its annual fundraising objective (one year plan or short-run plan), but it is also interested in surviving and being needed in the long-run.

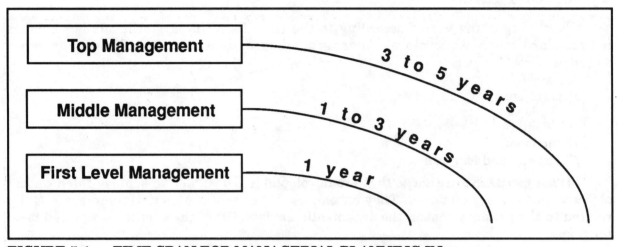

FIGURE 5-1:   TIME SPAN FOR MANAGERIAL PLANNING IN
                SMALL ORGANIZATIONS

Long-run plans may be from three to five years in relatively small organizations; while in large organizations, such plans may span twenty to thirty years or more. Top management usually formulates long-run plans along with setting long-run objectives.

Roger Smith, former Chairman and Chief Executive Officer of General Motors Corporation, stated in a speech to The Economic Club of Detroit how General Motors is preparing for the long-run future. In his speech, entitled "The 21st Century Corporation," Mr. Smith explained the acquisition of Electronic Data Systems and Hughes Electronics:

> ...A major reason for bringing our three firms together was to create a computer-integrated 21st Century Corporation such as I've described. Each of the entities—General Motors, EDS, and Hughes has unique properties and strengths which complement the others. We offer each other special synergies, which we hope to use for mutual competitive advantage.[3]

Long-run planning is essential if companies in a highly competitive environment wish to survive over the next twenty to thirty years. As one would expect, General Motors, the largest organization in the United States and in one of the highly competitive industries, is preparing now for the next century. Shouldn't every organization prepare for the long-run as well?

---

[3] "The 21st Century Corporation," speech by Roger B. Smith before The Economic Club of Detroit, September 6, 1985.

Organizational Guidelines

Regardless of the type of plan, the success of the plan depends on how well it is implemented by the personnel involved. Part of the responsibility of management when formulating plans is to provide guidance to the efforts at implementation. This is accomplished by introducing what is known as organizational guidelines as part of the plan.

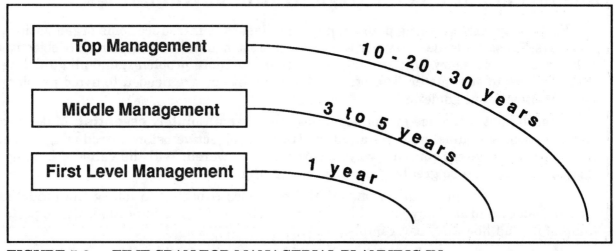

FIGURE 5-2:   TIME SPAN FOR MANAGERIAL PLANNING IN
LARGE ORGANIZATIONS

Organizational guidelines are anything managers introduce to influence the behavior of personnel working to achieve objectives. Organizational guidelines are popularly known as "red tape," and include such examples as rules, procedures, policies, systems, methods, codes, regulations, and many more. There are distinct differences in each of these types of organizational guidelines.

Rules are guidelines that demand certain employee action with no room for interpretation. Rules have no flexibility and are the most specific type of organization guideline. In effect, rules dictate certain employee behavior. Example: No employee shall smoke on company premises at any time.

Procedures are a series of job tasks or steps to be taken in chronological order to achieve a certain end result. Example: Purchasing requisition procedure which requires filing a form and completing steps in a sequence.

Policies are the most general of organizational guidelines. Policies are flexible, subject to interpretation, and are introduced primarily to influence managerial actions. Example: Promotion from within policy.

Systems are a group of coordinated procedures that are followed to achieve a major end result. Example: A manufacturing system such as automotive sub-assembly lines feeding into a final assembly line to produce a finished product—the automobile.

Methods are guidelines that specify an exact way to do a particular task. Example: The exact way an employee should perform one step of work in a procedure.

Codes are standards of professional practice or behavior. Example: An organization requiring employees to dress in a prescribed manner.

Regulations are an authoritative issue of guidelines for employees to follow originated by higher management or government. Example: Safety regulations issued by OSHA.

Recommendations for Organizational Guidelines

Effectively implementing plans requires managers to introduce some organizational guidelines. These guidelines, however, can create confusion and slow achievement of objectives if they are not necessary. Unclear guidelines generate more problems, and all guidelines are expensive to administer. Therefore, a few suggestions are needed to avoid problems with organizational guidelines.

First, do not introduce guidelines unless they are absolutely **essential**. Make sure that the proposed guideline is required to attain the objective before introducing it. The question of cost versus return always needs to be answered. Will the value of having a particular guideline be greater than the cost of administering it?

Next, keep the guidelines **simple.** All employees expected to follow the guideline should understand it. They should know why such a guideline is needed, the expected value of it, and how they can comply with it.

Third, put guidelines in **writing**. To avoid communication breakdowns, such as possible misunderstanding, put the guidelines in writing. Provide each affected employee a copy with an explanation of the value of the new rule, procedure, etc. Have meetings to explain the new guidelines. In effect, justify totally the addition of new guidelines (red tape).

Finally, **audit** guidelines periodically. Every year or two management should audit or review the guidelines in their area of responsibility. Anything that has been introduced over time to influence and control employee behavior should be inspected. If any of the prescribed guidelines are no longer serving the original purpose, they should be eliminated or modified. Sound managers work continuously to simplify work effort. Removing obsolete guidelines is an essential first step in simplification.

Planning and Control

In 1917, Henry L. Gantt, one of the scientific management pioneers (see Chapter 1 for more discussion), developed the Gantt Chart. The Gantt Chart is a control technique still used throughout the world today in more sophisticated form than his original. The original chart identified individuals and machines along the vertical axis, and measured individual and machine output along the horizontal axis. Also included on the horizontal axis was a time scale. By setting work or project standards for a set period of time and by posting work output for a set period of time, a manager could quickly determine whether the work standard was being met or exceeded, and in what period of time and by what quantity. The chart was relatively simple in form and use, but Gantt revolutionized American management's thinking about planning and control with its introduction.

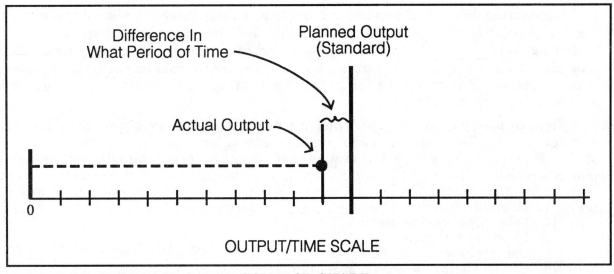

FIGURE 5-3: MODIFIED GANTT CONTROL CHART

Control programs are designed to measure performance against plans (standards). Therefore, the functions of planning and control are closely related. Control compares what is actually happening to what management hoped would happen when they developed their plans. Any significant deviation from planned results requires corrective or remedial action by management.

Managerial plans to product a produce of a certain quality, in a set quantity, and at a specific per unit cost may have programs of quality control, production (quantity) control, and financial (cost) control to guarantee that the planned objectives are met.

Another control device which is important to managers in all types of organizations is budgeting. Budgeting directly relates planning to control. Formalized budgets are part of the planning process and are used to determine expenditures for the allocation of resources in implementing plans. When planned budget allocations are exceeded, it is usually a time for managers to take some corrective or remedial action.

Theoretically, if the functions of planning, organizing, implementing and decision making were performed perfectly, there would be no need for the control function. This does not happen in the real world; however, sound planning does minimize the scope of the control function.

Steps in Planning

Suppose an organization wishes to double its revenues over the next five years, or an organization wishes to reduce its internal operating costs over the next three years. What are the steps to follow in achieving these goals? The first step is to develop a detailed plan of action that focuses on the goal.

Developing a detailed plan of action requires that management consider all the facts and variables that can affect future performance and make pertinent decisions based on this information. While a generalized plan can give some direction toward the achievement of goals, it is much better to develop a detailed plan of action that specifies who is to do what, when, where, how, and why. As stated before, sound planning will not eliminate all problems or guarantee success, but sound planning does increase the chances of success. The key is to consider a full range of possibilities and decide in advance how to deal with them within the plan.

Steps in planning, sometimes called **the planning process**, are not in a perfectly sequential order. The steps can be arranged in any order depending on the practicality of the situation. Here is a typical sequence of steps to follow in developing a detailed plan of action:

1. Generate ideas
2. Select tangible objective(s)
3. Inventory your resources
4. Conduct necessary research
5. Review alternative courses of action
6. Select a course of action
7. Establish a time standard
8. Anticipate major problems in advance
9. Determine your organization structure
10. Decide on essential organizational guidelines
11. Formalize a program of control
12. Blueprint your plan of action
13. Implement the plan
14. Evaluate the results

The Planning Process

These fourteen steps in planning are called **The Planning Process**. This process is extremely useful as a guide when developing specific plans. Students can use the process to plan vacations and fraternity parties. Managers use this process to plan the introduction of new products and/or services plus any other facet of organizational activity. Entrepreneurs use the process to plan opening their own businesses.

The planning process is a logical, common sense approach. Adhering to the process does not guarantee the success of your plan, but it does reduce the risk of failure. Each step is explained in detail.

Generate Ideas. This is probably the most overlooked step in formal planning. Higher management needs to encourage lower level managers to generate ideas from employees, customers, students, competitors and any other source available. If the organization has a system for reviewing ideas, through a refinement process the best ideas surface for consideration and intense scrutiny. Ideas which have realistic possibilities can be selected and put into tangible (written) form to become working objectives. Virtually every product or service used by organizations today or produced for consumers began with a new idea. Great organizations are not created by accident; they tend to do something better than their competitors. It all begins with ideas.

Select tangible objective(s). From a review of the ideas generated, tangible objectives are selected. Once selected, the idea(s) need to be approved by higher management and put in writing to avoid confusion about the planning effort which follows (steps 3 - 14). These objectives should be clearly described, concrete, achievable goals.

Inventory your resources. Planning efforts can be wasted unless a careful inventory of resources is conducted prior to the investment of much time or money. The purpose of the inventory is to determine the availability of monies, employee skills, materials, the state of equipment, what management talent is available, and much more. Essentially, the inventory analysis compares the resources available for undertaking a project against what will be needed for maximum success in reaching the objective.

Conduct necessary research. Research takes the form of investigation, review or study about the project or subject under consideration. When planning to reach set objectives, it may be necessary to conduct market research, financial analyses, review historical patterns of the organization, or simply read some literature on the topic. Fast food organizations such as McDonald's always test market new products prior to a full scale introduction. The purpose of research is to uncover potential problems, verify the feasibility of the planning effort, acquire facts pertinent to the subject or project, identify trends, and specifically to determine whether the objective of the plan is realistic or not.

Review alternative courses of action. There are always several possible directions to take in the pursuit of a planning objective. When planning a vacation in Florida, you consider whether to fly, drive, take the bus, or go by train. All can be viable options. The same viable options face managers in charge of planning. A necessary step is to list optional courses of action with the significant advantages and disadvantages associated with each option. The facts should be considered without personal bias or emotional whims when addressing the advantages and disadvantages of options.

Select a course of action. Unless there are announced restrictions that temper a choice of courses, an objective decision maker will select the course of action that appears to be the freest of problems. This will usually be the course of action for which the advantages most outweigh the disadvantages. Factors which influence this decision and do temper the choice are cost considerations, budget limitations, resources available, governance restrictions and requirements, organizational policies, and many other internal and external considerations, any one of which may limit the options it is feasible to take. An ever-present consideration for the planner is to select the course of action that most ideally will achieve the desired end result in the most efficient and effective way possible.

Establish a time standard. A critical step in planning is the determination of the period of time in which the desired end result must be reached. This is called the time standard. Time standards should be set at a level of excellence which focuses all effort in the proper direction, but some leeway must be allowed for the unexpected: breakdowns, bad weather, absenteeism, slow deliveries, etc. Personnel involved in implementing a plan will be more highly motivated if the time standard is tight. Implementing a plan and successfully attaining the desired objective in a shorter period of time than the standard is a measure of efficiency.

Anticipate major problems in advance. Failure by managers to anticipate major problems in advance is the primary cause of planning failure. Planners cannot anticipate every problem that might occur before implementing a plan; however, potential major problems that have a high probability of happening should be considered and preparations for the occurrence made. Managers deal with two types of problems in planning: **risks** and **uncertainties**.

Risks are events or occurrences that managers should be able to predict with reasonable accuracy and plan for so that if they do occur, the loss or damage can be offset. Routine risks that must be anticipated are death of key people, bad weather, a shortage of supplies, breakdown of equipment, trends in the economy, and hazards such as fires and burglary which can be covered by insurance.

Uncertainties are events or occurrences that a manager cannot anticipate with accuracy and plan for so that if they do occur, the organization will either be damaged or benefited. A benefit to the organization is called a **windfall**; damage, a **disaster**. Examples of uncertainties from history are the Persian Gulf Conflict in 1990-91, the oil crisis of the 1970s and its subsequent economic upheaval, the surprising recent outbreaks of measles on several college campuses, and the accidental discovery of penicillin. Perhaps many uncertainties should be anticipated, but the probability of certain events happening is so low that no one foresees them. Such things as earthquakes in an area previously not known for having them or a building's being hit by debris from outer space are examples of low probability uncertainties.

The significant point to remember about risks and uncertainties, is that the occurrence of an unanticipated risk reflects badly on management. But the occurrence of an uncertainty affecting the organization, either as a benefit or as a disaster, is not due to good or bad management.

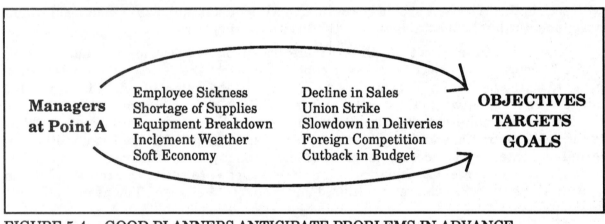

FIGURE 5-4:   GOOD PLANNERS ANTICIPATE PROBLEMS IN ADVANCE
AND ARE PREPARED FOR THEM

Determine your organization structure. The success of implementing a plan often relates directly to the way the effort is organized. Sound planning includes deciding who is to do what, when, where, and how. Assigning the critical jobs to people with the right qualifications; designing an open communication system; pinpointing responsibility; delegating appropriate authority to accompany responsibility; and coordinating all effort to develop a synchronized flow of work is fundamental to sound planning.

Decide on essential organizational guidelines. Organizational guidelines have been defined previously as anything management introduces to influence employee behavior toward the achievement of objectives. Some guidelines (red tape) may be established early in the planning stages to help control and influence the implementation of the plan. For example, certain rules may be set covering the purchase of equipment [No purchases exceeding $500.00 may be made without approval by a higher manager] or rules may be established regarding who can drive a company vehicle [No one with a speeding ticket or DUI in the past three years may qualify]. Some procedures, policies, rules, and systems incorporated into the plan can be of great value if they help expedite activity and minimize confusion or problems when a plan is implemented.

Formalize a program of control. Preventing the implementation of a plan from getting "out of control" is the purpose of this step. Control programs are designed to measure the actual progress against the planned or expected results. This kind of program should be carefully developed before introducing it as part of the implementation of a plan. Control programs can be costly, but they are valuable if they prevent major problems. Ideally, planners should decide on the control program, perhaps having several critical points throughout the plan where results are measured against the planned progress. The control program should be relatively simple, easy to administer, but still accurately measure the progress at critical stages. The lack of formal controls can cause small problems to blossom into major flaws and can destroy an otherwise good planning effort.

Blueprint your plan of action. When all decisions have been made about each of the steps in the planning process, it is time to write out the complete plan. Writing everything down so that the final plan clearly shows the sequence of steps, the timing of activities, who is to do what, etc. is good common sense. A plan in writing is easier to understand, easier to follow, and easier to change if conditions so dictate.

At this stage in the planning process, you have developed a **master plan** which is ready for implementation once approved by the necessary and appropriate management levels.

Implementation. Put the plan into action! This is easy to say, but may be difficult to do. Individuals involved in implementing the plan, no matter how sound the plan may be, may prove to be effective barriers to good end results. To make sure this is not the case, managerial planners must have competent, motivated individuals carrying out the plan. Those who will implement the plan must be convinced that the plan is the best approach to undertake, need to be totally supportive of the objectives, and should understand clearly the importance of the part they play in the plan. Without question, plans are only as good as the individuals who implement them.

Evaluation. The purpose of evaluation is to review the planning and implementation effort. From this process of evaluating, the strengths and weaknesses of the plan and its implementation will be revealed. Information which will allow managers to do an even better planning job in the future result from the evaluation step, regardless of the degree of success of the current plan.

Long-Term Planning

Another kind of planning is described as **long-term** or **long-range**. Upper level managers are more responsible for this kind of planning. Executives of large organizations often set goals and develop plans for the next five to twenty years. Part of their job is to provide direction to the efforts of all personnel so that there is a common purpose in the present as well as the future. Executives of smaller organizations view the long-term as three to five years, but they plan for the same reasons as those in larger organizations. This type of planning responsibility applies to top managers of **any kind of organization**: government, education, business, profit-seeking and nonprofit. The vision and acumen needed to plan effectively for the long-term are facets of the conceptual skill that characterize successful top managers.

In this section we take a closer look at the job of the executive who must formulate plans for the long-term. These people are called **strategic managers**.

Strategic Management

Strategic management can be defined as *the process of managerial decision making and implementation of plans that directly affect the quality of performance and survival of an organization in the long-term.*

Historically, the study of management has focused on the effective use of internal resources to achieve desired end results. This is still important today for operational managers and those responsible for reaching established short-run objectives. Over the last twenty years, however, top management has given much more attention to the environmental factors that affect an organization's future performance. This is necessary when formulating sound strategy.

Strategic management includes long-run planning, strategy formulation, strategy implementation, managerial decision-making, and the monitoring and control of implemented plans. Today, top level managers are often called strategic managers, while middle- and first-level managers are called operating managers. Every level of management is important; but those managers who are responsible for the quality of performance (and survival) of an organization in the long-run are the strategic managers who consider external or environmental factors as well as internal resources when they plan.

George Steiner and John Miner state that, "The emphasis on strategic management as distinct from operational management reflects the growing significance of environmental impacts on organizations and the need for top managers to react appropriately to them."[4]

Another view of strategic management is provided by Thomas L. Wheeler and J. David Hunger: "The study of strategic management emphasizes the monitoring and evaluating of environmental opportunities and constraints in light of a corporation's strengths and weaknesses."[5]

---

[4] George A. Steiner and John B. Miner, *Management Policy and Strategy* (New York: Macmillan Publishing Co. Inc., 1977), p. 7.

[5] Thomas L. Wheeler and J. David Hunger, *Strategic Management* (Reading, Mass.: Addison-Wesley Publishing Company, 1984), p. 4.

Both of these statements reflect the need for strategic managers to consider both internal and external factors as they plan for the long-term and formulate strategy.

A good example of strategic management where both internal and external factors have been considered in formulating plans involves Apple Computer, Inc. In early March, 1987, Apple Computer, Inc., introduced a second wave of Macintosh computers that are expected to intensify competition among personal computer makers and create a true alternative computer system to the IBM Personal Computer. These two machines—the Macintosh II and the Macintosh SE—are the first Apples that will be able to run programs written for IBM personal computers and compatible machines.

Many businesses and consumers had avoided Apple machines because they were not compatible with IBM and lacked special features found on other machines. When the new machines were introduced, Mr. John Sculley, Apple Chairman, President, and Chief Executive Officer, said, "There is no power on earth like an idea whose time has come."[6]

Strategic Planning Defined

Strategic planning is a job function of strategic managers which has many different meanings. Management literature abounds with various definitions of all management topics, including strategic planning. The variations result from semantics problems (different interpretations of word meanings).

Here are several definitions, from leading authorities in the field of management, of strategic planning:

Strategic planning involves an organization's most basic and important choices—the choice of its mission, objectives, strategy, policies, programs, goals, and major resource allocations.[7]

Strategic planning comprises the process of setting common purposes, goals, and objectives for the enterprise, breaking them up into specific plans and policies for the operating level and securing the necessary resources to put the plan into action.[8]

Strategic planning is the 'management of change.' It is a decision-making process, based on empirical evidence and analytical studies, that provides the basic direction and focus of the enterprise.[9]

Now look at the common elements in each of these definitions. All stress the importance of making decisions and choices today which will affect the organization in the future. Strategic planning is long-term in outlook and direction but is based on knowledge currently available.

---

[6] Robert Snowden Jones, "Apple Unveils Office-Market Computers," *Atlanta Journal*, March 3, 1987, pp. 1D & 8D.

[7] John H. Grant and William R. King, *The Logic of Strategic Planning* (Boston: Little, Brown and Company, 1982), p. 3.

[8] Alan J. Rowe, Richard O. Mason, and Karl E. Dickel, *Strategic Management and Business Policy* (Reading, Mass.: Addison-Wesley Publishing Company, 1982), p. 6.

[9] T. Mitchell Ford, *Long Range Planning*, Vol. 14, No. 6 (December, 1981), pp. 8-11.

The definition of strategic planning we will use in this text is the following:

Strategic planning is the process of determining an organization's long-term goals and objectives in compliance with its mission and formulating the proper plan of action (strategy), policies and programs which insure that sound decisions will be made about internal resources and environmental factors that affect all effort to achieve the desired end results over the long run.

Inherent in strategic planning is that the processes and plans should strive to meet goals and objectives in the most effective and efficient way possible.

Why Strategic Planning?

If you will review what happens to an organization over the long-term without strategic planning, then you can identify the reasons for it. Without strategic planning an organization is like a ship without a rudder, engine, sails, or compass. There would be no direction, no course to follow, no protection, and no goals or objectives to achieve. You would not know if you had achieved anything, and the organization would be adrift, subject to environmental factors that could not be controlled.

Strategic planners, like all planners, anticipate the future, but strategic planners look farther ahead. They define the purpose, set the course, anticipate problems, prepare for contingencies, evaluate the environment, formulate plans of action (strategy), structure the organization properly, and introduce the policies and procedures needed to implement the plans. Good strategic managers also evaluate and control strategies once they are implemented as an on-going part of the process.

The common sense objectives of good strategic planning are the following:

1. Increase the odds that the firm will survive over the long-term
2. Increase the probability that the firm will more nearly achieve its stated objectives
3. Increase the possibility of operating more efficiently and effectively
4. Provide a plan for harmonizing the activities of all elements within the organization toward its stated mission
5. Provide a long-run planning framework within which short-run plans can fit and be used to move the plan toward culmination
6. Become the model for continued organization growth and expansion.

It makes sense for managers to formulate short-term (operating) plans and follow them to achieve specific objectives. But these operating plans must conform to some type of overall scheme that leads the organization somewhere. This is the purpose of strategic planning: a grand plan that forms the boundaries which guide organizational activity toward the attainment of long-term goals and objectives (those set five or more years into the future).

An organization must have both kinds of plans to survive. Strategic planning by nature and purpose requires more conceptual skill of the manager. Thus, top level managers generally tend to be the strategic planners.

The Strategic Planning Process

While there is no sacred sequence of steps to follow in strategic planning, a practical approach is listed below. (Note that the steps might vary depending on the size and nature of the organization, the kind of industry, the organization's history, the volatile nature of the industry or environment, and many more factors.)

Step 1:   Define the goals and mission of the organization.
Step 2:   Identify the long-term objectives.
Step 3:   Review the existing strategy to achieve these goals.
Step 4:   Evaluate current environmental factors.
Step 5:   Inventory the organization's resources.
Step 6:   Identify strategic strengths and weaknesses of the organization.
Step 7:   Compare current strategy against current information.
Step 8:   Formulate new strategy if needed.
Step 9:   Develop policies, procedures, and programs to accompany new strategy.
Step 10: Implement and control the strategy.

Step 1: Define the goals and mission of the organization. Logic dictates that a firm know where it wants to go and why before it develops detailed plans and a strategy. Where a firm wants to go, we call **goals**. Goals provide the sense of direction that influences all organizational efforts. For example, the goal of a firm may be to become number one in industry sales.

Why an organization wants to achieve its goals relates to its **mission**. The mission of an organization evolves from its particular, unique characteristics; from its philosophy or culture, and is a function of its reason for existing. The organization may exist to achieve a reasonable net profit and to survive. But its mission may be to provide the finest possible product quality and services among competitors so that it not only will reach its goal (become number one among competitors), but will also achieve its purpose of existence (being profitable and surviving). To do this, the organization must establish a mission which all employees understand and endorse.

The goals and mission of the organization should be in writing. They should be formal statements that clearly focus the direction of all effort. The goals and mission should be based on the uniqueness of the organization. The uniqueness is the "edge" that the organization has or is trying to develop which will enable it to achieve its goals effectively and efficiently.

Written mission statements may be generalized and vague or formal and detailed. The latter is preferred so that employees, customers, patrons, members or other interested parties who read it have no questions about the direction of effort and the unique qualities of the organization that set it apart from others of its type.

A mission statement can be of particular help to an organization in recruiting employees from the lowest league level all the way through the top level. A mission statement for a health or fitness club should define its target market and encourage members to join.

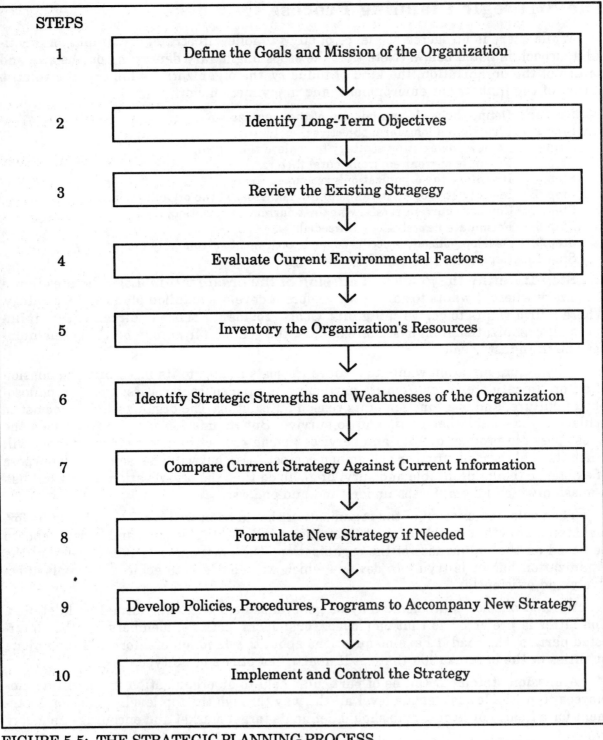

FIGURE 5-5: THE STRATEGIC PLANNING PROCESS

Step 2: Identify Long-Term Objectives. The purpose of strategic planning is to formalize long-term objectives. Then, through the process of analysis, research and strategy formulation, implement plans that allow an organization to achieve its objectives in an efficient and effective way. A major influence on the determination of specific long-term objectives is the mission of the organization.

The mission provides purpose and reason for the organization to exist, and it includes the general organizational goals. Objectives, however, are more specific than goals and can be more easily quantified to make measuring progress simpler.

Identifying long-term objectives is the second step in the strategic planning process.

Step 3: Review the Existing Strategy. A further step in formalizing strategic planning is to review the existing strategy. Questions such as these must be answered: What are the current objectives? What plans are being or have been implemented to achieve these objectives? Is this current strategy viable and compatible with existing resources, environmental factors, and current objectives? The answers to these kinds of questions tell the organization if conditions have changed enough to warrant formulating a new strategy.

One test strategic managers can use to evaluate the need for changing strategy is whether performance (end results) meets the original objectives. Any significant difference between the two suggests a review of the existing strategy and probable implementation of a new one.

Step 4: Evaluate Current Environmental Factors. A major step in strategic planning is evaluating the environmental or external factors that can affect management's plans and decisions. This activity is often called an environmental analysis.

Strategic managers who stay current on changes in the environment have a valuable attribute called **awareness.** That is, they know what is changing in the political, social, technological, and economic arenas. Collectively, all managers directly involved in strategic planning must have awareness. Knowing the current trends in the important environmental areas is critical to the formulation of sound strategy.

Major technological advances such as the development of microprocessors for computers a few years ago can have a major impact on the plans and long-term objectives of an organization. Certainly specific legislation enacted at the local, state or federal level can alter plans and decision. In the social sphere, the great influx of foreign-born people into the American work force and in the market place can affect everything from employee relations programs to advertising decisions. And economically, managers need to maintain a current sensitivity to economic indicators (such as the consumer price index, the prime rate, unemployment figures, inflation rates and more) as well as international factors (such as OPEC's actions and any trade or tariff changes with trading countries).

These are relatively simple examples to emphasize the need for managers to stay current on a wide variety of environmental factors. It is important to remember, however, that an organization's strategy cannot respond to every change or event in the environment. Critical factors must be identified and watched. Not every move or action will affect the organization, but those that impact the formulation of strategy must be monitored. This is where some managers become brilliant and others fail. Thorough analysis of the key factors in the formulation of strategy is a must.

Step 5: Inventory Organization Resources. Early in the strategic planning process, an analysis of internal resources must be conducted. This means taking an inventory of the strengths and weaknesses of the organization.

The purpose of inventorying internal resources is to isolate the significant strengths, often called the competitive advantages, which can be used more effectively in formulating future strategy.

Specifically, an inventory of internal resources should answer questions such as these:

1. What are the skills and capabilities of our personnel?
2. What is the state of our physical resources plant, equipment, etc.? Is it updated; properly maintained; and are we using it at full capacity?
3. Are our work layout and space needs being met in every functional area so that we can operate at maximum efficiency?
4. Do we have sufficient funds to support our efforts to achieve desired objectives? Is the cash flow adequate? Can and do we have sources available for additional funds for short-term and long-term needs without costly delays?
5. Are activities and resources properly controlled to insure conformance to whatever standards must be met (nondiscrimination laws, regulatory guidelines, safety standards, etc.)?
6. Have we clearly identified the organization's competitive advantages and disadvantages?

Step 6: Identifying Strategic Strengths and Weaknesses of the Organization. Strategy is also called a **master plan**. Reviewing the master plan that has been followed to achieve current results should identify the significant strengths and weaknesses of that strategy.

A list of strategic strengths of the organization might be in order. For example, during the past eighteen months the organization may have had personnel totally enthused about their activities; more than willing to work extra hard, if necessary; sensitive about the quality of their performance; and excited about the status and future of the organization. This major strength should be used by the organization in a positive way in formulating plans. But if a major weakness in the strategy is revealed by the organization's performance, an overall problem with the strategy may exist. The effort and enthusiasm of personnel may have resulted in little, if any, success to the organization if, for example, the organization is overmatched by its competition or severely underfunded.

An objective review and listing of all strengths and weaknesses of any strategy that have developed during operations explains why results have been good or bad. Organization strengths and weaknesses, however, are relative to that of the competition.

An effective analytical tool to implement this step in strategic management is "SWOT" analysis. In "SWOT" analysis, the planner lists the organization's internal **Strengths** and **Weaknesses** and external **Opportunities** and **Threats**; then, evaluates these factors.

Step 7: Compare Current Strategy Against Current Information. Results obtained by following current strategy suggest whether the strategy is adequate or needs to be modified. A wide difference between organization performance and strategic expectations emphasizes the need for new strategy. Changes in the environment or in internal factors may have prevented the attainment of expected or desired objectives.

Following the first six steps in the strategic planning process will provide much information about the organization's mission, goals, objectives, environmental factors, internal resources, strategic strengths and weaknesses, and more. When all this information is reviewed, strategic managers know what the current strategy is, what is good and bad about it, and how the organization has performed using it. Now the strategic managers need to know if a new strategy is needed.

In order to determine the overall effectiveness of the current strategy and the need or desirability of changing to a new one, the following questions must be answered:

1. Are the organizational objectives still the same?
2. Is there new information available today, environmental or internal, that has not been considered previously and may affect future performance?
3. Do we have any better means of analyzing current information than was available when the current strategy was formed and does sharper analysis affect the projections and/or conclusions reached earlier?
4. Are our competitors likely to change their strategies? Are we well-informed about the strategies used by our competitors?
5. Is current performance within acceptable deviations from desired results? Are we satisfied with our current performance under the current strategy?

Answering these questions compares current strategy with current information and indicates whether a new strategy is needed. Figure 5-6 summarizes the reasons for altering strategy.

Step 8: Formulate New Strategy if Needed. In Step 7, it was determined whether a new strategy is needed. If management decides performance has not met criteria or if changes in the environment or internal factors dictate a change in strategy, then managers must review alternatives and set a new strategy.

Choosing among alternatives must be related to maximizing organizational strengths or minimizing organizational weaknesses or related to objectives which, if achieved, will show improved organizational performance.

Strategic alternatives should be realistic options that parlay the strengths of the organization into greater success in achieving predetermined objectives.

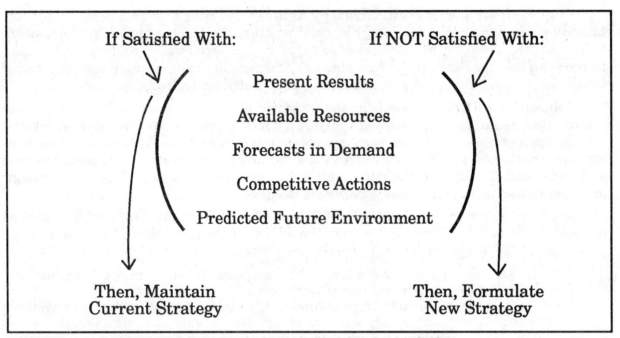

If Satisfied With: If NOT Satisfied With:

Present Results

Available Resources

Forecasts in Demand

Competitive Actions

Predicted Future Environment

Then, Maintain   Then, Formulate
Current Strategy   New Strategy

FIGURE 5-6: MAINTAIN CURRENT STRATEGY OR CHANGE?

When strategic managers must select among alternative courses of action, they should evaluate each option. New strategy should be right for the organization with regard to the following:

1. Internal consistency
2. Consistency with the environment
3. Appropriateness in light of available resources
4. Satisfactory degree of risk
5. Appropriate time horizon
6. Workability[10]

Internal consistency refers to the strategy's being compatible with internal policies and organization goals.

Consistence with the environment suggests that the selected strategy, which includes plans, policies, tactics, etc., be compatible with governmental regulations, industry trade practices, patron expectations, competitors' actions, and any other outside or external factors that influence strategic planners decisions including ethical and social responsibility considerations and union agreements.

Appropriateness in light of available resources refers to how realistic and appropriate the strategy is considering funding available, competency of personnel, physical facilities, and so forth.

---

[10] Seymour Tilles, "How to Evaluate Corporate Strategy," *Harvard Business Review*, Vol. 41, No. 4 (July-August, 1963), pp. 111-121.

Satisfactory degree of risk emphasizes that all strategy implementation has risk associated with it. How much risk management wishes to expose the organization to in pursuing the objective is the crucial question. Ideally risk is calculated for each strategic alternative under consideration. The degree of risk any organization takes with a particular strategy is a function of the soundness of the strategy and the resources of the organization. That strategy finally accepted should be the one that meets or most nearly meets the degree of risk which the organization defines as acceptable.

Appropriate time horizon means that every strategy should be accompanied by a time standard so all involved know when certain results are to be achieved. The time horizon or standard should be realistic in view of the internal resources and environmental factors but set at a level of excellence.

Workability means simply that if the strategy implemented produces the desired results, then it works. But how do you evaluate strategy for workability without encountering risks? The answer is that you will never really know until you apply the strategy.

Step 9: Develop Policies, Procedures, Programs to Accompany New Strategy. A strategy is composed of a plan or plans which, if followed, will provide direction toward the attainment of predetermined objectives. Strategic managers develop the plans which consist of programs, procedures, policies, and many more forms of organizational guidelines.

A program is a statement of activities that need to be implemented to accomplish a plan. Programs are the action oriented part of strategy.

Procedures are a series of steps or tasks in a logical order. Procedures detail how certain specific results are to be obtained. Procedures are parts of a program.

Policies are general guidelines to influence the behavior of all personnel. They have flexibility and room for interpretation built into them. Policies are important parts of programs which are the substance of strategies. Policies guide and influence management actions toward organization objectives but provide latitude for interpretation and adaptation to changing situations or conditions.

Other organizational guidelines (also called "red tape") may be essential to the formulation and implementation of a good program and sound strategy. Budgets, rules and systems are examples of guidelines that must be included in specific programs.

Step 10: Implement and Control the Strategy. The implementation of strategy activates its component plans and programs. Sound strategic planning should deliver excellent end results; however, managers can insure the performance of the strategy by reviewing all facets of the plan—programs, procedures, budgets, policies, objectives, tactics, etc.— before initiating action. In addition, management must answer such questions as these:

1. Are all personnel involved thoroughly educated and trained for implementing the strategy?
2. Is the proper organizational structure in place to generate coordination of effort and efficiency?
3. Are required resources on hand and readily available for effective utilization?

Once these points have been checked and compliance satisfied, the strategy can be implemented. Thereafter, the control function becomes the manager's chief role.

Control *is the function of measuring actual performance against the expected results or the desired standard.* Programs of control must be included in the formulation of strategy. At critical stages of progress, a quantitative evaluation should be made.

A comparison is made between results achieved and results desired, and any unusual deviation pinpointed. These lapses in the implementation of the strategy require managerial action.

Such managerial action may be a product redesign, an adjustment in ticket prices, a change in personnel or reassignment of personnel, a change in the time and/or location of an event to draw a larger crowd, or any number of other options.

Also, at critical stages of progress, management should evaluate whether the strategy is being implemented **as designed**. Failure to do this can generate poor performance without the strategy's being the reason and lead to faulting the strategy erroneously. One consequence of failing to implement the strategy properly is unnecessarily changing a strategy that has not been accurately tested first.

Summary

Planning is the management function that precedes all other functions. Sound planning is the basis for good organization, implementation, control and decision making. Poor managerial planning is the number one cause of organizational failure.

The purpose of planning is to formalize objectives and develop a plan to attain the objectives in the desired period of time with a minimum of problems and in the most efficient and effective way possible.

Overall benefits to the organization from sound planning are:

1. Sound planning gives direction to the efforts of employees.
2. Sound planning helps an organization determine its own destiny.
3. Sound planning is a key to effective control.
4. Sound planning is essential to managerial success.

There are many ways to classify plans. The most common classifications are by strategic, operational, functional, short-run and long-run. Operational plans may be single-use or standing.

Organizational guidelines, commonly called "red tape," can be defined as anything management introduces to influence employee behavior toward the achievement of objectives. Common examples of guidelines are rules, procedures, policies and systems. There are many more. Four suggestions are made to managers about introducing organization guidelines:

1. Do not introduce guidelines unless they are absolutely essential.
2. Keep the guidelines simple.
3. Put the guidelines in writing.
4. Audit guidelines periodically and eliminate any which are no longer needed.

The planning and control functions are closely related. Control programs are designed to measure performance against plans. When actual performance deviates significantly from planned performance, corrective or remedial action is taken.

There are fourteen steps in planning to achieve a specific objective. These **steps are:**

1. Generate ideas
2. Select the best ideas and make them tangible objective(s)
3. Inventory resources
4. Conduct necessary research
5. Review alternative courses of action
6. Select a course of action
7. Establish a time standard at a level of excellence
8. Anticipate major problems in advance
9. Determine your organization structure
10. Decide on essential organizational guidelines
11. Formalize a program of control
12. Blueprint the plan of action
13. Implement the plan
14. Evaluate the effort after implementation.

Evaluation is the review of what happened, good and bad, so that the managers can do an even better job of planning in the future. Together these fourteen steps are called The Planning Process.

Strategic management is long-term planning not operational or tactical planning which is relatively short-term. Upper level managers do long-term planning and are called strategic managers. Long-term planning usually covers three to five years, but it can be for as long a time period as ten to twenty years.

Strategic management is defined as the process of managerial decision making and implementation of plans that directly affect the quality of performance and survival of an organization in the long-run. Strategic managers, also called strategic planners, focus their attention on long-run planning, strategy formulation, strategy implementation, managerial decision making, and the monitoring and control of implemented plans.

Strategic planning is defined as a process which involves the following: determining an organization's long-term goals and objectives to conform to its mission and formulating the strategy, policies and programs that insure reaching the desired end results in the long-run. The strategy, policies and programs guide decision-making so that internal resources and environmental factors can be used in the most efficient and effective way to achieve predetermined goals and objectives.

A strategic planning process is outlined and discussed. This process, when followed by strategic managers, leads to the formulation of new strategy as required and includes the implementation and control of such strategy.

The steps in the strategic planning process are the following:

1. Define the goals and mission of the organization.
2. Identify the long-term objectives.
3. Review the existing strategy to achieve these goals.
4. Evaluate current environmental factors.
5. Inventory the organization's resources.
6. Identify strategic strengths and weaknesses of the organization.
7. Compare current strategy against current information.
8. Formulate new strategy if needed.
9. Develop policies, procedures and programs to accompany new strategy.
10. Implement and control the strategy.

New strategy formulated should be right for the organization and should be evaluated by these criteria:

1. Internal consistency
2. Consistency with the environment
3. Appropriateness in light of available resources
4. Satisfactory degree of risk
5. Appropriate time horizon
6. Workability

A generalization managers should heed is that sound long-term planning, using the strategic planning process, will produce sound strategy which, if followed, will yield the best possible results in the future based on information available today.

Review Questions

1. Define the purpose of planning.
2. Why is it stated that planning is the primary function of management?
3. Explain the close relationship between the functions of planning and control.
4. Operational plans may be standing plans or one-use plans. What is the difference between the two?
5. What are the four suggestions to managers about organizational guidelines (red tape)?
6. List the steps in planning (The Planning Process).
7. Distinguish between organizational "risks" and "uncertainties."
8. Explain how a "windfall" differs from a "disaster."
9. Outline a classification of types of plans.
10. What are the overall benefits to an organization from sound planning?

Assignments for Personal Development

1. Using the planning process, outline the steps to follow in planning your family's vacation to Disney World.
2. List four or five external conditions in the economy today which will have a direct impact on long-term planning by your organization's top management.

Incident

OPPORTUNITY UNLIMITED

Carlton Cabot, a bespectacled, slightly graying, thirty-eight-year-old native of Boston, is a middle management executive with the Global Reaper farm equipment manufacturing company. His primary field is finance (he holds an MBA in finance from a top Ivy League university), and his responsibilities in this company have largely been budgeting, forecasting and financial systems. Carlton is reserved, but aggressive and ambitious; and he has held the same position at Global for his entire five year tenure there. So far, he has been reasonably satisfied because his work suits his training and preference and the location of the home office (Hartford) is highly agreeable to his New York-born, socialite wife and their two children. Cabot is a little squeamish as he rushes into the President's office for an urgently called meeting.

As Cabot takes a seat in front of the President's desk, he glances around at other company top managers. Then, the President begins:

> Carl, we have been extremely impressed with your work in the controller's area. You have proven to be incredibly accurate in your planning, forecasting and budgeting. I am sorry we have taken so long to recognize your performance, but we have a challenging position for you now that has all the prestige and rewards you have earned. We have chosen you to be the head of the new Brute Tractor Division. You know what great hopes we have for this little home tractor. The possibilities for this equipment in suburban lawn care and rural gardening are unlimited! The division is based in Topeka, and you will need to go there immediately and begin to set up regional managers and organize your people—hire them, everything. Here are your tickets for Topeka on tomorrow morning's plane. Don't worry about the moving expenses—we'll sell your home here and pay for all the expenses. I'm sending Ed Leech from sales with you to help for the first few days. I am personally very proud of you! I know you want to get home and get started packing. Good luck!

Cabot picked up the ticket, shook hands with the President, and slowly headed back to his own office to sort out what had just happened. He realized that turning down such a chance would be like resigning from the company, and the job market was too tight even to consider that. He began to think of the thousands of details he needed to pull together and of all the work it would take to make the promotion successful. Then he picked up the phone to call his wife and prepare her.

Questions:

1. Do you think Cabot is qualified for this position? Why?
2. Put yourself in Cabot's shoes and develop a plan of action for his first few months in Topeka.

Suggested Readings

Carroll, Stephen J., Jr., and Henry L. Tosi, Jr. *Management by Objectives: Applications and Research*. New York: Macmillan, 1973.

Dyson, R. G., and M. J. Foster. "Making Planning More Effective." *Long-Range Planning* 16 (1983): 68-73.

French, Wendel L., and Robert W. Hollmann. "Management by Objectives: The Team Approach." *California Management Review*, Spring 1975, pp. 13.22.

Gluck, Frederick W., Stephen P. Kaufman, and A. Steven Walleck. "Strategic management for Competitive Advantage." *Harvard Business Review* (July/August 1980): 154-61.

Humble, John W. *Management by Objectives in Action*. New York: McGraw-Hill, 1970.

Naor, Jacob. "How to Make Strategic Planning Work for Small Business." *S. A. M. Advanced Management Journal* (Winter 1980): 35-39.

Steiner, G. A. *Managerial Long-Range Planning*. New York: McGraw-Hill, 1963.

Yavitz. Boris, and William H. Newman. *Strategy in Action: The Execution, Policy, and Payoff of Business Planning*. New York: Free Press, 1984.

CHAPTER 6

SOLVING PROBLEMS AND MAKING DECISIONS

After studying this chapter, **you will know**:
- The definition of decision-making
- The distinction between problem-solving and decision-making
- What are programmed and nonprogrammed decisions
- Three conditions of uncertainty
- Major decision-making approaches
- Steps in the rational decision-making approach
- Planning tools to aid problem-solving and decision-making (forecasting, MBO, budgets and ZBB)
- More about management information systems (MIS)

Introduction

Every manager confronts problems and makes decisions. Decision-making is the essential activity that justifies the existence of managers. Formulating plans, structuring an organization, implementing programs and controlling activities all involve continuous decision-making.

Solving problems is another expectation of managers. Without problems there would be no reason to have managers. Solving problems requires an analysis of facts and information that leads to determining a course of action (making a decision).

This chapter presents some tools and techniques which can aid a manager as he or she plans, analyzes and decides what action to follow. Typically, sound planning precedes sound decision-making, and most often the best managers are the most effective decision makers. They are the ones who achieve the desired results most effectively and efficiently.

A distinction should be made between problem-solving and decision-making although the two are usually grouped together.

Problem-solving involves determining the proper response to a situation which is judged to be nonstandard or unacceptable. Decision-making involves selecting a course of action among alternative choices.

Other subjects in the chapter are planning and decision-making aids including using management information systems (MIS).

This chapter is of special value to managers who interrelate with many different groups of people. "People relationships" often generate problems which require careful analysis of many factors as a prelude to making a decision to optimize results.

DECISION-MAKING RESPONSIBILITY

Within the formal organization, managers make a majority of the decisions. While individual nonmanagement employees may choose a best way to do a task from their available choices or workers may proceed with their work according to their own self-determination, managers make the significant decisions, including the decisions to allow the employees this type of freedom.

The autonomy to make decisions depends on the individual manager's level of authority; the nature and tradition of the organization; the personalities of bosses, peers and employees; and the expectations or pressure placed on a manager by his or her superior managers. One cardinal rule managers must remember is that every decision must be based on what is good for the whole organization. Making decisions that benefit one group of employees or oneself, but not the organization, are a good way to lose a job.

Perhaps the most difficult situation a manager faces in his or her career is determining a course of action when it is good for the organization or department but the choice conflicts with the action the manager would prefer personally. Nonmanagement employees must realize that when they become managers, they become the organization and every action they take should be for the benefit of the organization.

Managers make many different kinds of decisions. Some affect the entire organization and other decisions may be routine such as deciding if an employee can leave work early. Whatever the magnitude of the decision, all decisions are important and carry some degree of risk.

Types of Decisions

There are several ways to describe the types of decisions managers must make. Depending on the situation, decisions may be considered **programmed** or **nonprogrammed**.

Programmed decisions are those that are repetitive and routine. The decision is influenced by some traditional habit or practice, a defined rule or set procedure. "Red tape" in the organization dictates the decision to make when problems are routine. For example, when supplies must be ordered, a purchasing requisition procedure outlines the steps that one must follow. There is an employment process that a candidate for a vacant position must follow when under consideration for hiring. Programmed decisions based on predetermined **decision rules** allow managers to concentrate on the unusual problems and decisions rather than worry about handling these routine matters. Many of the decision rules are included in employee manuals which clearly state action prescribed in certain situations. Decision rules, carefully developed, can eliminate wasted time in the decision-making process.

Nonprogrammed decisions are those that apply to unusual problems or situations that are unique or have never occurred previously. Generally higher level managers handle these problems and decide what to do. Situations requiring nonprogrammed decisions are those that require special consideration. Most of the major problems managers face will require nonprogrammed decisions which incorporate risk.

Programmed	**Nonprogrammed**
When to pay overtime	How to overcome low employee morale
How to purchase supplies	Improving the organization's image
Determining employee holidays	Gaining support of the stockholders
Hiring new employees	Selecting the right product line
Who drives organization vehicles	Storm damage to facilities

FIGURE 6-1: EXAMPLES OF PROGRAMMED AND NONPROGRAMMED DECISION SITUATIONS

Conditions of Uncertainty

Managers are required to make decisions that affect the future based on today's climate and information. Managers attempt to achieve stated goals and desired end results at some future time with each decision made in the present time. Today's decisions do not always result in meeting the goals. The amount of information available to managers at any time varies widely. Circumstances change rapidly, and no person or organization operates in a static environment. The dynamics of the environment dictate that varying degrees of uncertainty accompany decision-making. The primary conditions of uncertainty are **certainty, risk** and **uncertainty**.

If a manager knows exactly what will happen when a decision is made, the manager operates under conditions of **certainty**. Under a condition of certainty, the manager has accurate, factual information on which to base a decision. The outcome is known in advance. While the condition of certainty may be more theoretical than actual since nothing in the future can be absolutely guaranteed, the probability of predicting the outcome relative to the other conditions of uncertainty is much higher (see Figure 6-2).

Risk is a condition under which a manager can predict with reasonable accuracy future occurrences and assign relative probabilities to them. Gathering information as a basis for predicting probabilities may be costly so some type of value analysis must be made by the decision maker to determine if the cost of information will be more than offset by the outcome. A reasonable probability can be assigned to most of these factors, and the decision maker can proceed.

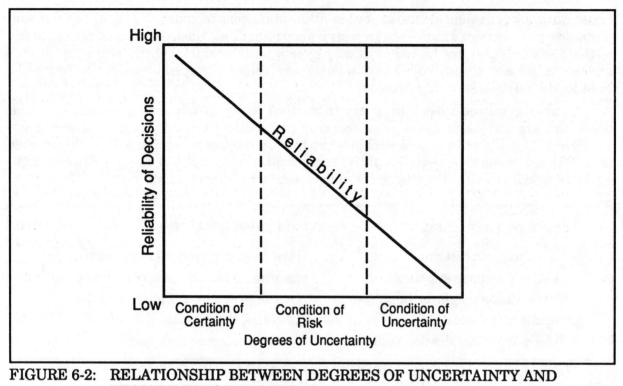

FIGURE 6-2: RELATIONSHIP BETWEEN DEGREES OF UNCERTAINTY AND
RELIABILITY OF DECISIONS

CERTAINTY	RISK	UNCERTAINTY
• Ordering office supplies	• Predicting the weather	• Employee resignations
• Granting a pay increase	• Life expectancy	• Acceptance of a new product
• Faxing a message	• Normal employee attrition	• Starting a new business
• Availability of monies in bank account	• Risk of injuries	• Anticipating revenues ten years in advance

FIGURE 6-3: TYPES OF DECISIONS UNDER CONDITIONS OF UNCERTAINTY

Uncertainty is a condition which exists under which the manager has little or no information. There is no accurate or totally reliable way to calculate objectively the probabilities. Managers, however, still must use subjective reasoning or a "feel" of the situation as a basis for decisions. Decisions made under conditions of uncertainty carry a high degree of unreliability (refer to Figure 6-2). It is a responsibility of managers to attempt to anticipate uncertainty as much as possible and prepare to offset its effect. Such ability to calculate and prepare for these situations is a reflection of the quality and capability of the manager and decision maker.

The Nature of Problems

It is clear that managers face existing problems that they must handle. Other problems, however, must be defined by the managers. Finding and anticipating problems can be an opportunistic activity. Preventing a problem from occurring may be a cost-saving action. Finding a problem may in reality be an opportunity to bring about gain to the organization beyond normal expectations.

Henry A. Mintzberg, Duru Raisingham and Andre Theoret distinguish among crises, problems and opportunities. Their research indicates that crisis decisions are usually triggered by a sudden, single event (a fire, death of a top manager, bankruptcy of a key supplier, for example) that requires immediate attention. Problems become evident through a stream of ambiguous and frequently verbal data stimulated by the accumulation of multiple events. Opportunities are often evoked by an idea or single, non-crisis event. When handling problems and opportunities, managers accumulate and process information until they reach a certain threshold. When that threshold is reached, the manager is prepared to make a decision. The threshold varies among managers and with the nature of the decision being made.[1]

Remember that problems not handled appropriately can prevent an organization from reaching its desired objectives.

DECISION-MAKING APPROACHES

Many decision making approaches are used by managers for the purpose of achieving desired results. Some are laughable; others are more objective. No approach to decision-making, however, can guarantee a correct solution to general management problems. A **general management problem** is any kind of problem within an organization about anything so long as people (the human element) are part of the problem. General management problems account for about ninety (90) percent of the kinds of problems that managers face daily versus technical or nonhuman problems which represent ten (10) percent of a manager's daily problems.

Where the variables in a problem can be quantified, often a **mathematical** or **quantitative** method of decision-making is used. Accountants, architects, engineers and quality control specialists are typical of personnel who employ quantitative methods in performing their daily tasks. Examples of quantitative decision-making methods are linear programming, queuing theory, simulation models, Program Evaluation and Review Technique (PERT) and Critical Path Method (CPM).

Another decision-making approach is the **intuitive approach**. Every manager has made decisions on the bases of hunches and/or feelings at some time. The decision to hire an applicant for a job usually is determined at the last stage of the personnel selection process by a manager who uses largely "feel," intuition or personal judgment. There is no information available that can absolutely predict whether any job applicant will become an outstanding employee if hired. Figure 6-4 lists some of the intuitive approaches to decision-making used on occasion by all managers.

---

[1] Henry A. Mintzberg, Duru Raisingham, and Andre Theoret, "The Structure of 'Unstructured' Decision Processes," *Administrative Science Quarterly*, 21, No. 2 (June 1976), 246-275.

Based on:

• Hunch	—	"We'll take the next exit."
• "Gut" feeling	—	"I've got a feeling this is wrong."
• Vibes	—	"Something tells me he is not be be trusted."
• Emotion	—	"I know we can't afford it but I want it."

FIGURE 6-4: EXAMPLES OF INTUITIVE DECISIONS

The Rational Approach to Decision-Making

Since decision-makers are people whose actions and decisions are influenced by many things (time of day, food intake, weather, attire and the environment in general), a rational decision-making approach is presented. The use of this approach does not guarantee a more correct decision or recommendation in every case. What the rational decision-making approach does guarantee is that, on average, a manager will make sounder decisions and recommendations with this approach than if he or she uses some other approach when confronting **general management problems**.

Decision-makers are people, and people are not totally rational and objective when analyzing problems every time. The use of the rational approach to decision-making is an effort to offset the influence of biases, tradition, emotion and all other personal and environmental factors which can warp decisions. The rational decision-making approach forces the manager to focus on a more logical and more objective method to making decisions. It involves the use of the scientific method, a seven-step approach which is mentioned in Chapter 2 "Science of Management" (the application of the scientific method to general management problems leading to problem-solving and decision-making).

These are the seven steps in the rational decision-making approach:

1. Clearly identify the fundamental management problem
2. List all the facts pertinent to the problem
3. List alternative courses of action to solve the problem
4. List advantages and disadvantages of each alternative (evaluate)
5. Review all of the above
6. Draw conclusions, make recommendations and/or decisions
7. Follow-up after the decision has been implemented to ascertain if the desired results have been achieved.

Step 1: Clearly identify the fundamental management problem. This is a critical step. No progress can be made in any organization unless the fundamental or causal issue is defined and overcome, eliminated or modified. Symptoms of causal problems must be separated from the fundamental problem in order to effect a conclusive solution. Employee absenteeism or tardiness may be causing delays and costly difficulties, but the underlying or cause problem leading to this symptom must be identified before corrective action can be significant and lasting. Fundamental management problems are those that have occurred in the past; are occurring now; and more than likely will show up again within the organization in the future. Threats or punitive action may temporarily stem the absenteeism, but no truly effective solution will be found until the fundamental reason for the employee's attitude is identified and addressed.

Step 2: All factual data and pertinent information should be gathered prior to continued analysis. Because factual data may be limited, the rational decision-making approach sometimes is called the subjective decision-making approach. Using factual data is important but facts can be scarce when analyzing general management problems.

Step 3: The identification of alternative courses of action refers to the choices of action a manager has to eliminate or overcome the fundamental problem. If a manager has difficulty finding alternative courses of action, it may indicate that the manager does not have a problem to solve. All real management problems have several ways of being handled. Situations which many people call problems, but where nothing can be done about them, are really conditions that exist that create a negative atmosphere. Each alternative carries risks and must be evaluated for its potential effect on all phases of the organization's effort. Many managers forget that doing nothing about an existing problem is always one alternative.

Step 4: Listing advantages and disadvantages of each alternative is something nearly every individual goes through when making a thoughtful personal decision. Questions such as to buy or lease; rent or purchase; keep a current job or try to find a new one or accept an offered one are examples. The purpose of Steps 3 and 4 is to force a manager or individual to review all sides of a problem and all consequences of any action before reaching a conclusion.

Step 5: Review all of the above is a suggestion for managerial decision-makers to slow down and carefully rethink everything one more time before implementing a decision. This step does not suggest a long delay, but it does emphasize that a conclusion drawn now may not be the same as one drawn tomorrow. Wise decision-makers allow a little time to pass before implementing important decisions. The old saying, "Haste makes waste" has some validity.

Step 6: After Step 5, if a manager feels comfortable with the analysis and review, he or she draws conclusions and makes a decision or recommends a course of action to higher management for implementation.

Step 7: Following up after a decision has been made is an act of a truly professional manager. Decisions should not be implemented and left unattended. It behooves the manager to check on the effect of the decision and measure results against expectations. In this step managers take corrective or remedial action if necessary.

Group Decision-Making

Most decisions are made by individuals although it is not uncommon to find groups making decisions. Examples of group decision-making include the United States Congress and state legislative bodies, committees, corporate boards of directors, trustees of nonprofit organizations and juries in the legal system. The great advantage of this approach is the pooling of thoughts, experience and ideas of many to provide a consensus. The major disadvantages are that the approach can be time consuming and the group decision nearly always is based on compromise, which may or may not be the best decision for the problem at hand.

Creative Decision-Making

Chapter 11 includes some of the creative problem-solving and decision-making approaches used in organizations. These include **brainstorming, synectics** and **The Gordon Technique**. Each approach is different, yet each is an effort to encourage participants to think creatively about solutions to problems without any advanced preparation.

Brainstorming, developed by Alex F. Osborn, involves the presentation of a problem to a group of employees. The employees are encouraged to present solutions or ideas about the problem off the "top of their heads." The purpose of this phase of brainstorming is to generate a large quantity of ideas. The second phase is a review of each idea and the elimination of those that have little merit. In the final phase one of the ideas is chosen as the best or most feasible.

Synectics is another technique used in creative problem-solving. It involves the participants' expressing their fantasies about how a particular problem could be solved if there were no constraints on action. Each wishful solution is critiqued carefully and often one or two of the solutions can become the basis for a realistic solution.

The Gordon Technique was developed by J. J. Gordon and differs from brainstorming and synectics. In this approach the group leader describes a problem area with one word and the participants use this word as a starting point in their discussions. For example the word could be **inflation**. Even though the group leader is the only one who knows the real problem, the discussion may eventually lead to ideas that have practical application to solving the problem.

PLANNING TOOLS TO AID DECISION-MAKING AND PROBLEM-SOLVING

Several decision-making approaches have been presented. All will be used at one time or another by managers. Deciding on hunch or intuition may be the preference of managers in some situations, but most managers prefer a more objective decision-making approach if they have valid information available to use as a basis.

Several of the most important planning tools (also called decision-making aids) will be discussed. These planning tools provide more objective data and guidance to managers when they make decisions.

Forecasts

Forecasting is an effort to help a manager anticipate future occurrences in light of current information and predictions. Forecasts tend to be one of these three types: (1) **Event outcome forecasts;** (2) **event timing forecasts;** and (3) **time series forecasts.**[2]

Event outcome forecasts are concerned with predicting the outcome of a highly probable future event such as what will be the final construction cost of a new building. Event timing forecasts are concerned with predicting when a given event will occur such as

---

[2] Leslie W. Rue and Lloyd L. Byars, Management—Theory and Application, Fifth Edition (Homewood, IL: Richard D. Irwin, 1989), pp. 204-5.

QUALITATIVE	QUANTITATIVE
Historical Trend Analysis (Review of past to predict future)	**Time Series Analysis** (Mathematical projection of future based on past)
Group Opinion (Consensus of a group)	**Regression Modeling** (Mathematical forecasting using independent and dependent variables)
Delphi Technique (Separated expert opinion)	**Econometric Modeling** (Sophisticated mathematical method to model an entire economy)
Polling (Participants' projection of future)	

FIGURE 6-5: FORECASTING TECHNIQUES

when will a major earthquake occur in downtown Log Angeles? Time series forecasts are used to project future trends based on historical data. For example, will blood donations to the American Red Cross continue to increase at five percent annually?

Forecasting methods are numerous and vary in their level of complexity (see Figure 6-5). The selection of a forecasting method depends on the importance of the subject, the expertise available, and the financial resources on hand for forecasting.

The most common forecasting methods are these:

(1) **Historical trend analysis.** This method projects the future based on experience and past patterns. The weakness of this method is that conditions in the past may not be representative of conditions in the future.

(2) **Group opinion.** This method takes place when managers and other employees exchange views and opinions and collectively forecast once a consensus is reached.

(3) **Statistical techniques.** Using a mathematical or statistical approach when forecasting may represent the most objective and reliable method. Not all organizations have the necessary funds for gathering and analyzing data, and they may not have on hand personnel with the required expertise in the field of mathematics, statistics and computers. The best known statistical methods are **time series analysis, regression modeling**, and **econometric modeling**. Econometric modeling is not realistic for a first-level manager because these models are used to predict activity in the economy as a whole and involve too many variables that do not pertain. Time series analysis and regression modeling, however, are possible methods for use. **Time series analysis** mathematically forecasts future activity based on what has occurred in the past. Seasonal and cyclical fluctuations are highlighted based on historical trends. This is a good method when external forces remain relatively stable and much historical data is available. **Regression modeling** is a mathematical method of forecasting where certain identified variables (known as independent variables) are used to predict another variable (known as a dependent variable). The objective of regression modeling is to determine how changes in the independent variables affect the dependent variable.

Management by Objectives (MBO)

Management by objectives (MBO) is a philosophical approach used in some organizations to help managers more effectively implement plans. MBO is a popular planning/decision-making aid because managers are able to use it to convert organizational objectives into group and individual objectives. Many people are reluctant to set personal objectives, but MBO helps to overcome this barrier. When individual employees discuss with managers their objectives and have significant input into establishing their own annual work objectives, they feel more committed and perform better. Managers must manage individuals, not groups, and should learn to know their employees so well that they can align the employees' goals and objectives with those of the department and the organization as a whole. Theoretically when all employees, all managers and all parts of the organization achieve their annual objectives under MBO, then the overall organizational goals will be met.

The major disadvantage of an MBO program is that much time must be committed to introducing the program, meeting with all employees, formalizing objectives, and monitoring performance throughout the year. Small organizations, however, find MBO a helpful planning/decision-making aid because the time requirement is much less in introducing and administering the program.

MBO or some similar program has had wide acceptance in every type of American organization since the mid-1950s. Not only does MBO influence management decisions, the program also becomes a control mechanism when actual performance of employees and groups is measured against the mutually derived and agreed upon predetermined standards.

Budgets

A budget is a financial forecast or plan that projects expected income and expenditures over a given period of time.

Budgets influence many managerial decisions such as the size of the labor force, wages, funds available for supplies and equipment, operating expenditures and much more. The most common budgets are operating budgets, capital budgets and financial budgets. Operating budgets are used to relate projected revenues to projected expenditures to determine adequate cash flow, the break-even point, and to project a net profit or loss. Operating budgets normally are for a one year time period. Capital budgets project the sources and uses of capital. Financial budgets are used to determine the cash flow and balance sheet items. Managers would be most interested in operating budgets and on occasion capital budgets when, for example, a new facility is being planned. Budgets, as a tool to aid planning/decision-making, become a major aid to managers as they address problems and formulate and implement decisions.

Zero-Base Budgeting (ZBB)

This approach to budgeting is nothing more than common sense but has received much attention since former President Jimmy Carter popularized it while Governor of Georgia and then President of the United States (see Figure 6-6).

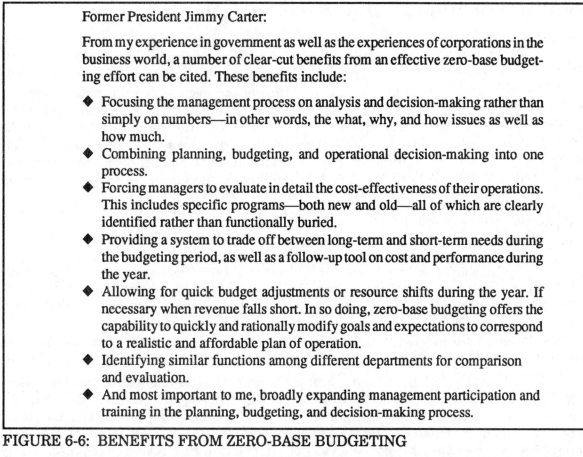

Former President Jimmy Carter:

From my experience in government as well as the experiences of corporations in the business world, a number of clear-cut benefits from an effective zero-base budgeting effort can be cited. These benefits include:

◆ Focusing the management process on analysis and decision-making rather than simply on numbers—in other words, the what, why, and how issues as well as how much.

◆ Combining planning, budgeting, and operational decision-making into one process.

◆ Forcing managers to evaluate in detail the cost-effectiveness of their operations. This includes specific programs—both new and old—all of which are clearly identified rather than functionally buried.

◆ Providing a system to trade off between long-term and short-term needs during the budgeting period, as well as a follow-up tool on cost and performance during the year.

◆ Allowing for quick budget adjustments or resource shifts during the year. If necessary when revenue falls short. In so doing, zero-base budgeting offers the capability to quickly and rationally modify goals and expectations to correspond to a realistic and affordable plan of operation.

◆ Identifying similar functions among different departments for comparison and evaluation.

◆ And most important to me, broadly expanding management participation and training in the planning, budgeting, and decision-making process.

FIGURE 6-6: BENEFITS FROM ZERO-BASE BUDGETING

Source: Jimmy Carter, "Jimmy Carter Tells Why He Will Use Zero-Base Budgeting," reprinted from *Nation's Business* 65 (January 1977): 26, published by the Chamber of Commerce of the United States, January 1977.

Zero-base budgeting was conceived by Peter A. Pyhrr in the late 1960s when he was employed by Texas Instruments. Then-Governor Carter, impressed with the concept, recruited Pyhrr to help install zero-base budgeting throughout state government in Georgia. Zero-base budgeting is an operating, planning and budgeting process which requires each manager to begin each budget period at zero expenditures and justify every budget request in detail. The pressure to support spending any money on any item rests with the manager/preparer. Budget requests are reviewed by higher managers, and through a participatory process, funds are allocated for those expenditures that are acceptable and judged appropriate. ZBB originates at the lower level of management and moves upward unlike MBO which begins at top management and spreads downward throughout the organization.

ZBB is especially useful in nonprofit organizations where funds are frequently scarce and must be budgeted among alternative uses carefully. In many organizations funds are limited and the supply of additional monies to supplement or cover budget overruns is nonexistent. Nearly all nonprofit organizations or service oriented firms could use ZBB, but large organizations such as manufacturers would find it difficult to implement.

Management Information Systems (MIS)

To succeed as planners, organizers, implementors, controllers and decision-makers, managers must have adequate information. The information must be timely and pertinent to the situation confronting the manager. Before computers were widely used, gathering such information was tedious and laborious. Much of the necessary information was out of date or inaccurate. Managers depended on staff personnel to do research in newspapers, trade publications, by interviews and so forth. Such information gathering efforts took time. Today managers have readily available more information than they can digest, and the focus is on determining what information to use and on managing the timely flow of the information. The key to a manager's success rests with determining what information to rely on and what to discard.

Professor James A. Senn wrote the following:

> If the aviation industry had developed at the same rate as electronic data processing, we would have landed people on the moon less than six months after the Wright brothers made their first flight at Kitty Hawk. If the cost of a 1955 Cadillac (introduced about the same time as computers were introduced in business) had been reduced as much as that of computer memories while efficiencies were raised to an equal degree, the Cadillac would now cost $5 and go 20,000 mph.[3]

MIS are not new in organizations, but technological progress in the evolution of electronic computer applications has magnified the importance of MIS.

Today, a Management Information System (MIS) is a computer-based network that integrates the collection, processing, storing and transmission of information.[4] This information is made available to managers who must make decisions. The computers do not make decisions! Experts view information as a resource available to managers to use as they see fit. One view of information as a resource is presented by John J. Connell:

> Information is not a resource in the same sense as people, money, materials and facilities. Information has no intrinsic worth as people do; its worth is entirely subjective. Information does not vary in value because of external factors, as money does; its value is in the mind of the user. Information is not consumed in its use as are materials. Information is not physical in nature, as are facilities. The mediums for recording and moving information may be physical, but the information carried is intangible and only useful to thinking human beings.
>
> If not a resource on its own, then, what is information? It is brain food. It is the feedstock used in the intellectual process of managing other resources.[5]

One should not confuse MIS with data processing. **Data processing is the capture, processing and storage of data** whereas MIS uses that data to produce information for management.[6] Data processing provides the database of the MIS. Data is composed of facts about places, things, people, events that have not been interpreted. Data, once interpreted for the benefit of managers, is called information.

---

[3] James A. Senn, *Information Systems in Management*, 2nd ed. (Belmont, Calif.: Wadsworth, 1982), p. 83.

[4] Robert Kreitner, *Management* 2nd ed. (Boston: Houghton Mifflin Company, 1983), p. 495.

[5] John J. Connell, "The Fallacy of Information Resource Management," *Infosystems* 28 (May 1981), 81-82.

[6] "Using MIS Strategically," *Management Review*, April 1984, p. 5.

Computers are the centerpiece of MIS. Computers have evolved from bulky pieces of equipment in the 1950s to the **mainframe** of the 1960s, to the **minicomputers** of the 1970s and on to the **microcomputers** (personal computers—PCs) of today. The personal computer, costing only a few hundred dollars, is capable of processing vast amounts of data and is no larger than a typewriter. They are widely available and versatile.

The most important components of MIS are hardware and software. **Hardware** includes the physical components such as the computer, printer, monitor (screen), keyboard and so forth. **Software** refers to the various programs which can run on the hardware and which include the instructions to a computer to perform certain tasks. Software can be standard or customized. Standard software can be purchased in any computer store. Customized software is written by consultants or computer specialists specifically for an organization to perform a special task. **Programmers** are the people who write instructional programs that tell the computer what to do. **System analysts** are people who investigate potential computer applications and determine the types of programs needed.

Summary

Every manager confronts problems and makes decisions. Decision-making is the essential activity that justifies the existence of managers. In the strictest sense decision-making involves selecting a course of action from alternative choices. Problem-solving involves determining the proper response to a situation which is considered to be nonstandard or not acceptable.

Decisions may be described as programmed or nonprogrammed. Programmed decisions are those that are repetitive and routine. Nonprogrammed decisions are those that apply to unusual problems or situations that are non-routine. Generally higher level managers handle non-routine problems.

Varying degrees of uncertainty accompany decision-making. The primary conditions of uncertainty are **certainty, risk** and **uncertainty**.

Major decision-making approaches include the mathematical or quantitative approach, the intuitive approach, the rational approach, the creative approach, and the group decision-making approach. The rational decision-making approach involves the application of the scientific method to general management problems.

Planning tools to aid decision-making and problem-solving include forecasts, MBO, budgets and MIS. Forecasts tend to be one of three types: event outcome, event timing, and time series forecasts. The most common forecasting methods are historical trend analysis, group opinion and statistical techniques.

Management by Objectives (MBO) is popular because managers are able to convert organizational objectives into group and individual objectives. Not only does MBO influence management decisions, but the program also becomes a control mechanism to measure actual performance of employees and groups against mutually derived, predetermined standards.

A budget is defined as a financial forecast or plan that projects expected income and expenditures over a given period of time. Major kinds of budgets are financial, operating and capital. Budgets such as those for printing brochures or event programs are calculated in time increments.

Zero-base budgeting is an operating, planning and budgeting process which requires each manager to justify every budget line item request in detail. Former President Jimmy Carter made ZBB popular when he introduced it in state government as Governor of Georgia and in the federal government when he was President.

Another tool of managers to aid in decision-making and problem-solving is MIS. A Management Information System is a computer-based network that integrates the collection, processing and transmission of information. Information is made available to managers who make decisions. One should not confuse data processing with MIS. Data processing is the capture, processing and storage of data (information) whereas MIS uses interpreted data to produce information needed by management. The important components of MIS are hardware (the computer) and software (the programs).

Review Questions

1. Make a clear distinction between decision-making and problem-solving.
2. Discuss why higher-level managers generally make the nonprogrammed decisions.
3. Clearly explain the three conditions of uncertainty which affect managerial decision-making.
4. Outline and briefly discuss each step in the rational decision-making approach.
5. Describe the major methods used in forecasting.
6. Explain the value of a participative approach when introducing an MBO program.
7. Review the potential value of an organization using Zero-Base Budgeting (ZBB). Why do you think many types of organizations do not use ZBB?
8. Management Information Systems (MIS) provide information to managers as a basis for decision-making. How does MIS differ from data processing? Explain fully.

Assignments for Personal Development

1. Some people feel that computers simplify the decision-making process while others claim it does not. Those saying it does simplify the process point out that computers provide access to much information quickly; data provided is more accurate, timely and reliable; and the use of computers gives managers more time for other things.

   Those who say it does not simplify decision-making point out that computers are of no help in making decisions about people; that information provided is no better than the computer program which is designed by humans capable of errors; and managers depend too much or too little on computers because they do not understand them.

   As a future manager, take a position on this issue. List all your reasons for viewing computers as valuable to decision-making or not and be prepared to support your position.

2. Select some type of organization and list all of the subjects that management should attempt to forecast. Discuss how the information obtained from forecasting would aid managerial decision-making.

Incident

FRUSTRATED SUPERVISOR

Wallace Ferguson was a newly appointed supervisor of the Accounts Payable Department. His first three months on the job had been a nightmare. He was working ten to twelve hours daily and getting more behind with the work. Most of his days were filled with problem situations and making decisions. It seemed that every staff member came to him for either a solution or recommendation about every problem, or they wanted him to approve or make a decision before they took action. He was flattered by the confidence and attention they showed him, but something was going to have to give!

Questions:

1. What's wrong with Wallace Ferguson as a decision-maker? List four things.

2. Would it make a difference if Wallace Ferguson understood the distinction between programmed decisions and nonprogrammed decisions? Discuss.

Selected Readings

Cowen, Scott S., Burton V. Dean, and Ardeshir Lorhrasbi. "Zero-Base Budgeting as a Management Tool." *MSU Business Topics*, Spring 1978, p. 29.

Edwards, Ward. "The Theory of Decision Making." *Psychological Bulletin* (1954), 380-417.

Heenan, David A., and Robert Addleman. "Quantitative Techniques for Today's Decision Makers." *Harvard Business Review*, May-June 1976, pp. 32-62.

Kepner, Charles, and Benjamin Tregoe. *The Rational Manager*. New York: McGraw-Hill, 1965.

Levin, R. I., and C. A. Kirkpatrick. *Planning and Control with PERT/CPM*. New York: McGraw-Hill, 1966.

Newman, William H., and James P. Logan. *Policy, and Central Management*, 9th ed. South-Western, 1985.

Shull, Fremont, Andre Delbecq, and L. L. Cumming. *Organizational Decision Making*. New York: McGraw-Hill, 1970.

Small, John T., and William B. Lee. "In Search of an MIS." *MSU Business Topics*, Autumn 1975, pp. 47-55.

Srinivasan, C. A., and Paul E. Dascher. "Information Systems Design: User Psychology Considerations." *MSU Business Topics*, Winter 1977, p. 51.

CHAPTER 7

THE FUNCTION OF ORGANIZING

After studying this chapter, **you will know**:

- The Purpose of Organizing
- The Benefits of Organizing
- The History of Organizing
- Some Theories of Organizing
- The Definition of a Formal Organization
- How to Structure Departments
- Types of Organization Structures
- Steps in Organizing

Introduction

All formal work effort requires good organization if success is the objective. Lack of sound organization brings about disorder, confusion, frustration, duplicated effort and often chaos. Good organization generates efficiency of effort and harmony in the combination of resources, both human and nonhuman, involved. Defects in the organization become the primary cause of daily management problems.

Coordination of effort does not happen by accident. Managers should learn that only good organization leads to the proper level of coordination required to reach objectives. Sound organization provides two benefits to management that are essential for the success of any type endeavor: first, the right people will be in the right jobs; and second, the proper amount of resources (human and nonhuman) of the right quality will be available at the time they are needed.

The responsibility to organize effectively is a function of management. Comments you will hear that reflect on the organization skills of managers are similar to these:

- They really work well together.
- Everyone knows their job and when to do it.
- Have you ever seen such team effort?
- There are no weak links.

As you study Chapter 7, remember that practicing managers probably know less about the subject of organization than any of the other subjects in management.

The Importance of Organizing

"Organizing" comes from the word "Organism" and refers to parts separate in function which are interdependent. Applied to today's organization, **organizing is a managerial effort to assign work and allocate resources; then, arrange the work and resources in such an orderly way that a group's effort generates the desired end result in the most efficient manner possible.**

Organizing is a main function of management which is often not a separate managerial act. Organizing may be part of planning or mixed with other management functions as well. Collectively, the activities of planning, organizing, deciding, implementing and controlling are called **managing.** Students should view organizing as the managerial effort to create order from chaos in the workplace, generating operating efficiency in the process.

Organizing is important in management because of the following benefits:
1. Generating effective group action
2. Synergizing resources
3. Pinpointing individual responsibilities
4. Facilitating the functions of implementing and control.

Generating effective group action. Reaching desired work objectives requires the efforts of many individual employees. When employees' efforts are coordinated so that the group reaches its goals and individual employees fully use their knowledge and skills, the organization as a whole benefits as well as individual employees.

Synergizing Resources. Sound organization leads to the proper use of resources (people, money, inventories, supplies, equipment, etc.) so that over time the value of end results is greater than the combined starting values of the resources (refer back to the synergistic management concept in Chapter 2). This point reflects on efficiency of effort which is the primary purpose of organizing work.

Pinpointing individual responsibilities. A major reason for organizing is to specify the duties and responsibilities of individual employees. Doing this eliminates doubt about any employee's purpose and relationship to other work being performed. Lines of authority and accountability (reporting relationships and dependencies) are defined and clarified. Every member of the work unit wants to know who is in charge of what; where to go for answers of each kind of question; how each employee's actions affect others; and who judges work performance.

Facilitating the implementing and control functions. Today, good organizing considers interpersonal relationships, the work environment, and the control of results. It is well accepted that the majority of workers perform best when the following conditions are met: (1) Their job skills and knowledge are right for the job; (2) working conditions are pleasant, and (3) they have a clear understanding of their duties and responsibilities. Organizing efforts support the implementation of plans and programs and facilitate the control function by communicating work expectations that become a standard of evaluation of performance.

History of Organizing

Organizing has a long history as a recognized function of management. Whether studying the prehistoric era or ancient civilization, it is clear that there were organization structures, there were superior/subordinate relationships, there were centers of authority, and there were duties delegated to subordinates.

Construction of the pyramids in Egypt from 5000 to 525 B.C. provides a vivid example of good organizational technique:

> During the New Empire under the reign of Ramses IV, one expedition to quarry stone at Hammamat was carried out in quite a regal style. The expedition was under the titular leadership of the high priest of Amon (because the monuments were for a god) and other attendants of the king, none of whom made any consequential contribution. The men who, in effect, were in charge were military officers inasmuch [sic] work of this nature usually fell on the army. On this expedition one hundred ten officers of each rank, fifty civil officials and ecclesiastics, one hundred thirty stone masons, two painters, and four engravers furnished the leadership. The work of transport was done by five thousand common soldiers, two hundred members of the king's court, eight hundred barbarians, and two thousand bondservants of the temple. Altogether, the expedition consisted of 8,368 men.

> By using masses of organized labor the Egyptians were able to accomplish tasks that astonish us. While their system of organization may appear unwieldy, cumbersome, and even wasteful, they actually had no reason to economize on labor since more peasants, mercenaries, and slaves were always available simply for the asking.[1]

In Chapter 1, you will find the contributions of many individuals, civilizations and governments to the subject of organization. This includes the feudal organization, the organizational genius of the Romans, Alexander the Great, Niccolo Machiavelli and many more.

In more modern times, Sir James Steuart, Adam Smith, Thomas Jefferson and Eli Whitney introduced important organizational concepts in the eighteenth century. Steuart developed a source of authority theory based on dependency; Adam Smith introduced the principle of work specialization in 1776 (also known as the "division of labor" principle).[2] The concept of interchangeable parts was one of Thomas Jefferson's suggestions,

---

[1] Adolf Erman, *Life In Ancient Egypt*, trans. from the German by Helen M. Tirard (London: MacMillan and Company, 1894), p. 472, as quoted in Claude S. George, Jr., *The History of Management Thought* (Englewood Cliffs, N.J.: Prentice-Hall, Inc., 1968), p. 5.

[2] Adam Smith, *An Inquiry into the Nature and Cause of the Wealth of Nations* (London: A. Strahan and T. Cadell, 1793), Vol. 1, pp. 7-8.

and Eli Whitney was the first American to apply the concept of interchangeable parts and the specialization principle when he manufactured muskets for the government in the 1790s.

During the late nineteenth century and early twentieth century, the subject of management took on new importance. The so-called "pioneers" of modern management emerged with their writings, theories and practical applications. People like Frederick W. Taylor, Frank Gilbreth, Henry L. Gantt, Harrington Emerson and others applied their management ideas successfully and became nationally famous.

Taylor introduced an organization structure called **functional foremanship** which exchanged multiple accountability for intense specialization to support the work of individual employees. This contribution, while not universally popular in Taylor's day, is the basis of matrix organization as practiced today in multi-project organizations.

In 1931, James D. Mooney and Alan C. Reiley published *Onward Industry*.[3] This represented the first effort in the United States to present a systematic approach to organization. Many principles or "universals" of organization were included.

Theories of Organizing[4]

Historically speaking, organization theory is identified as **classical, neoclassical** and **modern**. None of the theories is complete or neatly packaged. None is totally accepted by researchers in management; however, the theoretical approaches provide students some insight into the evolutionary development of management thought about organizing.

Classical theory. Classical organization theory or doctrine relates to the early work of Taylor, Fayol, Mooney and Reiley and others. Importance is placed on organization structure or the hierarchy. Principles of organization have been developed to provide guidance to practicing managers. The main elements of classical organization are the division of labor, the scalar principle, the functional management process, organization structure, and the concept of span of management (control).

The division of labor principle refers to breaking work down into basic components and emphasizing specialization of effort. Workers become expert at one job and output and efficiency increase. This element directly influences the others, and thus is considered the foundation of classical organization.

The scalar principle pertains to vertical growth of an organization (the hierarchy or chain of command), while functional process pertains to horizontal growth (the functional processes of management). Within these elements in classical organization you find the subjects of delegation of authority and responsibility, unity of command, accountability, and the separation of the organization into specialized (functional) parts, from which evolved line and staff activities.

---

[3] James D. Mooney and Alan C. Reiley, *Onward Industry* (New York: Harper and Brothers, 1931).

[4] Many of the points and ideas presented are drawn from William G. Scott, "Organization Theory: An Overview and an Appraisal," *Journal of the Academy of Management*, Vol. 4, No. 1, April, 1961, pp. 7-26.

The organization structure refers to clearly established lines of authority, responsibility, accountability and communication that logically relate work functions to each other. A sound organization structure is a system that balances functional activities and creates consistent relationships between work groups. The goal of organization structure is to achieve an end result in the most efficient, effective manner.

Span of management (sometimes called span of control) defines the number of employees a manager can effectively supervise. There is no set number, but the number for any given management situation depends on four factors: (1) the talent of the manager; (2) the type of work being performed by subordinates; (3) the worker's skill at the job, educational level, background and work ethic; and (4) physical factors in the work area. The importance of this concept is that the span of management directly affects the organization structure. A wide span of management creates a flat organization structure; a short span, a tall structure. The shape of the organization structure affects human and departmental interrelationships and organizational complexity.

Neoclassical theory. The neoclassical theory of organization is an effort to offset some of the shortcomings of the classical theory by expanding into the behavioral sciences. The underlying elements of classical organization theory are modified by emphasis on the importance of individual behavior and the impact of the informal organization which operates within the framework of the formal organization. Earlier contributors to this approach were Henry L. Gantt and Lillian Gilbreth. Most researchers agree, however, that the Hawthorne Studies led to the evolvement of the neoclassical school.[5]

The neoclassical approach focuses on problems such as employee monotony, fatigue, isolation and insignificance (which results from specialization of work). Neoclassical theory stresses subjects such as motivation, coordination and leadership as responsibilities of managers.

While classical organization theory implies perfection from assignment of duties (delegation), communication, control and other managerial and employee functions, the neoclassical school identifies human frailties and expects some errors in managerial judgment. Neoclassical theory views classical theory as sound but impossible to apply perfectly because of the human element. Neoclassicists have devised tools, techniques and additional theory to overcome the problems which result from delegation of duties; interpersonal conflicts between workers and between managers and nonmanagers; employees' job frustration and boredom; motivation of employees and many other troublesome areas.

Neoclassicists also pay special attention to the informal organization. The informal organization is an indigenous grouping of employees in the work place. Informal organizations, which will not show up on an organization chart, are created around work locations, around similar work being performed, by common interests of the employees (the company softball team), or by special problems or issues affecting a group of employees (such as a group of older employees who believe they are being discriminated against in pay increases).

---

[5] For review see F. J. Roethlisberger and William J. Dickson, *Management and the Worker* (Cambridge: Harvard University Press, 1939).

Management's recognition of the informal organization and accepting it as an important part of the formal organization are part of neoclassical theory. Each informal organization has its own leaders, communication system (grapevine) and standards.

The formal and informal organizations are distinct entities which may or may not work well together. Collectively, the two organizations along with individuals, jobs, the work environment and more make up the social system which can be studied as a whole.

Modern organization theory. The uniqueness of this theory is that it studies the organization as a system. Modern organization theory goes beyond classical and neoclassical approaches and treats the organization as a system of interdependent variables.

According to William G. Scott, the key questions to ask are these:
1. What are the strategic parts of the system?
2. What is the nature of their mutual dependency?
3. What are the main processes in the system which link parts together and facilitate their adjustment to each other?
4. What are the goals sought by systems?[6]

While these are important questions to answer, the student should realize that there is no unified body of thought. Researchers stress and analyze different segments of the system depending on their special interests.

Modern theorists consider the organization to be a system composed of the following strategic parts: the individual; the formal structure; the informal organization; status and role patterns; and the physical environment of work. All together these parts compose the organizational system.

The Formal Organization

Traditionally the formal organization is described as **a group of people working together toward common objectives with a clearly defined hierarchy** (i.e., clear-cut lines of authority, responsibility, accountability and communication).

But, the question arises: How do you group people and develop a sound hierarchy? The answer is by formally structuring the organization's departments into efficient and effective work groups, divided according to **function, product or service, location, customer** or some other criteria.

Functional Departmentation. This is the most basic form of structuring an organization. The word **function** here refers to an activity like sales, production or finance. Employees who do the same or similar jobs are brought together in one department. A manager heads each functional department and is responsible for seeing that the departmental goals are achieved. Often small organizations are structured functionally, and every employee is considered a line employee. **Staff** employees do not appear until the organization grows larger.

There are four major advantages of functional organization by departments: Each employee can be a specialist or expert in his or her job; the managers' tasks are more

---

[6] Scott, "Organization Theory," pp. 7-26.

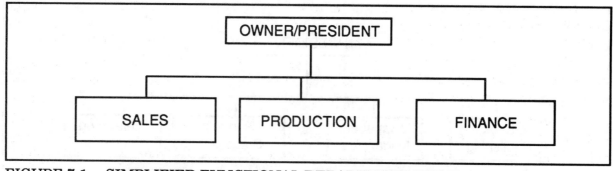

FIGURE 7-1:   SIMPLIFIED FUNCTIONAL DEPARTMENTATION
ORGANIZATION STRUCTURE

narrow and limited to more specific duties and responsibilities; the job of coordinating work and talents is relatively easy; and the success or failure of a department's efforts can be measured more precisely. An example of structuring an organization by functions can be seen in Figure 7-1.

Product Departmentation. In large organizations with a diverse product line most departments are structured around major products or products of a similar nature. This includes large service organizations as well. Employees identify with their departmental product line such as General Motors employees who work in the Pontiac Division. Within the product departments, managers are assigned to functional duties and pursue the objectives of that department. Often the structuring of an organization by products provides the basis for identifying the revenue generating areas, usually called profit centers. Being a manager of a profit center provides an unusual opportunity for managers to demonstrate managerial competency (or incompetency). Organizing by product often is the forerunner of decentralizing authority, responsibility, decision making and control in management The ultimate authority and responsibility, however, never leaves top management.

The four major advantages of organizing by product departmentation are the relative ease of coordinating all of the work and activity associated with the isolated product or product line; the promptness in decision-making associated with that product area; the work and results achieved by product departments are more visible and readily available for objective evaluation; and product managers have the opportunity to demonstrate their functional skills.

The inherent weakness in product departmentation is that managers can become so engrossed in the success of their part of the organization that department goals and needs may take precedent over what is good for the organization as a whole. In addition, organizing by product or product line leads to the creation of multiple line specialists since each department must have its own specialists. The result is an increase in overall operating costs. Figure 7-2 shows a typical product departmentation organization structure.

Location Departmentation. Some large multiunit organizations tend to structure their departments, divisions or plants around the locations they serve. These locations may be small geographic areas such as the northwest side of a city, or they may be con-

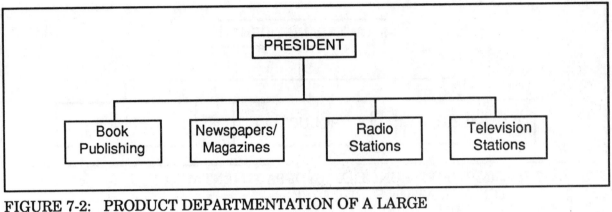

FIGURE 7-2:   PRODUCT DEPARTMENTATION OF A LARGE
              COMMUNICATIONS COMPANY

tinents such as Europe, Australia or North America. Usually these sub-organizations
have corporate line support from the home office but function independently on a daily
basis. Much like product departmentation, each geographic area can be viewed as a revenue generating part of the whole, and individual managers can be held responsible for
the results in their location. Again, there can be some duplication in providing line specialists in each geographic area, but normally this occurs only when distance between
markets is large.

The major advantage of organizing by location departmentation is that managers
can respond quickly to problems that occur in their geographic area. These managers
are nearer the action; control is more assured; and problems can be pinpointed more
accurately, leading to quicker resolutions.

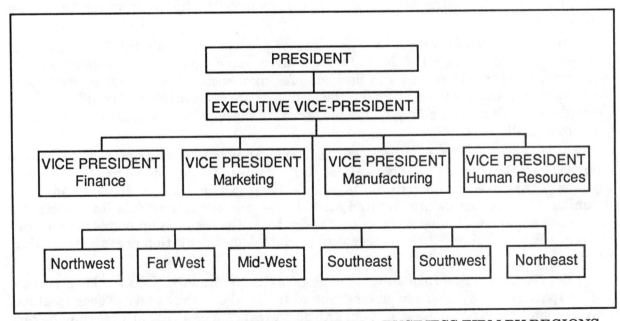

FIGURE 7-3: LOCATION DEPARTMENTATION IN A BUSINESS FIRM BY REGIONS

Customer Departmentation. Sometimes there are advantages to structuring an organization around identifiable customer groups or target markets. This allows the personnel in that customer area to specialize in meeting the unique needs and demands of that group. In an international sporting goods company, major customers may be separated and identified by the particular sport's equipment they use such as skiers, tennis players, golfers, etc. A manager becomes a specialist in that sport's total equipment line. See Figure 7-4 for an example of customer departmentation in a large commercial bank.

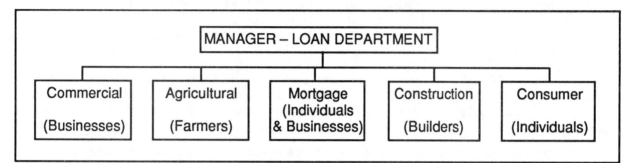

FIGURE 7-4: CUSTOMER DEPARTMENTATION IN LARGE COMMERCIAL BANK

Other Types of Departmentation. Two other types of departmentation are used occasionally to group jobs in organizations. The first is departmentation by **time**. Many companies operate on work shifts such as airlines; nurses and other staff in a hospital; utility companies that operate some services (such as telephone operators) on a twenty-four hour basis; and manufacturers which operate more than one eight-hour work crew daily. Each shift will have its own personnel, supervisors and organization structure.

A second type of additional departmentation is by **number** or **sequence**. For example, an elementary school may limit the number of children in a single class to twenty; in the army, the number of soldiers in a squad, a company or battalion may be fixed.

Summary Comments. The word **departmentation** has been used repeatedly to denote the grouping of jobs by functions, products, location, customers, time, sequence and numbers. Students should understand also that **departments** may refer to divisions, plants, sections, branches, bureaus, regions or other synonyms. The selected word depends on the growth, size or nature of the organization.

Finally, depending on the size and nature of the organization, departmentation of jobs may be grouped in one area or at one level by product and in another area by function, etc. There can be departmentation mixes within the same organization to gain advantages of specialization and control.

Major Organization Structures

The field of management, especially in the area of organization, is full of jargon. When studying the major forms of organization structure, students may be perplexed to read about so many types. Writers identify major organization structures as line, line and staff, matrix, classical, tall, flat, functional and more. In addition, organizations are called highly centralized or highly decentralized. To students this can become confusing.

To clarify this subject, this text will discuss three major types of organization structure: line, line and staff, and matrix. Nearly every type of organization structure is one of these or a variation of one of the three. A fourth major type, committee organization structure, will be discussed in detail in Chapter 12.

The Line Structure. The line structure is built around activities essential to the attainment of the primary objectives of the organization. All work of all employees in all departments directly relates to the production, financing and marketing of goods and/or services produced. The goods and/or services produced are designed for a market; and in the case of a profit-seeking business, the output is intended to generate revenues which will cover costs and produce a profit. Profit becomes the primary objective of a business so that it can survive.

Those organizations which do not have profit as the major goal, called nonprofit or not-for-profit organizations, must clearly define primary objectives so that all employees and all customers/clients (who may be supporters, members, users of services, volunteers, etc.) know why the organization exists and what it should achieve.

Every organization should have a written statement expressing the primary reason for its existence. Every employee and participants in the organization's activities should be familiar with this statement. Sometimes this is called the **mission statement**. See Figure 7-5 for an example of a mission statement of a large medical center.

The mission of our medical center is to contribute to the well being and the quality of life of our community by providing in partnership with our physician practices high value health and wellness services for those whom we serve.

FIGURE 7-5: MISSION STATEMENT OF A MAJOR URBAN MEDICAL CENTER

The line structure is used primarily by small organizations. It is relatively simple to construct with vertical lines connecting the various levels of the organization (see Figure 7-6).

The major advantage of the line structure is the clarity associated with pinpointing authority and responsibility. Decision-making can be quick in response to a problem, and responsibility for results is clear. A major disadvantage is that line managers may not possess all the special skills needed to run an organization. The talent and ability of the line managers are often limited, but they are frequently required to perform many jobs whether qualified to do so or not.

The Line and Staff Structure. As organizations grow in size and complexity, staff positions and departments evolve. **Staff functions relate indirectly to the primary purpose of an organization.** Prior to the creation of "staff," line managers or line employees performed the now-called staff activities. Typical staff functions are personnel, indus-

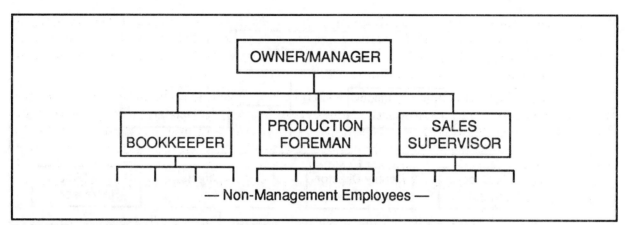

FIGURE 7-6: SIMPLE LINE STRUCTURE ORGANIZATION CHART

trial relations, research and development, public relations, control activities, and the technical assistance or "how-to" positions. Except in unusual cases, staff personnel have no direct authority over "line" employees. The job of staff personnel is to support line managers by providing assistance, advice, counsel, coordination, specialized knowledge or technical skills. Figure 7-7 shows a simple line and staff organization chart.

Staff positions are created by higher line managers to enlarge knowledge and skills in specialized areas. Once staff positions are added to line positions, the organization structure becomes line and staff. Most organizations beyond the smallest in size are structured this way.

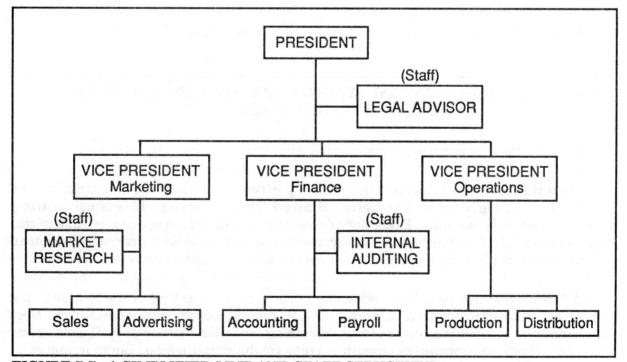

FIGURE 7-7: A SIMPLIFIED LINE AND STAFF STRUCTURE

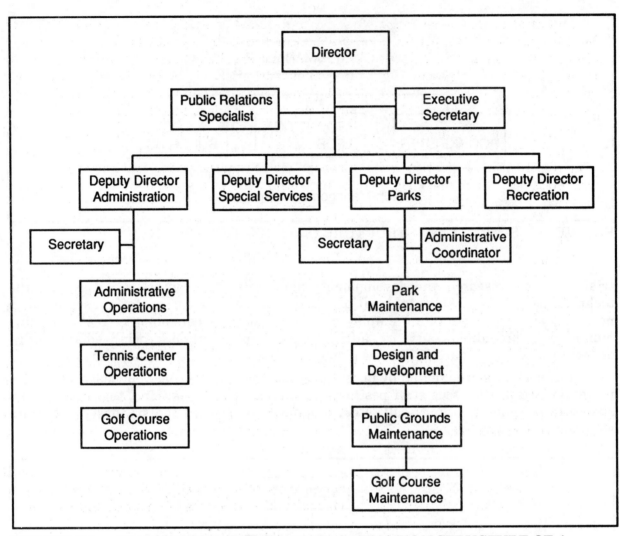

FIGURE 7-8:   PARTIAL LINE AND STAFF ORGANIZATION STRUCTURE OF A
COUNTY RECREATION AND PARKS DEPARTMENT

Functional Staff. A special kind of staff position or department is sometimes created by higher line managers and given **limited line authority**. This is called **functional** or **specialized staff**. Examples of specialized staff are inspectors in quality control, plant maintenance personnel, safety specialists and security personnel. They operate as pure staff (described above); but in special situations, they can exert "limited line authority."

Advantages and problems with staff. The major advantage of the line and staff organization structure is that of providing specialized support to line managers. Staff personnel free the line managers to concentrate on immediate issues as well as long-run problems. Staff positions allow more flexibility in the organization. Line managers do not have to become specialists in every area of the organization's operations.

Potential conflict does arise when staff is added to a line organization structure. There is opportunity for contention between line managers and staff managers over who is in charge of what. For example, staff personnel specialists have no authority to hire new employees for a line manager. The job of personnel may be to advertise, interview, test and screen applicants on behalf of line managers, but the line manager interviews and approves the applicant before employment.

Staff personnel make suggestions to line managers as part of their function, and they may become upset if line managers do not accept and follow these suggestions. Being highly specialized then having expert advice ignored can irritate staff personnel. Often staff people are regarded as internal consultants who are sensitive to their area of expertise. If line managers do not understand the staff person's point of view, and the staff person does not fully understand the function of the line manager; trouble will develop.

Figure 7-8 shows another simple line and staff organization structure. In this example, the Public Relations Specialist, all secretaries, and the Administrative Coordinator are staff positions. Two points are important about staff positions or departments in an organization. One, staff is always offset from the line of authority with the staff person or department head reporting directly to a line manager above the staff position. Second is that the staff person or department is located on an organization chart in the area that it serves. The Public Relations Specialist serves the Director and is located below and offset from the line directly under the Director. The Executive Secretary does the same. Each staff person in this example serves administrators and participants under the direction of his or her higher line manager. The position of staff on an organization chart does not reflect its relative importance, but the location of line positions on a chart does reflect power, status and importance.

The Matrix Structure. The matrix organization structure is two directional, based on the mathematical concept of **matrix** (an array of both vertical columns and horizontal rows). Large companies that are involved in multi-projects often structure part of the organization as a matrix.

These are the characteristics of matrix organization:
1. Employees are assigned to work on a project while maintaining entity in a functional department.
2. Employees have accountability to more than one boss.
3. Specialized knowledge and skills are more readily available to assist in project work.
4. Communication is more open to access information.
5. Managers are more flexible and better able to adjust to changes in technology and in the market.

Large companies engaged in several major projects found it difficult to set up a line and staff organization structure for each project. Furthermore, they were duplicating staff skills and not fully utilizing the talents of line employees. Matrix organization evolved primarily at the insistence of government. When projects involved government contracts, the government wanted a means to fix responsibility for progress and performance. The outcome was matrix organization structure.

Several of the characteristics of matrix organization structure have roots in Frederick

W. Taylor's functional foremanship organization structure. Functional foremanship created multiple accountability to provide intense specialization to workers on the line.

Matrix organization structure has proved valuable to many companies, but its popularity has waned. The major disadvantages are the violation of the scalar principle, parity principle and unity of command.

The scalar principle is violated because the matrix structure encourages lateral or horizontal communication in addition to or in place of vertical (chain of command) communication. When authority and responsibility is divided between project and functional managers, the parity principle is violated. Anytime an employee reports to more than one supervisor (boss), the unity of command principle is violated; and the matrix structure is based on multiple accountability.

The matrix structure can also create problems between line managers and project managers over the control of employees and resources. Power struggles sometimes arise over the final source of decision-making.

Figure 7-9 shows a simple example of matrix organization. Note the vertical columns and horizontal rows, multiple accountability, and the identity of functional departments and projects.

Some large companies that have abandoned matrix organization structure have gone toward a decentralized structure of independent units. These units operate much like subsidiaries or profit centers and concentrate on specially assigned projects. This approach eliminates some of the disadvantages of matrix organization structure but often increases operating costs due to duplication of skills and personnel.

Steps in Organizing

Now that we have discussed the importance of organizing, reviewed some history of organizing, sampled organization theory and learned major organization structures, the question arises: Just how do you organize group effort? The process of organizing involves five steps:
1. Dividing work
2. Grouping tasks
3. Activating authority and responsibility
4. Determining spans of management
5. Coordination of organizational resources

Step 1: Dividing Work. The cornerstone of organizing is the division of work into smaller parts. Smaller parts of the overall task then can be performed by an individual employee or by a group of employees. The concept of **work specialization** is based on Adam Smith's division of labor principle. Without dividing work into smaller parts, an individual employee would have to perform all the tasks associated with any function (all the production, or financing or marketing of a product or service). This would not be efficient nor would it mesh with the definition of a formal organization.

There are many advantages to work specialization. One employee doing the same task repeatedly develops great skill, leading to an increase in overall efficiency. Total organizational productivity increases sharply.

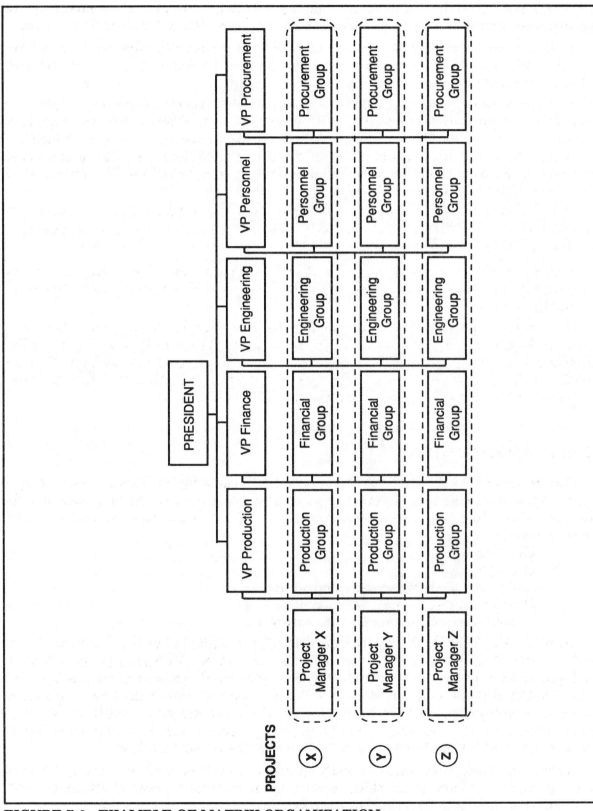

FIGURE 7-9: EXAMPLE OF MATRIX ORGANIZATION

Historically, the United States became the world's greatest economic power through the application of work specialization and the division of labor principle. This concept is the basis of mass production which creates standardized parts and end products, low unit costs of production, and reasonable prices of finished goods.

Criticism of work specialization has surfaced in recent years and centers on the attitude of the workers who perform the same specialized jobs continuously. These workers, as revealed by closer scrutiny of the human factor in organizations, can become bored, dissatisfied and resentful. The work may lack challenge and eventually fail to stimulate high productivity. There is a problem with workers in these jobs thinking they are perceived as "units of production" rather than as people. These problems led to progress in redesigning highly specialized jobs to make them more interesting and stimulating (see Chapter 12 for a discussion of job enlargement and job enrichment). It appears certain, however, that work specialization will not disappear.

Step 2: Grouping Tasks. The second step in organizing is to group jobs in a logical way so that managers can more soundly supervise employees in identifiable departments. This is called **departmentalization**. Departmentation can be by function, product, location, customer and, less frequently, by time, number or sequence (as we have already discussed).

In a small organization an individual manager may oversee all activities and be in complete control of all work effort. As growth occurs, however, it is necessary to appoint managers to supervise the work of parts of the total organization. Called departments in small organizations, they may be divisions, plants, regions, districts or overseas markets in large ones.

Step 3: Activating Authority and Responsibility. After dividing work into smaller parts through the application of the division of labor principle and after grouping tasks in some logical way with a manager assigned to each department, the next step in organizing is to activate the authority and responsibility of each manager.

Authority in management is associated with **power**. Alvin Brown, a pioneer in the study of modern organizations wrote

> That aspect of responsibility which represents its power of performance has been called authority. In common usage, the word is not always given so broad a sense, being often limited to the power exercised by one member of enterprise over another. It is also defined, however, as the right to act officially—the personal power that commands influence, respect, or confidence—so that it is not confined to its exercise toward particular persons. In this sense, as has been said, authority is the exact reciprocal of responsibility. It cannot be less in extent since responsibility without authority would be an empty duty. It cannot be greater in extent, since authority without responsibility would be an empty power.[7]

While there are many interpretations of authority, the **right to act officially** is most often associated with managers. Managers have **formal authority** which is a form of power. This authority or power originates from higher up and is legally passed downward one level at a time. In business individuals have the legal right to incorporate, elect directors, select a president, appoint people as managers, etc. The authority or

[7] Alvin Brown, *Organization of Industry* (Englewood Cliffs, N.J.: Prentice Hall, Inc., 1947), p. 61.

power of the manager originates from above the position. According to many writers authority is power that has been formalized by the organization.

A second view of the origin of formal authority comes from Chester I. Barnard who advocated the **acceptance theory.**[8] This view holds that the employee, the subordinate or the influencee determines whether the manager has any authority or not. If employees below do not comply with the manager's request, demand, order or directive, the manager has no authority or power.

In American organizations the vast majority of workers accept the legitimacy of authority which a manager has and they willingly comply with the manager's directions. In practice, however, there are two tests to determine if a manager has any real authority:

> First, is the manager being accepted from below? That is, are the employees responding positively to the directions and orders delegated to them by the manager? (This is the Acceptance Theory.)

> Second, is the manager being supported from above. A manager has no authority whatsoever if the boss above does not back him or her. (This is the Authority Theory—source of power from the top down.)

Responsibility accompanies authority. There is no need to delegate authority unless there is a job to do, an obligation to meet, and you wish to accomplish more work by assigning part of it to subordinate employees. **Responsibility** is an acceptance of accountability for doing a particular job. In the case of the manager, the job is to achieve desired goals and objectives working with and through employees and other resources.

Delegating is the assignment of authority and responsibility to a person or group of people at the next lower level in the organization. The Chair of a committee may appoint a subcommittee and assign part of the overall committee's work to it. A manager may tell an employee what to do, when to do it, and why the work is important. In each of these cases, there is an assignment of authority and responsibility from one management level to the next lower level to do specific jobs. This is **delegating**.

In management, the process of delegating involves these four steps:

1. **Assign responsibility.** A person or group is told exactly what to do verbally or in writing or both.
2. **Assign authority.** A person or group is given the power needed to get the job done.
3. **Assign a time standard.** A person or group is told exactly when the job or task is to be completed.
4. **Assign accountability.** A person or group must accept the assignment and report to the manager above (the delegator) on progress and problems.

Delegation of authority and responsibility flows downward in a formal organization. Some writers argue that responsibility cannot be delegated. This view is based on the concept that ultimate responsibility for results below is never relinquished by managers at the higher level. This is true! It is also true, however, that any manager or employee

---

[8] Chester I. Barnard, *The Functions of an Executive* (Cambridge, Mass.: Harvard University Press, 1938).

who has a job to perform has responsibility for that job. The question arises: Where did the employee get that responsibility? And the answer is from someone at the level above him or her. The responsibility for accomplishing the assignment was delegated downward along with the authority needed to do the job. Employees at one level work on behalf of bosses above them. Both have responsibility for the work assigned. But the employee's responsibility is limited to specific tasks and jobs, while the boss' responsibility encompasses many tasks assigned to various different employees. The boss still retains the ultimate responsibility that the work delegated to employees will be done properly and on schedule.

Step 4.: Determining Spans of Management. In the logical sequence of developing an organization which will generate efficient group effort and reach common objectives, we have divided the work into smaller parts, departmentalized tasks, and activated authority and responsibility. Now, we must discuss how many employees should be assigned to individual managers.

The number of employees reporting to a single manager is called the **span of management**. Because the number also affects supervisory effectiveness, the question of **control** also arises. The ideal number of employees a manager can effectively supervise and control has been debated for many years.

It is important to recognize that if a manager supervises too few employees, inefficiency can be the result. If the manager supervises too many employees, inefficiency and ineffectiveness can result due to the loss of control.

Determining the span of management directly affects the shape of the organization structure. If there is a wide span of management, the structure will be flat with fewer levels of management. Also, the organization will most likely have decentralized its decision-making, authority, responsibility and control. If the span of management is narrow, the organization structure will be more vertical or tall. This indicates more levels of management and more centralization of management functions. See Figure 7-10 for a graphic representation of these two extremes.

General Ian Hamilton of the British Army (post-World War I), Lyndall F. Urwick and V. A. Graicunas (both in the 1930s) were management pioneers who researched the span of management question. Hamilton and Urwick suggested an executive span should not exceed six subordinates. V. A. Graicunas developed a mathematically sound theory in 1933 which is pertinent to this question today. Called Graicunas' Theorem, it says as you add employees to an organization arithmetically (1 + 1 + 1), the organizational relationships increase at a much faster (geometric) rate (4, 16, 64).[9] The impact for managers is that by increasing employees one at a time, the complexities of management increase at a much faster rate because of the increase in relationships. Interactions between individuals, between managers and individuals, and between groups of subordinates are all expanded for each additional employee added.

The question of a limit to the number of subordinates any one manager can effectively supervise remains unanswered. Some organizations, like the military, have a set

---

[9] V. A. Graicunas, "Relationships in Organizations," *Bulletin of the International Management Institute*, March 7, 1933, pp. 39-42.

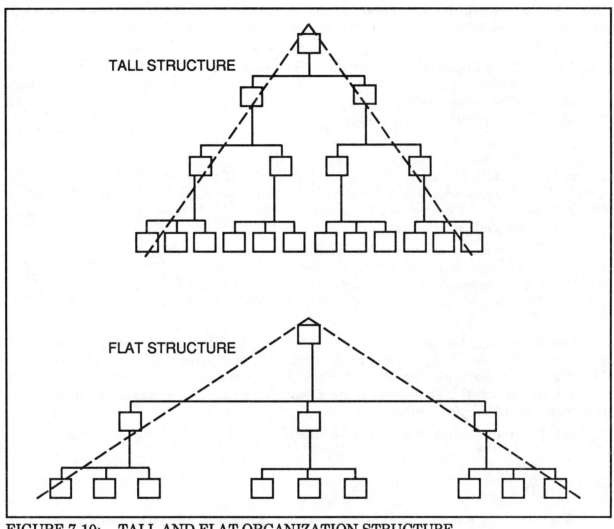

FIGURE 7-10:   TALL AND FLAT ORGANIZATION STRUCTURE
SHOWING DIFFERENT SPANS OF MANAGEMENT

number; most other organizations base the limit on four significant factors. These factors involve the nature of the work, the skills of the manager and the worker, and the physical work environment.

The exact number of subordinates any given manager can effectively supervise is not fixed, but it should be apparent that there is a theoretical limit even if it cannot be precisely calculated. When this theoretical limit is exceeded the result is ineffectiveness. The symptoms are results not realized, frustration for the managers, wasted resources, loss of control, and poor overall performance by employees.

Step 5: Coordination of Organizational Resources. The last step in organizing group effort is coordinating the use of resources so that organizational objectives can be met in the most efficient way possible. When work is divided into smaller parts and grouped logically (Steps 1 and 2), these separate work components must be coordinated. Coordination refers to the blending, matching or synchronizing of individual and group effort. Without coordination individuals and departments would act independently with no regard for the effort of others or for overall organizational objectives.

Coordination is needed when there is a high degree of interdependence among departments. If one department's work directly affects another's in a sequential manner, good communication is the key to effective coordination. Providing knowledge about schedules, expected quality, costs, problems, etc., to each interdependent department is essential. This is called **sequential interdependence**.

Another type of departmental interdependence which requires coordination occurs when one department works directly with another department. This is called **parallel interdependence**. An example is the food services unit of a hospital which must coordinate patients' meals with doctors instructions. Each must keep the other informed and follow directions and procedures to coordinate and control departmental activities (or the safety and well-being of patients suffers).

The least amount of required coordination occurs when departments do not work directly with each other and do not depend on the work of each other. These departments are **autonomous** in their efforts to achieve organizational goals, but the lack of productivity and efficiency within each unit can affect the well-being of other departments.

Coordination is best achieved when all managers and all employees in departments understand the overall objectives, the departmental objectives, their own objectives, the importance of their work, the time schedules, the organizational guidelines (rules, procedures and policies) influencing their actions, and when all receive adequate information to support their work efforts.

Good communication is essential to effective coordination and sound organization.

Summary

Organizing is a managerial effort to assign work and allocate resources; then arrange work and resources in an orderly way so that group effort generates the desired end result efficiently.

Organizing is a primary function of management but is not usually a separate managerial act. Organizing may be part of planning or mixed with other management functions.

Organizing can be viewed as a managerial effort to bring order to the work place and generate efficiency of effort.

Organizing is important in management because of the following benefits: It generates effective group action; it synergizes resources; it pinpoints individual responsibility; and it facilitates the implementing and control functions.

Recognition of the organizing function has a long history. Organization structure existed in prehistoric and ancient civilizations which had superior-subordinate relationships, centers of authority, and duties delegated to subordinates.

Organization theory is identified as **classical, neoclassical** and **modern**. None of the theories are complete nor totally accepted by researchers in management. The theoretical approaches do provide students some insight into the evolutionary development of management thought about organizing.

Traditionally the formal organization is described as a group of people working together toward common objectives with a clearly defined hierarchy (lines of authority, responsibility, accountability and communication). A sound hierarchy results when the organization's departments are structured into efficient and effective work groups or units. Departmental work groups can be categorized by function, product, location, customer, time, number and/or sequence.

The major types of organization structure are line, line and staff, matrix and committees (not discussed in this chapter). Nearly all small organizations are line structured. Large organizations tend to be structured line and staff, and very large, multi-project organizations may have some form of matrix structure as part of the formal organization.

Delegating is a major activity of a manager. The process of delegating involves four steps: Assign responsibility, assign authority to accompany responsibility, assign a time standard, and assign accountability.

The steps in organizing group effort are the following:
1. Dividing work into smaller parts based on the concept of **work specialization**
2. Grouping tasks in a logical way so that managers can more soundly supervise employees in identifiable departments, called **departmentalizing**
3. Activating authority and responsibility by delegating both downward
4. Determining spans of management (the number of employees which should report to a single manager) without losing any efficiency and effectiveness of effort
5. The coordination of organization resources between departments that have a high degree of interdependence.

Review Questions

1. Why is organizing so important to the managerial functions of planning and implementing?
2. Can you name the important managerial benefits of organizing? Which of the benefits do you consider most important?
3. What subject of interest did Adam Smith, Thomas Jefferson and Eli Whitney have in common? Explain.
4. Is the classical theory of organization still in vogue? Discuss completely.
5. Matrix organization is widely used in multi-project organizations. What are the advantages and disadvantages of this form of organization?
6. How do you go about organizing group effort? Name and explain each step.

Assignments for Personal Development

1. Visit any kind of organization and ask a manager to list the ten most common daily problems that he or she has to handle. Identify which of the ten occurs because of defects or weaknesses in the existing organizational structure.
2. Some major companies reorganize every four or five years. Why? Present the reasons you find or think of and exchange points of view in a class discussion.

Incident

DISGRUNTLED EMPLOYEES

Ms. Pam Petite had just returned from lunch with several of her colleagues. The luncheon was a celebration of her first year of employment with a large public relations firm. Her division concentrated on the promotion of trade shows, exhibitions and holiday events.

She was disgusted with the conversation around the lunch table. Instead of talking about her and her experiences during this past year on the job, her colleagues spent most of the time complaining about the management of the organization. Everyone at the luncheon had a few choice complaints!

Pam decided to write down the complaints she could remember:

*   Communication misunderstandings
*   Ineffective delegation of work assignments
*   Jurisdictional disputes over work responsibilities
*   Conflicts between line and staff personnel
*   Bosses failing to support employees when problems arise
*   Employees bypassing their managers
*   Failure of employees to report everything that happens to their bosses
*   "Fuzzy" job descriptions
*   Lack of excitement in the workplace.

The more Pam thought about the complaints, the more she realized that she was part of a badly organized organization which is managed by some less than competent managers.

Questions:

1. Is there anything Pam Petite can do to help the public relations firm become better organized?
2. Assuming Pam Petite was appointed to an employee committee to come up with recommendations for improving the organization—what should she recommend? (List five things as a start.)

Suggested Readings

Argyris, C. *Integrating the Individual and the Organization*. New York: Wiley, 1964.

Drucker, Peter F. "New Templates for Today's Organizations." *Harvard Business Review*, January-February 1974, pp. 45-53.

Fink, Stephen L., R. Stephen Jenks, and Robin D. Willits. *Designing and Managing Organizations*. Homewood, IL: Richard D. Irwin, 1983.

Goddard, Robert W. "The Rise of the New Organization." *Management World* 14 (January 1985): 7-11.

McCaskey, Michael B. "An Introduction to Organizational Design." *California Management Review*, Winter 1974, pp. 13-20.

Nash, Michael. *Managing Organizational Performance*. San Francisco: Jossey-Bass, 1983.

Ouchi, W. G., and A. M. Jaeger. "Type Z Organization: Stability in the Midst of Mobility." *Academy of Management Review*, April 1978, pp. 305-14.

Pugh, D. "Effective Coordination in Organizations." *SAM Advanced Management Journal*, Winter 1979, pp. 28-35.

CHAPTER 8

THE CONTROL FUNCTION

After studying this chapter, **you will know**:

- The meaning of control
- Steps in the control process
- The need for control
- How much control organizations should have
- The relationship between planning and control
- The types of controls
- Characteristics of effective control
- Why employees resist control
- Methods to overcome employees resistance to control
- How to control (minimize) control

Introduction

Theoretically control is the only management function you could eliminate. If managers were perfect at planning, organizing and implementing, there would be no reason for them to follow-up activities with control programs. We know that this is impossible; so, the control function exists in some degree throughout every organization

It would be difficult to overstress the importance of the control function in the management profession. Any time customers, clients, employees of personnel or any kind are involved in organizational activity, control to some degree becomes necessary. Many organizations require employees to adhere to a dress code when working. The dress code becomes a control program.

Controlling financial expenditures and maintaining desired quality of performance are other major areas saturated with control programs. All "red tape" or organizational guidelines are introduced to influence (control) the behavior of employees or personnel for whom management has responsibility. Employee handbooks tend to put in writing some of the most important standards of personnel behavior. Much of what is in a handbook is part of a control program.

You should read the chapter carefully. It is possible to over control. That is, the benefit from the control program does not exceed the cost of implementing the control program. Costs may be measured in dollars, but costs also include low morale, personnel turnover and lagging performance. As this chapter indicates, you need some control activities to insure conformity of activities, output and behavior; but managers must guard against imposing excessive controls.

A control activity is not a substitute for sound management. In a way a control activity is a result of sound planning that attempts to prevent or avoid negative outcomes before they occur. Failure to plan and control all organizational activity properly is a major cause of management turnover.

Origin and Meaning of Control

Control is a management activity that originates from **need**. Managers need to insure that work is performed properly; that a quoted price is correct; that the quality of an end product is guaranteed and consistent. The control function also provides managers with information they need for making decisions. And control activities originate from the need organizations have to provide satisfactory services and products to customers at reasonable prices. Without the function of control, the managers of an organization would, in effect, be "flying blind."

The essence of control is to adjust work activity to predetermined standards which are based on data obtained from that same work activity.

It is important to note that managers who develop sound strategy, viable objectives, achievable mission statements, clear organization charts, reasonable schedules, etc., are vulnerable to serious consequences if they confuse these activities with **control**. Control is the step added to assure that desired objectives are met in an efficient manner.

Control should not be viewed as a negative activity which is introduced to punish, restrain or confine individuality or creativity within or outside the organization. Control programs have a positive purpose: to insure conformity of activities, output and behavior.

The control function generally pays for itself many times over unless the program is so complex and cumbersome that costs of implementation override the benefits.

The Control Process

Any control process involves these three steps:

1. Setting standards
2. Appraising conformance to the standards
3. Taking appropriate corrective or remedial action if the standards are not met or are exceeded.

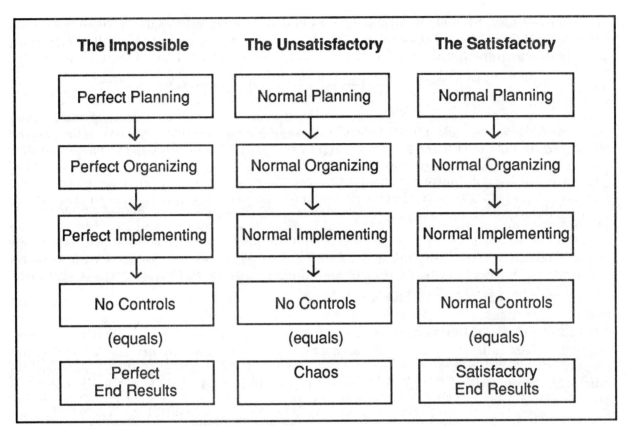

The Impossible	The Unsatisfactory	The Satisfactory
Perfect Planning	Normal Planning	Normal Planning
↓	↓	↓
Perfect Organizing	Normal Organizing	Normal Organizing
↓	↓	↓
Perfect Implementing	Normal Implementing	Normal Implementing
↓	↓	↓
No Controls	No Controls	Normal Controls
(equals)	(equals)	(equals)
Perfect End Results	Chaos	Satisfactory End Results

FIGURE 8-1: APPROACHES TO CONTROL

Step 1. Setting Standards. Standards originate from managerial planning and are based on the goals and objectives of the organization. Standards may pertain to everything from the quality of products to the number of days of employee sick leave; from sales quotas and inventory levels to the length and number of breaks an employee gets during the working day. For standards to have value, they must be expressed in measurable and understandable terms that are accepted by the people affected. For example, if American motorists do not accept 55 miles per hour as the standard speed limit on highways, this standard has little value. If employees routinely take thirty minute breaks rather than the allowed fifteen, the standard is meaningless. Standards should be objective, easily measured and relevant to the goals of the organization. Managerial subjectivity and judgment should be limited in the implementation of standards, and standards should be expressed in quantifiable terms whenever feasible. An organization's philosophic ideal, such as "We're going to provide the best quality and service in the industry," is a noble target, but not a good standard because it is difficult to measure results.

Step 2. Appraising Conformance to the Standards. Often called **monitoring** or **inspecting,** appraising conformance to the standards is done in two stages. First, measure performance; then, compare performance to the standards.

Measuring performance requires determination of when, where and how measurement will take place. How often performance is measured can determine control and cost effectiveness. Also managers need information on a timely basis to make sound decisions. The frequency of repetitive measurement depends on the nature of the work activity being controlled.

Methods used to measure performance can be quantitative, qualitative or a mixture of both. Measuring the amount of work produced that meets quality standards is quantitative. Measuring a worker's ability to get along with co-workers by observing and judging their interactions is solely qualitative. A manager's performance over a year may be measured by how well he or she stays within budget in his or her area of responsibility and by improvement in employee morale in the work area. This evaluation combines quantitative and qualitative methods.

Comparing performance to standards is the second stage of appraising conformance. Performance may match the standard, fail to meet it, or it may exceed the standard. The need for corrective action depends on the allowable deviation from the standard. When the organization allows employees six days of sick leave per year without a doctor's explanation, no action is necessary until an employee misses that seventh day.

Step 3. Taking Corrective or Remedial Action. If the standard is satisfied by performance measured in Step 2, there is no need for Step 3. But is the performance does not meet the standard, some type of corrective or remedial action should be taken. When a driver fails to meet the 55 mile per hour speed limit by driving 70 and being stopped and ticketed, corrective action has identified the problem (failure to match the maximum standard) and issued a remedy. A manufactured part that fails to meet the quality standards may be thrown out or reworked until it does conform to the standard. Correcting a deviation from the standard requires an evaluation by the manager in charge. The manager focuses on the planning (Was it faulty?); on the standard itself (Was it unrealistic?); or perhaps on the personnel involved (Were they trained and qualified to perform the task?). Whatever the source of the problem, it will continue to occur unless appropriate corrective action resolves the underlying problem.

The case study in Figure 8-2 concerns one of the critical problems facing the United States today, widespread insolvency in the savings and loan industry. The case shows the consequences of an activity getting out of control. The same sort of impact, on a smaller scale, could adversely affect the operations of any organization. Without question, control is an essential function of management.

The Need for Control

The need for control depends on answering this question: How expensive would operations be without controls? In very small organizations the control activities may be informal and largely unplanned. The managers react when a problem appears. But in well-managed organizations, control activities are planned, implemented, regularly reviewed and changed when conditions warrant.

These major factors affect the need for controls:
- The way organizations are structured
- Types of employees and the nature of their work
- Changes in the internal and external environment

Controls Fail in Thrifts

A major problem in the United States today, one that affects everyone, is the scandal about insolvent thrifts. How did such a problem occur when these financial institutions are audited regularly and governed heavily by legislation and the Federal Home Loan Bank Board? And how can this crisis be solved so that similar problems do not arise in the future?

Banning K. Lary[1] reports that, by the end of 1988, nearly 1,000 of the 3,400 thrifts in the U.S. were losing money. His figures come from a U.S. House of Representatives Government Operations Committee Report. What went wrong? Some people blame the deregulatory reforms of the early 1980's which allowed the savings and loan industry to diversify, reduced its restrictions and made competition fairer. Many experts say this deregulation has backfired. Others say the causes are high inflation, new competition for home loans, and fraud and mismanagement by officers of the insolvent thrifts. Regional economic problems, such as the real estate and oil busts in the Southwest during the 1980's, have also been cited.

Without question corrective action had to be taken. On Friday, August 4, 1989, Congress passed the most far-reaching restructuring of the nation's financial institution industry since the Great Depression of the 1930's. The thrift bill is designed to bolster thrifts and remedy the insolvency problems in the savings and loan industry caused by poor—and in some cases fraudulent—loan practices. The bill will pump $50 billion in cash into the ailing thrift insurance fund. The total cost to taxpayers starts with a minimum of $159 billion over the next ten years. The bill requires thrifts to concentrate more on traditional business; requires more of the owners or investors cash as part of capital requirements; and mandates that at least seventy (70) percent of their loans must be housing-related.[2]

[1]Banning K. Lary, "Insolvent Thrifts: A National Crisis," *Management Review*, March, 1989, Vol. 78, No. 3.
[2]James A. Mallory, "S & L Bill Considered Important First Step," *Atlanta Journal and Constitution*, August 6, 1989, p. 1E.

FIGURE 8-2: CASE STUDY

Organization Structure. Organizations that are highly centralized (tall structures)[3] concentrate authority, responsibility, decision-making and control near the top of the hierarchy. These organizations are more bureaucratic, with more "red tape," than decentralized firms (flat structures). More rigid control programs exist in highly centralized organizations, such as banks, to assure that all employees conform to the same standards, procedures, rules and policies. When we say managers make decisions "by the book," we acknowledge they operate in a tightly controlled, highly centralized organization that allows little room for individual initiative or creativity. The control function in these organizations becomes extremely important due to the sensitive nature of the work activities. Examples of highly centralized organizations with many rigid control programs are commercial banks, government agencies, the military and some educational institutions.

[3] For a complete discussion of organization structures, see Chapter 7.

Organizations that are highly decentralized (flat structures) are relatively less controlled at the top of the hierarchy. The control function is pushed downward to lower level managers. Examples of major control programs at lower management levels are conformance to budgets and achieving desired objectives (such as projected anticipated sales) over the set period of time.

Types of Employees and Their Work. Employees who are relatively unskilled and those in the process of acquiring more skills normally must be more controlled until they have achieved the level of competency which matches the desired quality and quantity standards. Thereafter, minimum control programs may be implemented to insure their conformance to standards. Highly professional employees such as researchers in a pharmaceutical laboratory may need little control over their activities whereas those who produce the pharmaceutical product need strict quality control programs. Obviously the nature of the work has as much effect on control activities as the type of employees. Getting the space shuttle ready to launch or preparing a new public stock offering dictate tight control programs. A creative team working on a new advertising campaign may require few controls (perhaps only a time deadline) until they present their work. Building a house in a residential neighborhood may require strict controls in selecting the craftsmen hired for the project; then, little control as they work except for observation of physical progress and conformance to the plans each day. Other factors that influence the need for control programs are age of employees; educational background; certified skills possessed; complexity of the work; dollars invested in work activities; geographic spread of the workers; time constraints for completion of work; and budget restrictions.

Changes in Environment. Change is inevitable. Managers must be alert to changing internal and external factors that precede a change in the way activities are controlled. Examples of internal changes are unionization of the work force; budget cutbacks; an expansion of the services offered; introducing new equipment; or a change in ownership or top management which brings a new philosophy or different techniques to the job. External environmental changes can include new legislation or rules and regulations; a slumping economy; higher than expected inflation; unusual weather conditions; a change in the prime rate or a gasoline shortage.

Sometimes information generated by current control programs influences managers to change the way activities are controlled. A new need arises which can only be met by changing the control program. An example of this is the professional sports leagues' responses to the growing problem of drug and alcohol abuse within their industry over the past decade.

How Much Control?

Control programs must have a "pay off." There is no need to control an activity if the cost is greater than the benefit. Economic considerations play an important role in deciding the amount of control. For example, no organization can afford to inspect the quality individually of thousands of items as they are received or shipped. Instead sampling based on probability theory is used to monitor the items. Inspectors of the U.S. Department of Agriculture use this approach when inspecting products under their jurisdiction.

How much control should an organization have over its activities? Like the old question, how long should a person's legs be; the answer is just enough (whether to reach the ground or to accomplish the desired results)! Anything beyond "just enough" is pure waste. Organizations should have just enough control to meet desired objectives. Control programs should be audited regularly to make certain that they are current and not obsolete, and to determine that they are functioning as designed.

Additionally, organizations should consider the impact of control programs on employees. If employees resent tight control programs and their productivity and morale are affected, the cost of control may be greater than the value. Many organizations today involve their employees in the design and implementation of control programs which affect them. One technique which allows this participation is Quality Control Circles.

Quality Control Circles originated in the United States; then became popular in Japan. In a Quality Control Circle (QCC) a small group of individuals meet to discuss and resolve quality control issues. The concept of allowing employees input in decisions affecting them is a form of participative management. As already discussed, participating in the problem-solving and decision-making process tends to make employees identify with the outcome and lessens their resistance to any change.

QCCs were introduced many years ago and failed to draw much attention until the Japanese implemented them and became renowned throughout the world for the high quality of their products in world markets. American firms noticed and many have introduced QCCs. The popularity of QCCs in Japan is not without exception, however; Japanese hospitals have been reluctant to experiment with QCCs despite their acceptance in some American hospitals.

Health Care Management Review reports that all the elements required for the success of QCCs are inherent in Japanese organization structure, i.e., cooperation, ethical goals, commitment and lifetime employment. But resistance to QCCs exists because the medical staff occupies a very dominant position and is not committed to the goals of QCCs. The report says U.S. hospitals are organizationally better suited to QCCs even though they do not have the underlying favorable cultural factors present in Japan.[4]

Planning and Control

The purpose of planning is to reach objectives in the proper period of time, as efficiently and effectively as possible, with a minimum of problems. It is highly unlikely that this can occur without introducing a planned control program. Managers plan, organize, implement and then control. Sound control programs alert managers to time delays, quality defects, poor employee performance, schedule problems, and much more. The opposite is also true. Good performance, being ahead of schedule and other positive indicators are valuable to managers, and such data results from using controls.

Planning involves the determination of necessary control programs. Since planning is future-oriented, and the future involves risks and uncertainties; controlling becomes an essential activity. There is a balanced dependency between planning and controlling as shown in Figure 8-3.

---

[4] Quality Circles: The Myth and Reality of Hospital Management," *Health Care Management Review*, Summer 1985, Vol. 10, No. 3, pp. 45-53 (no author identified).

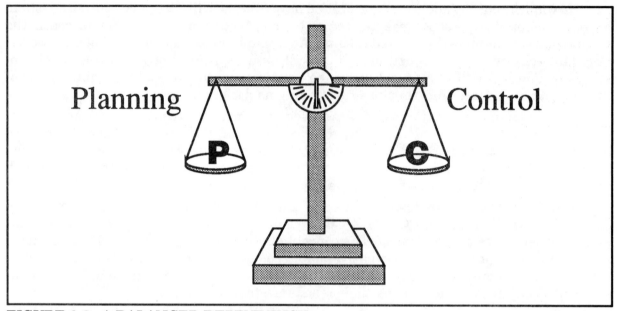

FIGURE 8-3: A BALANCED DEPENDENCY

Types of Controls

Managers can introduce control anywhere along the continuum of work activity: at the beginning, during the process, or at the end. The placement of control relates to the timing of work activity and the importance of each phase of the work. Figure 8-4 illustrates the three types of control commonly used in organizations.

Incoming or Screening Control. If control is introduced at the beginning, it is called **incoming** or **screening** control. The purpose of control at this stage is to prevent problems from occurring. This is a positive approach to control. Checking everything about a new car before you purchase it is one example. Commercial airline pilots who checklist the equipment and its systems before takeoff are another example.

In-process Control. When manufactured goods are subjected to quality checks (against standards of excellence) during the manufacturing process, the manager is using **in-process control**. This type of control also uncovers problems with time delays, quantity output, and employee performance before the end of the work cycle. In-process control does not prevent problems, but it does spot deviations from the standard before work activity is completed. In-process control provides an opportunity to adjust performance to the standard prior to incurring major problems. For example, if in-process control checks prove production is not meeting quantity standards, the production line can be accelerated. If a quality control check in-process reveals that two parts do not fit together as they should, it can be fixed before the integrity of a whole unit is threatened. If a baseball pitcher with a one run lead walks two batters and throws three straight balls to the third he faces in the fifth inning, he may be removed from the game before it gets out of hand. These are examples of in-process controls.

Final-stage Control. Final-stage controls review the results of the final product or service. Information obtained about deviations from the standard or plans can be used in controlling and improving performance in the future. Final-stage control also can provide information to support major management decisions such as to cancel offering advertised services; to scrub a shuttle lift-off; to add or discontinue a product; or to approve continuing past work practices.

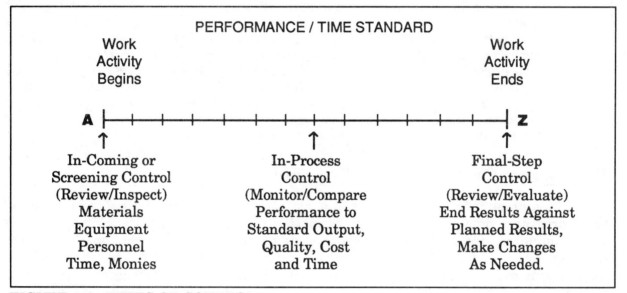

FIGURE 8-4: TYPES OF CONTROL

Characteristics of Effective Control

The control function is essential to insure that work performance matches the standards and to uncover the reasons for any deviations. Also, we know there is a balanced dependency between planning and control. Without sound planning and effectively designed control programs, the control function is ineffective.

Certain points must be remembered when designing control programs. These points may be considered the characteristics of effective control.

1. **The details of each control program should be tailored to fit the needs of individual organizations.** Every organization's products and services, work environment, types of employees and objectives are different from every other's. Establishing the control function must include consideration of all the variables which make that organization unique.
2. **The establishment of controls must have the complete support of top management.** Without such support it will be difficult to convince either managers or employees that controls are essential.
3. **Control programs must be cost-effective.** There is little cost justification to introduce controls if the cost, either in dollar value or in employee upheaval, is greater than the benefit.
4. **Control activities should possess enough flexibility to adapt to change.** When new standards are needed, it is better to modify the existing control program than to create an entirely new system.

5. **Control programs should provide information in a timely way.** Through a carefully designed system of communication pertinent information generated by the control function must be available to managers as needed. Sometimes data must be reviewed hourly; or it can be needed daily, weekly, quarterly or yearly. Generally information is needed less often when the work setting is stable, but needed more often when the work situation is subject to unpredictable changes and uncertainty. Timeliness means providing usable information exactly when needed.

6. **Objective information is the essence of sound control.** Often employees complain of management's showing favoritism: that one employee gets better treatment or a better evaluation than another without justification. Management's objectivity comes under question. Objective information is a must if control programs are to function properly. This is true whether the source of information is employees at work stations, computers, sales representatives in the field, or from managers evaluating personnel. It can become a legal issue if the information gained in a control program is not as objective as possible. Even cybernetic controls that are self-regulating must be designed to provide useful and objective information.

Employee Resistance to Control

It is common for the introduction of a control program to upset employees. After all these programs represent change, which most people resist by nature. Employees may resent implementing a new procedure or system, changing long-established work patterns; or they may balk at closer supervision, with each move questioned, and their performance measured against a nebulous standard. The result of too much control is to suppress and stifle individual flexibility, creativity and originality. This may be a purpose of the control program, but overcontrolling quickly generates a cost greater than the value of the control.

According to Jaeger and Baliga the Japanese have been able to introduce bureaucratic and cultural controls effectively which have enabled them to produce quality products at reasonable prices. Much of the credit is given to the use of their cultural control systems and the technology with which they are working.[5] Japanese managers consider the "total" employee as an integral link in successfully implementing a control program. They minimize employee resistance to controls and involve employees in the planning and implementation of control.

Overcoming Employee Resistance to Control

There are four recommendations to overcome or prevent employee resistance to control. Consider each recommendation a step to take to overcome or prevent resistance.

Step 1: Sound Planning

Ideally well planned control will avoid any employee resistance to control. Managers need to establish the objectives of the control program; then create a program that possesses all of the characteristics of effective control.

---

[5] A. M. Jaeger and B. R. Baliga, "Control systems and Strategic Adaptation: Lessons from Japanese Experience," *Strategic Management Journal*, April/June 1985, Vol. 6, No. 2, pp. 115-134.

Step 2: Employee Involvement

Allowing employees to participate in the development of a control program through ideas, suggestions and feedback eliminates a lot of resistance once a control program is introduced. Their input can be valuable throughout the planning stage. Since they are the ones to be directly affected by the control and often they are more knowledgeable about the situation needing control, their views and suggestions must be encouraged, reviewed and recognized in all cases.

Step 3: Careful Implementation

This step deals with the actual introduction of the control program. Careful implementation is a three phase process: First, employees must be **educated** about the control program. The employees directly affected by the control understand how the program works, its purpose, and the impact of it on them and the whole organization. More importantly they must be **sold** on the control program. This requires stressing the value of the control program to them, the benefits which will accrue, and the cost-effectiveness of the control. Finally, the control program should be **demonstrated**. A live demonstration presents a point more effectively than any other method. After the demonstration, questions should be encouraged and answered, once again involving employees in the control program.

Step 4: Follow-Up

Once a control is introduced, all employees involved should be encouraged to report their reaction to it. Each verbal or written comment should be recognized by management positively. Sometimes a follow-up group meeting is helpful in providing a forum for evaluating control. Some organizations use quality circles as a forum for continuous follow-up. When management identifies problems with the control which prevent achieving desired objectives, corrective action should not be delayed.

If these four steps are followed, management should be able to minimize or prevent employee resistance to control.

Organization and Control

Top management has the ultimate responsibility for the control function. In small organizations each employee may be assigned the duty to control his or her own work activities according to management's instructions. As organizations grow larger, staff persons and positions emerge, created by higher line management, to assist all employees in performing their duties. Often the new staff personnel are directly involved in control activities such as internal audits, safety, quality and scheduling. As growth continues and more complex organization structures evolve (such as organization by divisions, geographic regions or product lines), control departments may be created to function as specialized staff units. The most common of these deal with quality, inventory, budgets, production, forecasting, maintenance and safety. Staff control personnel are advisory to line managers but are delegated limited line authority in some specialized areas such as inspectors in quality control. Staff control specialists or departments, as shown in Figure 8-5, are located in the area where they advise line managers, but the placement of the staff, position or department on the organization chart does not indicate the relative importance of the work.

The fact that staff departments are created to assist and advise line managers about control does not decrease the line manager's responsibility to control.

The larger organization usually have a position entitled controller. The controller is a manager whose full time job is to control activities throughout the organization. The controller assists all line managers with their control activities and gathers and interprets data for the benefit of higher line management. Recently other job titles have been coined which reflect similar duties and responsibilities as that of a controller. In the healthcare industry the job title of Quality Assurance Director is popular. A quality assurance director in a large hospital deals with facts, data, trends, costs, etc., that are relevant to the control of services provided and their costs. This information is measured against the projected standards.

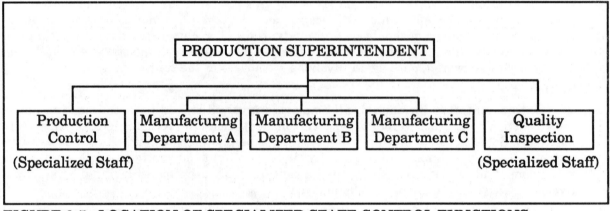

FIGURE 8-5: LOCATION OF SPECIALIZED STAFF CONTROL FUNCTIONS

Controlling Controls

As essential as the control function is, organizations can become overcontrolled. Control programs are a form of red tape and are expensive to administer. Control should be a result of a formulated control strategy developed by top management and should not be introduced out of crisis. Periodically management should audit all control programs to make sure they are still useful, current, and continue to possess all of the characteristics of effective control. Excessive control contributes to inefficiency which reflects directly on top management.

New Trends in Controlling

Total Quality Management (TQM) is the most widely known movement in the United States designed to control quality and improve all aspects of an organization's activities. While many dismiss the movement as faddish and even destructive, others describe it as a continuous process that will lead to improved quality, greater efficiency and higher employee morale. All these features are contributors to increased productivity in American organizations which is the key to economic growth without inflation and to competitiveness in expanding world markets.

The four key points of TQM are described as a continuous process in which an organization does the following:

- Statistically analyzes how jobs are done.
- Disposes of procedures that do not work.
- Uses all employees' broadest expertise and rewards it meaningfully.
- Purges itself of stereotypical thinking.[6]

TQM has its origins in the work of George Edwards, Walter Shewhart, W. Edwards Deming and A. V. Feigenbaum. These men advocated the concept of quality control in every functional area of an organization from design to sales. They stressed a preventive (proactive) approach to control of quality rather than relying on corrective (reactive) activities.

---

1. Create constancy of purpose toward improvement of product and service with a plan to become competitive, stay in business, and provide jobs.
2. Adopt the new philosophy. We are in a new economic age. We can no longer live with commonly accepted levels of delays, mistakes, defective materials, and defective workmanship.
3. Cease dependence on mass inspection. Require, instead, statistical evidence that quality is built in to eliminate the need for inspection on a mass basis.
4. End the practice of awarding business on the basis of price tag. Instead, depend on meaningful measures of quality, along with price. Move toward a single supplier for any one item, based on a long-term relationship of loyalty and trust.
5. Improve constantly and forever the system of production and service, to improve quality and productivity, and thus constantly decrease costs.
6. Institute modern methods of training.
7. Institute modern methods of supervision.
8. Drive out fear, so that everyone may work effectively for the company.
9. Break down organizational barriers—everyone must work as a team to foresee and solve problems.
10. Eliminate arbitrary numerical goals, posters, and slogans for the workforce which seek new levels of productivity without providing methods.
11. Eliminate work standards and numerical quotas.
12. Remove barriers that rob employees of their pride of workmanship.
13. Institute a vigorous program of education and training.
14. Create a structure which will push the prior 13 points every day.

FIGURE 8-6:   THE PHILOSOPHICAL BASIS FOR TOTAL QUALITY MANAGEMENT OF THE 1990s—The "Deming of the United States"

Source: Gitlow and Gitlow, *The Deming Guide*, pp. 29-31.

---

[6] Susan Harte, "Total Quality," *The Atlanta Journal-The Atlanta Constitution*, Section R, p. 1, October 11, 1992.

W. Edwards Deming is the most well-known of this group. Dr. Deming gained fame for influencing Japanese industrialists after World War II. His ideas and methods, which were not well-received in America at that time, appealed to the Japanese, and they used his methods to improve the quality of their products so that they could become the best in the world. Based at least in part on the success of Japan since the introduction of the Deming ideas and the loss of competitive advantages by the United States, the Deming methods have gained new attention and acceptance and are spreading throughout the United States. Dr. Deming's philosophy is the foundation for most TQM programs today. His management philosophy is outlined in his Fourteen Points detailed in Figure 8-6.

Once management accepts and understands these fourteen points, they have developed a philosophical basis for effectively using statistical quality control. Using the Deming methods of TQM to improve and control quality requires a total commitment by management, from the top to the lowest level. In order for the system to provide the right framework for positive action and successful results, the commitment must permeate the entire organization. A "quality culture" evolves which encourages teamwork, open communication, joint problem-solving, pride in workmanship, and an acceptance that the efforts to improve and sustain quality and performance will be an on-going, never-ending goal. According to Gitlow and Gitlow, these are the advantages of TQM as promoted by Dr. Deming:

> To improve quality, management must demonstrate its commitment to quality and accept responsibility for improving it. The "quality environment" encourages teamwork, communication, joint problem-solving, trust, security, pride of workmanship, and never-ending improvement. A true cooperative spirit prevails in this type of atmosphere, as teamwork is a prerequisite for the firm to function and constantly improve the extended process. The corporate culture changes so that workers are no longer afraid to point out problems in the system, and management is actively involved in the never-ending improvement of the extended process with the workers. Workers and management learn to speak the same language, the language of statistics and process control. Workers are responsible for communicating to management the information they have about the system so that management can act. Never-ending improvement of the process (not just within the organization, but of all aspects of the extended process, including vendors, customers, the community, and investors) eventually leads to higher quality, reduced costs, and greater profitability.[7]

Summary

Control is a managerial activity that originates from need. The need to insure that work is performed correctly; the need to assure that quoted prices are accurate; the need to guarantee the quality of goods and services and much more.

The essence of control is to adjust work activity to preset standards based on information obtained from monitoring work activity.

Theoretically control is the only function of management that could be eliminated, but only if planning, organizing and implementing were performed perfectly. Such is never the case.

---

[7] Howard S. Gitlow and Shelly J. Gitlow, *The Deming Guide to Quality and Competitive Position* (Englewood Cliffs, NJ: Prestice-Hall, Inc., 1987), p. 7.

Control activities originate from the need organizations have to provide customers with satisfactory products and services at reasonable prices.

The control process has three steps: setting standards; appraising conformance to the standards; and taking corrective or remedial action if the standards are exceeded.

Major factors affecting the need for control are these: the way organizations are structured; the types of employees and the nature of their work; and changes in the internal and external environments.

Quality Control Circles (QCCs) are widely used by Japanese firms and are popular in the U.S. QCCs are small groups of individuals who meet to discuss and solve quality control issues. The idea of QCCs originated in the U.S., but the value of having employees participate in solving control problems was not fully appreciated nor practiced much in the U.S. until the past decade.

Sound planning includes the determination of needed control after objectives have been formulated. There is a balanced dependency between planning and control.

Three types of control are incoming or screening; in-process; and final-stage.

Characteristics of effective control are these:

1. The details of each control program should be tailored to meet the needs of individual organizations.
2. The establishment of controls must have the complete support of top management.
3. Control programs must be cost effective.
4. Control programs should possess enough flexibility to adapt to change.
5. Control programs should provide information in a timely way.
6. Objective information is the essence of sound control.

Employees often resist new control programs. Four recommendations to overcome or prevent employee resistance are through sound planning; employee involvement; careful implementation, and managerial follow-up.

Top management has the ultimate responsibility for the control function. It is an essential activity, yet organizational activities can be overcontrolled. Management should audit all control programs periodically to make certain they are still useful and current and that they continue to possess all the characteristics of effective control. Excessive control contributes to inefficiency and reflects on top management.

Review Questions

1. Under what conditions could an organization do without the control function?
2. What are the essential steps in the control process? Explain each.
3. Discuss the balanced dependency between planning and control.
4. There are three types of controls. Each type serves a unique purpose. Clarify the purpose of each.
5. List and briefly discuss the characteristics of effective control.
6. Review options management has to overcome or prevent employee resistance to new control.

Assignments for Personal Development

1. Take a few minutes and list the control programs in your organization that directly affect your behavior as an employee. Some examples might be punching a time clock; parking in a designated area; going to lunch at a certain time, etc. (The number of control programs can overwhelm you!) How many of these control programs might be eliminated without harming organization efficiency and, in fact, might produce cost savings?

2. Identify two or three problem areas in the organization. Is there a need for improved controls in these areas? If so, what do you recommend that would replace the existing controls? Justify your recommendations.

Incident

A SMOKING GUN!

Ms. Fitzgerald, recently promoted manager, directly supervises five women in the administrative services area of a large health maintenance organization. At the time of her promotion her immediate superior, who was an Associate Director, told her she had a real challenge on her hands. The women employees were accustomed to a boss who had a laidback style of management because she was about to retire and was congenial and friendly to everyone. The former boss was extremely popular with her employees who all considered her a friend.

Her boss told Ms. Fitzgerald that the time had finally come when change was necessary to improve productivity and efficiency. Furthermore, he told her the socializing throughout the day had to stop. All employees had to realize they were there from 8 to 5 to work; and coffee breaks morning and afternoon as well as the lunch period were to be kept to their strict time limit. Ms. Fitzgerald was cautioned to expect trouble from these employees when she tried to straighten them out, but her job was to control their behavior enough to produce a sharp improvement in productivity and performance.

Questions:

1. Recommend ways to control employee work behavior in this situation so that employee productivity and efficiency will improve.

2. What advice would you give to Ms. Fitzgerald to overcome or prevent employee resistance to new controls?

Selected Readings

Dewelt, Robert L. "Control: Key to Making Financial Strategy Work." *Management Review* (March 1977): 18.

Howard S. Gitlow and Shelly J. Gitlow. *The Deming Guide to Quality and Competitive Position.* Englewood Cliffs, NJ: Prentice-Hall, Inc., 1987.

Hutchins, David. *Quality Circles Handbook.* New York: Nichols Publishing, 1985.

Lawler, Edward E., III, and John Grant Rhode. *Information and Control in Organizations.* Santa Monica, CA: Goodyear, 1976.

Mockler, Robert J., ed., *Readings in Management Control.* New York: Appleton-Century-Crofts, 1970.

Rhodes, David and Mike Wright. "Management Control for Effective Corporate Planning." *Long-Range Planning* 17 (August 1984): 115-21.

Shetty, Y. K. "Product Quality and Competitive Strategy." *Business Horizons* (May/June 1987): 46-52.

Tannenbaum, A. *Control in Organizations.* New York: McGraw-Hill, 1968.

Vancil, Richard F. "What Kind of Management Control Do You Need?" *Harvard Business Review.* March-April 1973, pp. 75-86.

CHAPTER 9

STAFFING THE ORGANIZATION

After studying this chapter, **you will know:**
- The Meaning of Staffing
- The Personnel Management Process
- How to Audit Human Resource Planning
- Steps in Human Resource Planning
- Major Legislation Affecting Staffing
- Recruitment Sources and the Process
- The Personnel Selection Process
- About Assessment Centers
- The Value of New Employee Orientation
- Types of Training Programs
- The Importance of Compensation

Introduction

This chapter stresses the importance of staffing positions with the most qualified personnel available. Whether an organization has a personnel department or not, the responsibility to hire, integrate, develop and maintain employees rests with the management. There is no shortage of applicants for open positions. The important point to remember is that every job should be filled by a competent, motivated professional individual. Often the new employee is less than the "best," but with management's guidance, training, encouragement, and support, the new employee may develop into the "best." Many consider the development of employees to their full potential the number one responsibility of managers.

No activity is more important in management than **staffing. Staffing is the acquisition and placement of qualified employees in jobs that fully utilize the talents and skills of the individual.** The staffing activity is essential because it directly impacts the economic success of the organization.

Managers may structurally organize soundly, design jobs effectively, and even develop an impressive organization chart; but no aspect of organization can work well if jobs are not filled with qualified people at the right times.

The business world historically has relied heavily on the "buddy system" to fill jobs such as administrators and management personnel. This often-criticized networking approach, however, has been tempered somewhat with the advent of government regulations on employment discrimination. In many cases a **search committee** is formed to recruit, screen, interview and recommend applicants for vacant positions. Search committees tend to consist of people from a cross section of functional areas, appointed by someone in higher administration, to perform the functions of a personnel department for a specific job opening. The search committee will advertise the job and the desired experience, qualifications and skills needed; screen applications; interview selected applicants; check references and work histories (as well as personal and academic histories in some cases), and recommend candidates to higher management. Search committees are in common use in the field of education but are used by other types of organizations as well. The creation of search committees is in part due to legal and public pressure to encourage the active recruitment of a cross-section of applicants. Also, members of a search committee may be more objective in the evaluation of applicants since they have no personal ties to the applicants.

Regardless of the method used to choose personnel to fill vacant jobs, each job should be filled by a qualified person.

Personnel Management

Staffing is a function of personnel management. Usually organizations that have one hundred or more employees create personnel management positions. These positions tend to be filled by personnel management specialists who assist line managers in performing all of the personnel functions. When organizations grow larger, personnel management departments (sometimes called human resource departments) are created and perform all of the personnel functions on behalf of line managers. Personnel managers and personnel management or human resource departments are traditional staff activities and have no direct line authority in the organization.

Line and Staff Conflict. Ultimate responsibility for the success or failure of any organization rests with line managers. As discussed in Chapter 7, staff persons and departments are internal specialists employed to provide some form of specialized aid to line managers. Line managers should make the actual hiring and firing personnel decisions, not personnel managers or departments. Personnel managers and departments provide the necessary skills and expertise to assist line managers in staffing decisions. Confusion can occur about the role of personnel because line managers become dependent on the skills of personnel managers while they perform their line responsibilities. All managers are, in fact, "personnel managers."

Staffing and Personnel Management. Personnel management is the process of supporting the accomplishment of organizational objectives by continually **acquiring** human resources; **integrating** employees into the organization; **developing** employee potential; and **maintaining** the work force.[1] Staffing involves the acquisition of human resources. This is the first step in building a strong organization, but new employees also must be integrated, developed and maintained to build a "great" organization.

Human Resource Planning (HRP). Human resource planning includes two steps. One is a projection of future human skills and talents that the organization will need to meet its strategic objectives. The second is the formulation of a detailed plan to recruit and staff the jobs so that the organization can satisfy its strategic objectives.

Knowing the strategic objectives is essential to HRP. Human resource planners must coordinate their efforts with higher management (who develop strategy) so that they are informed about changes in goals or direction of the organization. Internal and external environmental factors that may directly affect staffing needs must also be considered. For example, changing technology in the industry may make existing equipment and current job skills obsolete (internal environment); or a declining national economy may affect revenues, resulting in personnel cutbacks (external environment).

Auditing Human Resources. Essential to HRP is an audit of existing talent and skills of current employees. Information about each employee can be obtained from interviews, questionnaires, and a review of personnel files. Audit results show whether new employees with different job skills should be sought or if, with training, present employees can meet the future needs of the organization. An audit can indicate the need for both. In addition, HRP should focus on turnover trends, normal attrition rates, and expected retirements in some defined time period (say, two to five years). Normally it would be wise to project or forecast human resource needs for the next twelve months (short run) and also for the next five years (long run). The audit should include a review of management personnel as well as nonmanagement employees.

Step 1:	Determine Strategic Objectives
Step 2:	Establish the Time Standard for Reaching Objectives
Step 3:	Review Internal and External Environmental Factors That Affect Staffing Needs
Step 4:	Project Human Talents/Skills Needed for Achieving Strategic Objectives
Step 5:	Audit Human Resources in the Organization
Step 6:	Determine Human Resource Needs in the Short-Run and Long-Run to Meet Projected Needs
Step 7:	Plan a Program of Recruitment and Selection to Fulfill Human Resource Needs

FIGURE 9-1: STEPS IN HUMAN RESOURCE PLANNING (HRP)

[1] Donald P. Crane, *Personnel, The Management of Human Resoources*, 3rd ed. (Boston: Kent Publishing Company, 1982), p. 11.

Staffing and the Legal Environment

Many local, state and federal laws affect personnel management decisions, especially those decisions which pertain to staffing the organization. A brief review of the more important federal legislation is presented to indicate the complexity legal constraints add to management's staffing activities.

Social Security Act of 1935. This act established a federal tax on payrolls and provides disability and retirement benefits. The rate of the tax has been changed many times, and employers are responsible for collecting the portion paid by employees and depositing this amount into the employee's account with the Social Security Administration.

Fair Labor Standards Act of 1938. This law set minimum wages (amended many times), overtime pay and child-labor standards.

Labor-Management Relations Act of 1947 (Taft-Hartley Act). This act was an amendment to the National Labor Relations Act of 1935 (the Wagner Act) and was designed to balance some aspects of the Wagner Act, which guaranteed employees the right to self-organization and to bargain collectively. The Taft-Hartley Act lists unfair labor practices by labor unions; provides management more rights to speak against unions during an organizing campaign (as long as employees are not threatened); and established the National Emergency Strike provision (an eighty-day cooling off period invoked by Presidential court injunction if a strike endangers the national health and safety).

Equal Pay Act of 1963 – Amended 1972. This prohibits wage discrimination on the basis of sex when the jobs require equal skills, effort and responsibility and are performed under similar working conditions.

Civil Rights Act of 1964 – Amended 1972 and 1978. Title VII of the Civil Rights Act of 1964 prohibits discrimination in employment (hiring, discharge, recruitment, assignment, compensation, and other terms and conditions of employment) on the basis of race, color, religion, sex or national origin in organizations that conduct interstate commerce. As amended in 1972, the Act extended coverage to state and municipal employees and to employers in educational institutions. In 1978, the Act was amended to prohibit discrimination in employment because of pregnancy, childbirth or related medical conditions and to reduce the number of employees necessary to comply with the Civil Rights Act (to fifteen or more). The Act created the Equal Employment Opportunity Commission (EEOC) and the Office of Federal Contract Compliance Programs (OFCCP) to hear complaints filed under the provisions of the Act and to enforce equal opportunity legislation.

Age Discrimination in Employment Act of 1967 – Amended 1978 and 1986. This act prohibits employers from discriminating in employment against individuals on the basis of age between ages 40 and 65. A 1978 amendment extended the age to 70; and in 1986, the Act was amended to remove the age limitations.

Occupational Safety and Health Act of 1970 (OSHA). OSHA mandates that employers provide their employees with a healthy and safe work environment that is free from recognized hazards that cause or are likely to cause death or serious physical harm. In addition, employers must conform to the safety and health standards set by the Occupational Safety and Health Administration, established by the Act.

Vocational Rehabilitation Act of 1973. This act prohibits discrimination in employment against individuals who are mentally and/or physically handicapped. It requires government contractors to take affirmative action to employ and advance in employment physically and mentally handicapped individuals who are qualified. Employers must also make reasonable accommodations to provide accessibility for handicapped employees (i.e., ramps and elevators rather than stairs and aisles wide enough for wheelchairs to move freely). Employers must also allow applicants and current employees to self-identify themselves as handicapped. The government's affirmative action requirement means organizations must not only cease any form of discrimination in employment practices but also actively seek handicapped employees in recruitment programs. This Act is administered by the OFCCP (refer to Civil Right Act of 1964).

Federal Privacy Act of 1974. This act applies only to the Federal Government and its contractors. It provides certain safeguards for an individual against invasion of privacy. The Act requires that individuals be permitted access to any personal records concerning them.

Employee Retirement Income Security Act of 1974 (ERISA). This act was designed to protect the interests of participants in employee benefit plans and their beneficiaries. The Act establishes standards of conduct, responsibility and obligations for fiduciaries of employee benefit plans.

Vietnam Era Veterans Readjustment Assistance Act of 1974. This act requires government contractors to take affirmative action (actively seek) to employ and advance in employment qualified disabled veterans and Vietnam-era veterans (who may or may not be disabled). Those prospective employees and current employees who are eligible to be classified under this Act may be given special consideration. It is administered by the OFCCP.

Immigration Reform and Control Act of 1986. This law seeks to protect jobs for those who are legally entitled to hold them, specifically American citizens and aliens who are authorized to work in this country. To enforce the hiring provisions of the law, employers must verify employment eligibility of anyone hired after November 6, 1986, and complete and retain a form (titled I-9, see Figure 9-2) on each employee for three years from the hiring date or for one year after termination (whichever is longer). The Act creates a tremendous record-keeping burden for employers. If you examine the form reproduced in Figure 9-2, you will see the various documents which may be used to verify eligibility. The Department of Justice and the EEOC administer this law.

Acquiring Human Resources

Once human resource needs are determined, personnel managers must develop a program to attract people with the desired skills, experience and talent to apply for job openings. This is called **recruitment**. Once a pool of applicants has been assembled, the right person must be chosen for the job. This activity is called **selection**.

Recruitment. A recruitment plan requires a job analysis which leads to job descriptions and job specifications, if they do not already exist.[2]

---

[2] For a complete definition and discussion of job analysis, job description, and job specification, see Chapter 12.

1 EMPLOYEE INFORMATION AND VERIFICATION: (to be completed and signed by employee.)

Name: (Print or Type) Last	First	Middle	Birth Name

Address: Street Name and Number	City	State	ZIP Code

Date of Birth (Month/Day/Year)	Social Security Number

I attest, under penalty of perjury, that I am (check a box):

☐ 1. A citizen or national of the United States.
☐ 2. An alien lawfully admitted for permanent residence (Alien Number A _____).
☐ 3. An alien authorized by the Immigration and Naturalization Service to work in the United States (Alien Number A _____ .
or Admission Number _____ expiration of employment authorization, if any _____).

I attest, under penalty of perjury, the documents that I have presented as evidence of identity and employment eligibility are genuine and relate to me. I am aware that federal law provides for imprisonment and/or fine for any false statements or use of false documents in connection with this certificate.

Signature	Date (Month/Day/Year)

PREPARER TRANSLATOR CERTIFICATION (To be completed if prepared by person other than the employee) I attest under penalty of perjury, that the above was prepared by me at the request of the named individual and is based on all information of which I have any knowledge.

Signature	Name (Print or Type)
Address (Street Name and Number)	City	State	Zip Code

2 EMPLOYER REVIEW AND VERIFICATION: (To be completed and signed by employer.)

Instructions:
Examine one document from List A and check the appropriate box, *OR* examine one document from List B *and* one from List C and check the appropriate boxes. Provide the Document Identification Number and Expiration Date for the document checked.

List A — Documents that Establish Identity and Employment Eligibility	List B — Documents that Establish Identity	and	List C — Documents that Establish Employment Eligibility
☐ 1. United States Passport	☐ 1. A State-issued driver's license or a State-issued I.D. card with a photograph, or information, including name, sex, date of birth, height, weight, and color of eyes. (Specify State ____)		☐ 1. Original Social Security Number Card (other than a card stating it is notvalid for employment
☐ 2. Certificate of United States Citizenship			☐ 2. A birth certificate issued by State, county, or municipal authority bearing a seal or other certification
☐ 3. Certificate of Naturalization	☐ 2. U.S. Military Card		☐ 3. Unexpired INS Employment Authorization Specify form # ____
☐ 4. Unexpired foreign passport with attached Employment Authorization	☐ 3. Other (Specify document and issuing authority) ____		
☐ 5. Alien Registration Card with photograph			
Document Identification # ____	Document Identification # ____		Document Identification # ____
Expiration Date (if any) ____	Expiration Date (if any) ____		Expiration Date (if any) ____

CERTIFICATION: I attest, under penalty of perjury, that I have examined the documents presented by the above individual, that they appear to be genuine and to relate to the individual named, and that the individual, to the best of my knowledge, is eligible to work in the United States.

Signature	Name (Print or Type)	Title
Employer Name	Address	Date

Form I-9 (05/07/87)
OMB No. 1115-0136

U.S. Department of Justice
Immigration and Naturalization Service

FIGURE 9-2: EMPLOYMENT ELIGIBILITY VERIFICATION (FORM I-9). Federal form to be completed on every employee hired after November 6, 1986, must be retained in files and reverified if documents list expiration.

The most useful tool in planning a recruitment program is the **job specification**. Job specifications detail the human traits, education, experience and skills an individual must have to qualify for a particular job. **Job descriptions** are a written explanation of all the duties and responsibilities of a job. As Wendell L. French points, "...one use of job descriptions is in the development of job specifications. These specifications, in turn, are useful in recruitment, hiring people with appropriate skills, in promotion and transfer decisions, and in job evaluation.[3]

The last step in planning a recruitment program is to review sources of applicants that may have the desired qualifications to fill the jobs. Two general sources of supply are available: People from within the organization and people from outside the organization.

Sources from Within. Promoting or transferring employees from within the organization to fill job openings is an excellent source of people. Using existing personnel to fill jobs has many advantages:
1. It tends to boost employee morale.
2. It provides incentive to others.
3. You already know the work habits of the employee.
4. The organization is using an individual's skills to the fullest.
5. It minimizes new employee orientation and training.
6. It benefits both the employee and the organization.

Many companies post job openings to allow any employee who thinks he or she is qualified to apply for the position. Sometimes managers nominate employees for the position, or individuals may be chosen by management after a complete assessment of the individual's work record, training received, experience, potential and personal motivation.

Outside Sources. There are an abundance of outside sources for recruitment. But good human resource planners must pick sources carefully so that they may attract enough applicants of the right qualifications without overdoing it. Advertising in the newspaper "Help Wanted" section may bring in a torrent of applicants; however, the cost of processing applications may offset any benefit from the size of the applicant pool. Recruitment programs must involve sources which will supply job candidates with the desired skills.

For nonmanagement or nonprofessional jobs recruitment may be through newspapers; "word-of-mouth;" the union; employment agencies; vocational or trade schools, or local magazine ads. One of the best sources of applicants is from friends of current employees. This type of "word-of-mouth" recruitment tends to attract potential employees whose values, life style and work ethic are similar to existing employees.

For the more professional or technical jobs, including middle and top management, major sources of applicants would be graduate schools, specialized employment agencies, other companies, trade association journal ads, and friends of current employees who are in professional positions.

---

[3] Wendell L. French, *The Personnel Management Process*, 5th ed. (Boston: Houghton Mifflin Company, 1982), p. 189.

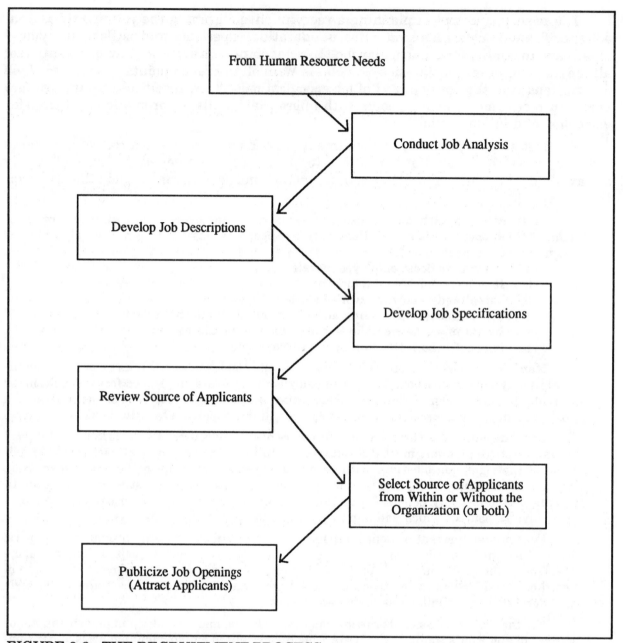

FIGURE 9-3: THE RECRUITMENT PROCESS

Selection. Selection is the process of reviewing the qualifications of applicants for specific jobs and hiring those that appear most qualified to do a particular job.

The personnel selection process is not a solution to all the problems that may plague a labor force. Hiring better qualified people is one step in the right direction. But the reception a newly hired employee gets once on the job can offset the benefits of a good selection process. New employees must be properly integrated into the organization, properly developed to their full potential, and properly maintained while on the job.

Selection processes vary with organizations. Some are detailed, elaborate, and expensive to administer. Other selection processes are so simple that they do not justify the title "process." When a person is hired, regardless of the complexity of the selection procedure, it means that someone in management has made a judgment, based on some criteria, that the applicant will be able to perform the job. He or she has been **selected.**

The Selection Process. Three points need to be emphasized about the selection process:

1. The selection process is not scientific. The use of the process does not guarantee that the person selected for employment will be the best available for the job; nor does it guarantee that the new employee will be steady, dependable, a self-starter, loyal, able to work well with colleagues and bosses, ready to accept responsibility and handle pressure well, and much more.
2. The last step in any selection process is "personal judgment" by the hirer. The various criteria used in selection do not guarantee that information obtained will accurately predict future performance. The person doing the choosing reviews the selection process data and makes a final personal judgment about the applicant for the job.
3. Every step in the selection process is a point that can disqualify an applicant. When an applicant under consideration for employment reaches the final interview stage, it means that the applicant has not been disqualified at any step in the selection process. Reaching the final stage in the process does not mean that the applicant should be hired, only that he or she is still available to be hired.

One interesting point of view about the selection process was presented years ago by Eli Ginzberg. While at Columbia University in New York, he was coordinator of a major project studying manpower resources in the United States. Dr. Ginzberg studied how men were selected for the military and how these selected personnel performed once in the service. One conclusion of the study was that about one of every three individuals show an unstable pattern of performance at some time in their lives, and there is no reliable way of predicting when it will occur. Dr. Ginzberg wrote that the most important lesson to management concerning the selection of employees is the need to establish a modest objective for screening. Management must realize that one inherent limitation of the selection process is that people's performance is likely to change over time.[4]

Steps in the Selection Process. The traditional steps in the personnel selection process are **reception, initial screening interview, application form, testing, background investigation, in-depth selection interview, physical examination, and final interview/job offer.**[5]

Reception. Whenever an applicant contacts an organization about employment, the reception should be positive. Each applicant should be treated fairly and honestly in a respectful manner. First impressions are important to both parties, and the applicant should be told if job positions are available. This step emphasizes the importance of the person within the organization who handles this initial contact.

---

[4] Eli Ginzberg, "The Ineffective Soldier," *Advanced Management*, Vol. 24-26, June, 1960, pp. 16-21.
   [5] Comments based on selected material from Robert L. Mathis and John H. Jackson, *Personnel, Contemporary Perspectives and Applications* (St. Paul: West Publishing Company, 1982), pp. 194-216.

Initial Screening Interview. Prior to an applicant's completing the application form, the interviewer can conduct an initial screening by asking certain questions. These questions would pertain to job interests, nature of skills, experience, desired location, salary expectations, and other general information. This is the time to inform the applicant about job openings, benefits, work schedules, salary, and other things. The purpose of the initial interview is to compare the job applicant's interests and skills with any job openings to justify moving to the next step in the selection process.

Application Form. Application forms, also called application blanks, must be completed by job candidates. The forms provide the organization biographical data about the applicant. The information on the forms is useful to an interviewer and also important in performing a background investigation. Today's forms request applicant information about work interest, work location desired, work skills possessed, education, previous work history, list of references or former supervisors, citizenship status, any disabilities, and possibly other miscellaneous items relating to the job. It is illegal to ask questions about sex, race, age, religion, marital status and number of children, native language, and national origin because application forms must comply with EEOC (Equal Employment Opportunity Commission) guidelines. An identification document with a photograph is now required to establish citizenship (see discussion of Immigration Control and Reform Act of 1986), but no information that might be used to discriminate against applicants is allowed.

Data provided by the applicant on the application form determines whether the selection process continues.

Testing. Tests may be used to help select new employees. Not all organizations use them; however, because tests are legally subject to requirements of validity and reliability and because tests are controversial as predictors in the selection process.

Test Validity occurs when performance on the job closely relates to performance on the tests. **Test reliability** exists when the individual taking the test scores about the same on the test when taken a second or third time.

Tests that measure ability, skill, aptitude, or knowledge relevant to a particular job best predict the performance of a new or prospective employee. Tests, properly validated, can be of great value in the selection process.

Background Investigation. Before an in-depth selection interview, a background investigation of the applicant should be conducted. This step insures that information provided in the initial interview and on the application form is correct. It is an important, precautionary measure.

Reference checking is the most common way to verify background information. Organizations can run credit checks, contact school references (obtain transcripts), contact personal references, or verify prior work experience with former supervisors. Information from personal references is probably the least important source to check because applicants will not list people who may write or say anything negative about them.

Conducting a credit check and verifying educational information are routine steps that take some time and cost money, but the information obtained may be valuable in evaluating an applicant. It is more difficult to investigate work background.

Employers are aware of the various federal and state laws which protect the privacy of personal information. The major law, already discussed in this chapter, is the Federal Privacy Act of 1974 which applies to government agencies and units; however, some states have similar laws.

Before contacting former employers, an organization should obtain written releases from the job applicant giving the organization permission to request personal information about his or her work experience. When contact is made with a former employer, only information that relates to the job performance should be requested. Information received in writing from former employers should be available for the applicant to see, if he or she desires to do so.

In-Depth Selection Interview. The in-depth selection interview should concentrate on the information provided by the applicant (during the prior steps in the process) and the information obtained from the background investigation. All this information should be compared with the requirements of the job by the interviewer in this step. There should be a "match" between the skills and abilities of the applicant and the job needs of the organization. A skilled interviewer provides a positive picture of the organization, yet is realistic in describing job expectations. The applicant should objectively "sell" himself or herself based on work experience and actual ability. Any additional information gained from tests may be discussed during this interview.

The interview may be highly structured, semi-structured, or unstructured. Semi-structured interviews may be the best at this stage in the selection process. In the semi-structured interview, the interviewer plans major questions in advance; but, depending on the responses of the candidate, other subjects and questions may arise which were not preplanned.

If the interviewer finds no cause to disqualify the applicant and all information appears accurate, the selection process proceeds to the next stage.

Physical Examination. Physical examinations may be at the expense of the applicant or provided by the organization. Public school teachers in many states must provide evidence of a physical examination, at their expense, annually to qualify for continued employment. Most business organizations pay for a required physical examination for a job applicant.

Among the purposes of a physical examination are these:

1. To make sure that workers are physically able to perform the work required on a job
2. To detect any contagious diseases
3. To have the health record of each employee
4. To identify injuries and illnesses, past and present, to protect against invalid worker's compensation claims in the future.

Many jobs have physical standards that can be met by a majority of job applicants. Some jobs, however, require lifting, strenuous physical activity, or working in areas with extraordinary temperatures. The work environment of some organizations may be dirty, with a heavy concentration of dust or fumes. Physical restrictions that prevent satisfactory job performance or endanger the health of an applicant (such as asthma to a person who will work in a dusty area) must be identified.

The physical examination can also provide vital information in projecting health care costs of employees under a medical insurance benefit program. The cost of medical insurance programs is escalating, and more organizations provide such benefits to their employees. According to Richard I. Henderson, Chrysler, Ford and General Motors spent over $3 billion in 1983 on medical insurance for its employees.[6]

If an applicant successfully passes the physical examination and matches the physical requirements of the job, he or she moves to the last step of the selection process.

Final Interview/Job Offer. Managers who hire employees often allow personnel specialists to process an applicant for employment up to the point of hiring. Then, the manager reviews all of the information obtained from the steps in the selection process, hears the findings and recommendations of personnel, and reaches an agreement on the position to be filled, starting salary and benefits to be provided, and date employee will report. The final interview and job offer should be handled by the new employee's immediate supervisor.

In some organizations the manager is involved throughout the selection process, but the above scenario is also common.

The final interview is intended to clarify job questions about work expectations, pay, benefits, starting date of employment, opportunity in the organization, and the importance of the work. The interview is open for free discussion and complete understanding of the job situation by both parties.

If the manager is satisfied with the information on the applicant and the responses from the applicant, then a job offer is made. If the applicant understands the conditions of employment and the work expectations and is satisfied with the offer, then the job offer is accepted.

Assessment Centers. Assessment centers are a special method of selecting managers for employment or promotion. Originated by the military in World War II, assessment centers have grown in popularity and are used extensively in large organizations. The purpose of assessment centers is to predict management potential of participants through a variety of techniques such as in-basket exercises, role playing, incident analysis, and gaming simulations.

Information gained about management potential from assessment center exercises should be reviewed along with other sources of information in the selection process before a final decision is made about hiring or promoting a manager.

---

[6] Richard I. Henderson, *Compensation Management: Rewarding Performance*, 4th ed. (Reston, VA: Reston Publishing Company, Inc., 1985), p. 454.

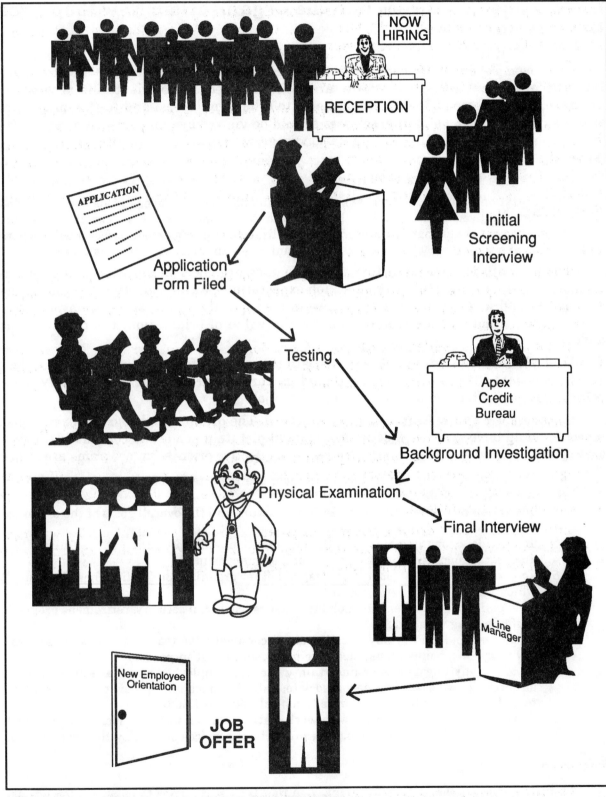

FIGURE 9-4: THE EMPLOYMENT PROCEDURE

Integrating Employees into the Organization: New Employee Orientation

Although it is often overlooked, **orientation** of new employees makes a significant difference in employee performance. **Orientation is a process of integrating the employee into the organization, work group, and job.** Included in the orientation program is an introduction to members of management, to other employees, and to the immediate supervisor. Orientation of new employees should be viewed by management as one of its most important responsibilities. Orientation programs should be carefully conceived and planned to be effective.

According to Kanouse and Warihay:

> ...Organizations determined to meet both their own and their employees' goals need a method for systematically addressing the way they deal with their human resources. Concerned members of management can initiate a change in their utilization of human resources at a point where it will make the greatest impact—at the beginning—with effective employee orientation.[7]

Some orientation programs in small companies are short in duration and often informal. A brief discussion of work rules, job expectations, an introduction to some of the employees, and a few questions and answers may qualify as the orientation program. But in organizations where managers know the value of orientation, the program has added importance.

Well planned and administered orientation programs for new employees may last one or two days. The new employee should go through orientation immediately upon being hired, not after two or three weeks on the job.

Objectives of New Employee Orientation. The orientation program for new employees should have specific objectives which will dictate much of the content of the program. The most common objectives/components of effective orientation programs are these:

1. To convey fully the importance of the job, the importance of being selected, and the work expectations
2. To explain and clarify the organization structure and the overall goals of the organization
3. To provide a complete history of the organization and a projection of the future
4. To describe opportunities for growth and advancement
5. To review all company policies, rules, and other organizational guidelines ("red tape") which will affect job performance
6. To explain employee benefits (holidays, insurance, social security, retirement program, profit sharing plan, etc.)
7. To discuss and answer any question about compensation (rates of pay, wage and salary programs, bonus plans, incentive plans, and merit increases)
8. To offset any uneasiness or uncertainty the new employees may have about the job situation, new bosses and new associates (also includes telling new employees where to go for advice or to seek answers to job-related questions)
9. To familiarize new employees with work stations, layouts, offices, locations of departments and activities, and to explain products or services offered by the organization

---

[7] Daniel N. Kanouse and Philomena I. Warihay, "A New Look at Employee Orientation," *Training and Development Journal*, 1980, p.38.

10. To introduce new employees to their fellow workers and immediate bosses as well as to other selected personnel who may have a relationship to their job performance

Potential Benefits of New Employee Orientation. While the administration of an effective orientation program for new employees may take some time and will cost an organization money, the potential benefits far outweigh these costs. The primary benefits are as follows:

1. Reduced start-up costs because less time is involved in workers' reaching standard levels of performance
2. A more positive attitude toward work and the organization which creates more loyalty, less absenteeism, and less turnover
3. Good orientation reduces new employee anxiety and increases feelings of self-worth and dignity
4. New employee operates with more confidence, based on acquired knowledge of the organization, clear work expectations, familiarity with operations, and introduction to fellow workers and bosses

For many companies the development of an organization **handbook**, sometimes called a policies and procedures manual, is helpful to use in an orientation program. A **handbook** contains, in writing for future reference, much of the same information given the new employee orally during orientation. The employee receives a copy to refer to any subject for review at any time. Other organizations distribute the handbook and many other written documents for employees to use as well (i.e., company newsletters, directory of employees, maps of physical layout, etc.). Altogether such items constitute an **orientation kit**.

Orientation Follow-Up. Initial orientation, before new employees actually begin work, should be followed with a continuing or follow-up orientation in the future. To integrate the employees fully into the organization a follow-up orientation session should be held within three to six months of employment. After the employee has been on the job for this length of time, there may be a need to answer questions, listen to problems, explain any changes, and offer continued support. This would provide continuity to the integration process and insure that new employee orientation programs are effective.

Developing Employee Potential

Human resource effectiveness depends largely on developing the capabilities of employees. Rapid change in all aspects of business, from technology to social interaction, demands constant efforts to keep employees informed of new policies, techniques, and developments in the organization and in the economy. Because of the variegated composition of the work force, management faces a real challenge and responsibility in developing the full potential of every employee.[8]

We have discussed the importance of staffing; the legal environment; the recruitment and selection of employees; and the integration of employees into the organization through orientation programs. Now, we look at developing employees through training, performance appraisals, promotions, transfers, and disciplinary action.

---

[8] Donald P. Crane, *Personnel, The Management of Human Resources*, 4th ed. (Boston: Kent Publishing Company, 1986), p. 283.

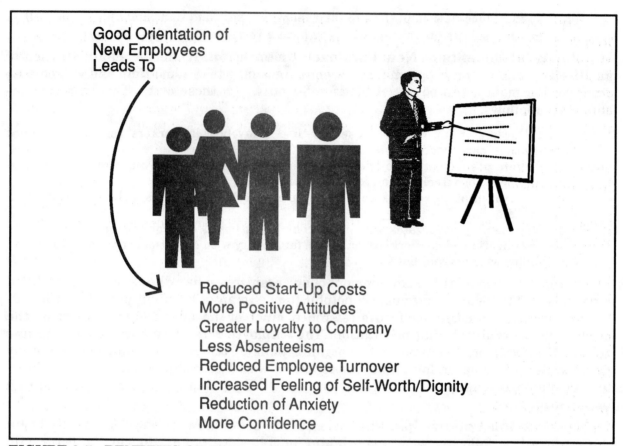

Good Orientation of
New Employees
Leads To

Reduced Start-Up Costs
More Positive Attitudes
Greater Loyalty to Company
Less Absenteeism
Reduced Employee Turnover
Increased Feeling of Self-Worth/Dignity
Reduction of Anxiety
More Confidence

FIGURE 9-5: BENEFITS OF EMPLOYEE ORIENTATION PROGRAMS

Training. Training is a process in which employees acquire new skills and knowledge that will enable them to be more effective in the performance of their jobs. The management responsibility to train employees and develop them to their full potential is the number one job of American managers, according to Crawford Greenwalt, former President and Chief Executive Officer of DuPont.[9]

Training efforts are directed at both nonmanagement and management employees. Nonmanagement training usually concentrates on teaching technical skills. Management training centers on teaching or developing personal and conceptual skills.

Determining Training Needs. Training needs can be established through observation of individual employee performance, group performance, and overall organizational performance. If individuals have difficulty meeting work quantity standards on a consistent basis, they may need additional training. If a department as a whole fails to generate quality work, there may be a need for training. If the whole organization misses its desired annual goals or objectives, there may be a need for training. Poor results can be a clue to encourage further investigation of individual, group, and total organizational performance to evaluate the need for training.

---

[9] Crawford H. Greenwalt, *The Uncommon Man* (New York: McGraw-Hill Book Company, Inc., 1959), p.32.

Training needs of individual employees can be assessed through **performance appraisals. Performance appraisals compare the employee's work against the work standards or the objectives of the job (for management).** If work standards or objectives do not exist, then managers are wasting time evaluating employees. If an employee's work performance repeatedly fails to match or exceed the standard, he or she becomes a candidate for training. Since other factors, both personal and organizational, can affect job performance, more training may not be the answer in every case.

Another method for determining training needs is to conduct a questionnaire survey or personal interviews of selected personnel to determine the problems they have and their suggestions for overcoming them. Often, more training is the solution.

When training is indicated, management has several options for types of training programs: on-the-job training (OJT), apprenticeship training, vestibule training, programmed training, and classroom training.

On-the-job training (OJT) is the most common form of training, occurring daily under the direction of an experienced employee or the immediate supervisor. The employee performs his or her work assignment while the "trainer" watches and teaches.

Apprenticeship training dates back to ancient times and is often related in today's organizations to unions. Apprentices work under a skilled craftsperson who teaches the trade to the individual who performs the work (normally at a lower wage level). Apprenticeships vary in length of time, but usually last from two to five years.

Vestibule training takes place in a separate work environment that simulates real working conditions. Under these conditions, using identical equipment and supplies, the trainer stresses correctness of technique, procedure, and quality rather than quantity of output. Once an employee is properly trained, he or she fills a job as part of the regular work force.

Programmed training includes correspondence courses available through colleges, trade associations, and educational organizations. Also included are study courses on video and/or audio cassette tapes and computer video displays. Programmed training is a process of studying material and being tested at periodic intervals to check satisfactory progress. It is a sequential process of going through stages of learning and satisfactorily acquiring knowledge until the course is completed.

Classroom training is normally conducted away from the work location, but many organizations today maintain their own classroom facilities. Groups of employees can be trained at one time; they receive the same information; and they have the opportunity to participate in question and answer sessions on topics of shared interest. Usually classroom training is part of orientation, a management development program, safety seminars, technical training programs on new equipment, and so forth. Training may be done by company personnel or by outside specialists.

Management Training. Management training is introduced when a need is established at the supervisory, middle management, or top level. Managers tend to need technical, human or personal, and conceptual skills (refer to Chapter 2) in varying combinations at each different management level. First level managers or supervisors need much technical knowledge plus good human or personal skills. Middle managers tend to need even more human or personal skills, some technical knowledge, and a growing amount of conceptual skill. Top managers primarily need conceptual skill with the amount of technical knowledge required based on the nature of the organization. Management training programs are structured with these skills in mind to provide or reinforce the skills managers need.

Supervisory training is growing in popularity today because of the manner by which most new supervisors are selected. They are primarily promoted from within the organization based on technical knowledge and skills but without confirmed management knowledge or skill. Training for supervisors often is conducted in a classroom setting on or off the premises by company personnel or by a professional management trainer. The major topics covered in a typical supervisory management seminar are the basic functions of management (such as planning and control, principles of communication, concepts of organization, and the management of people).

Middle managers and top level managers have opportunities to attend advanced management training programs. Many major colleges and universities offer these programs at off-site locations. Training time varies from one week to two months. Subjects stressed in these programs are centered on the conceptual skills needed by top managers in areas such as strategic planning, policy formulation, and corporate finance.

Promotions. Competent individual performance over a sustained period of time deserves recognition. Sometimes that recognition takes the form of a promotion. Promoting an employee, whether a manager or nonmanagement employee, can be a development technique that benefits the person and the organization. Moving into a position that requires new skills or talents with added responsibilities becomes a growth experience. Caution should prevail, however, because not every excellent employee at one level will perform as well at a higher level. It is important that the person under consideration for promotion have the experience, talent, and skills needed to do the new job.

Transfers. Transfers (sometimes called rotation) can provide a development opportunity for individuals. Relocating to a new work environment with new responsibilities and new associates can be stimulating. While some transfers occur because an individual is not being considered for promotion, most occur for the benefit of the organization and the individual. An opportunistic person should view a transfer as a chance to demonstrate competency in another area, showcasing his or her multiple talents and skills and confirming his or her value to the organization.

Disciplinary Action. Disciplinary action can be a verbal or written reprimand, a suspension, or a demotion. It must be carefully considered before applied. Many employees resent such action especially when they think they are being singled out, unfairly treated, or have a personality conflict with the manager. If disciplinary action is fair and based on known rules of the organization, however, the individual may learn from the experience and become a better employee.

Written reprimands are a form of **documentation**. Documentation is important today because of the growing number of lawsuits filed against former employers by discharged employees. To document properly, a manager should objectively write exactly the situation involving the employee as it occurred (time, date, place, etc.) and have a statement at the bottom of the page which reads: "I have read the above and have been given a copy." The employee signs this document and receives one of the copies. Other copies go to the manager, the manager's boss and possibly personnel (for filing in the employee's personnel records).

While disciplinary action is justifiably viewed as negative, the results gained sometimes are not. Often it provides the stimulus needed by an employee to snap out of the destructive work behavior before it is too late.

Maintaining the Work Force

Two things that work best to maintain a competent work force are compensation and benefits. Compensation programs enable organizations to attract, maintain, and develop the best available talent. Benefits are a form of supplementary compensation and one that grows in importance constantly.

Compensation and benefits together form what is called monetary income received by an individual employee. The fundamental purposes of compensation are to do the following:

1. Obtain qualified talent
2. Retain good employees
3. Provide equal pay for equal work
4. Reward performance
5. Provide incentive.[10]

High compensation "attracts" applicants and "holds" employees in the work force, but there are other factors important to the maintenance of the work force. These factors (discussed more fully in Chapter 10) revolve around the concept of "psychic income" and are some of the more important job needs, wants, and desires of employees. These factors include job security, opportunity for advancement, recognition, better supervision, safe and pleasant work environment, and many more.

It is important to properly recruit, select, integrate, and develop employees. But all these activities are useless if employees are not maintained. Maintenance of the work force should follow a well planned and carefully constructed program balancing the best interests of the organization and the employees. This planning effort should be based on a fair compensation program, with desirable benefits, and a reasonable satisfaction of basic employee job needs, wants, and desires beyond monetary income.

Summary

Staffing is the acquisition and placement of qualified employees in jobs that fully utilize the talents and skills of the individual.

Staffing is a function of personnel management and normally is performed by staff specialists operating under the authority of higher line management.

Human resource planning is essential to the effective achievement of desired staffing results. Human resource planning includes two steps: projecting human skills and talents needed to satisfy strategic objectives and forming a detailed plan to recruit and staff the jobs so that strategic objectives are met.

---

[10] Crane, *Personnel*, 3rd ed., p. 538.

The staffing function is directly influenced by state, local, and federal laws. Major federal legislation includes the Social Security Act of 1935; the Fair Labor Standards Act of 1938; the Labor-Management Relations Act of 1947 (Taft-Hartley Act); the Equal Pay Act of 1963, amended 1972; the Civil Rights Act of 1964, amended 1972 and 1978; the Age Discrimination in Employment Act of 1967, amended 1978 and 1986; the Occupational Safety and Health Act of 1970 (OSHA); the Vocational Rehabilitation Act of 1973; the Federal Privacy Act of 1974; the Employee Retirement Income Security Act of 1974 (ERISA); the Vietnam Era Veterans Readjustment Assistance Act of 1974; and the Immigration Reform and Control Act of 1986.

Recruitment is the task of attracting people with the desired skills, experience, and talent to fill jobs. The recruitment process requires the development of job descriptions and job specifications from job analyses. Job specifications refer to the human traits such as education, experience, and skills an individual must have to qualify to perform a certain job. Sources of qualified applicants for jobs come from within and from outside the organization. Promoting from within has many advantages if the people are fully qualified for the job. Major outside sources include "friends of employees," newspaper ads, campuses, employment agencies, the union, and other companies.

Selection is the process of reviewing the qualifications of applicants for specific jobs and hiring those that appear most qualified. The selection process is not scientific nor does it guarantee that the person selected will be the best available for the job. The last step in any selection process involves "personal judgment." Traditional steps in the personnel selection process are reception, initial screening interview, application form, testing, background investigation, in-depth selection interview, physical examination, and final interview/job offer.

Assessment centers are special methods of selecting managers for employment or promotion. The purpose of assessment centers is to predict management potential of participants through a variety of techniques such as in-basket exercises, role playing, incident analysis, and gaming simulation.

Orientation is a process of integrating the employee into the organization, their work group, and their jobs. It is often overlooked by organizations but can make a significant difference in employee performance and attitude. Good new employee orientation programs can lead to reduced start-up costs, more positive attitudes, greater loyalty to the organization, less absenteeism, and much more.

Training is the process in which employees acquire new skills and knowledge that will enable them to be more effective in the performance of their jobs. The management responsibility to train employees and develop them to their full potential is the number one job of American managers. Types of training programs are on-the-job training (OJT), apprenticeship, vestibule, programmed, and classroom training. Management training typically is classroom training. In addition to formal training efforts, employees can be developed through promotions, transfers, or disciplinary action.

Two things that best maintain a work force are compensation and benefits, which together comprise monetary income. Other factors, which generally revolve around "psychic income," have a maintenance influence, too. These factors include job security; opportunity for advancement; recognition; and other job needs, wants, and desires of employees.

Review Questions

1. Name the steps in the personnel management process. How does each step relate to the other steps?
2. How is a futuristic projection of human skills and talents needed in an organization determined?
3. Are you familiar with steps in human resource planning (HRP)? List them.
4. Starting with the passage of the Social Security Act of 1935, identify the major federal legislation enacted which affects the staffing of personnel.
5. Recruiting from within an organization is an excellent source of people. Explain the advantages of this source of personnel.
6. Discuss the personnel selection process. Why is the process not considered scientific and why is it not an absolute predictor of future performance?

Assignments for Personal Development

1. Everyone who holds or has held a job write out the steps he or she remembers in the selection process prior to being offered the job. Compare experiences in open discussion and relate what occurred with the steps in the selection process in this chapter.
2. "The Peter Principle" originated by Laurence J. Peter says in essence: The incompetents who hold high level positions in all kinds of organizations were probably competent in jobs at lower levels, but were finally promoted to a level of incompetency. Do you agree with this concept? As applied to you, is this concept positive or negative as an influencing factor on whether to accept a promotion or not?

Incident

HOW TO RECRUIT!

Pete Gray was elated! After a month of interviews, reference checks and a physical exam, he had been offered the position of City Recreation Director. He quickly accepted the offer even though he had never held a management position. The small town of 20,000 people had grown overnight from a "sleepy" town of 5,000 because of several major construction projects in the vicinity. The town had never had a formal recreation department, but the citizens demanded recreational services as part of a package to help justify increased local taxes.

When Pete was offered the job, the town fathers pointed out the budget constraints and the need to develop a quality program quickly. Five staff positions were funded in the budget, one of which was to be a receptionist/secretary. The other four positions and job titles would be left up to Pete. Pete realized he needed to do some planning and organizing quickly. Additionally a couple of other problems faced him: (1) The starting salaries of the four positions were fixed and were relatively low; and (2) the small town was over 100 miles from a major metropolitan marketplace and people with the job skills he needed were not in the small town.

Questions:

1. What should Pete Gray do before he starts trying to attract applicants for the open positions?

2. What recommendations can you give Pete Gray on how to recruit applicants for jobs in a small town when the pay is low and the location not the most desirable in the world?

Suggested Readings

Foulkes, Fred K. "How Top Nonunion Companies Manage Employees." *Harvard Business Review.* (September/October 1981): 90.

Higgins, James M. "The Complicated Process of Establishing Goals for Equal Employment." *Personnel Journal* (December 1975): 631-37.

"Job Analysis." *Bureau of Intergovernmental Personnel Programs* (December 1973): 135-52.

Lopez, Felix M., Jr. *Personnel Interviewing: Theory and Practice.* New York: McGraw-Hill, 1964.

McGuire, Joseph W. "The 'New' Egalitarianism and Managerial Practice." *California Management Review*, Spring 1977, pp. 21-29.

Rowland, Kendrith M., Gerald R. Ferris, and Jay L. Sherman. *Current Issues in Personnel Management.* Boston: Allyn and Bacon, 1983.

Teel, Kenneth S. "Performance Appraisal: Current Trends, Persistent Progress." *Personnel Journal* (April 1980): 296-301, 316.

Thomas, William G. "Training and Development Do Make Better Managers." *Personnel* 65 (January 1988): 52-53.

CHAPTER 10

MOTIVATION, MORALE AND LEADERSHIP

After studying this chapter, **you will know**:

- The meaning and goal of motivation
- The major theories of motivation
- Practical motivational approaches and techniques
- Why employee morale is of such great interest to managers
- Why the Hawthorne Studies represent the beginning of the Human Relations Movement in management
- About job satisfaction and employee performance
- About job enrichment and its impact on job satisfaction
- The definition of leadership and the major types
- Characteristics of effective leaders
- The value of leadership theory

Introduction

The most common problems managers face is how to stimulate certain employees to do a better job. Over a period of ten years managers throughout the nation and from every type of industry, have submitted to this book's author "My Most Difficult Management Problem." The most common type of problem described pertains to employee motivation. Employees tend to do enough to hold their jobs, but few employees work near their full capacity and ability. Highly motivated employees can effect significant increases in performance and significant decreases in problems that plague management such as absenteeism, tardiness, chronic complaining and low morale. Managers strive hard to get employees to perform near their full ability. The sports pages regularly include stories about highly-paid professional athletes who perform well below their potential or cause continuous problems for professional teams.

The subjects of motivation, morale and leadership blend together. Generally employees who are highly motivated have high morale. Employees who have high morale usually have bosses who are effective leaders as well as excellent managers.

MOTIVATION

Knowledge of what motivation is and how it can be applied effectively is important in managing people. Seeing the results of motivation is easier than explaining how it works.

The Meaning of Motivation

The word motivation comes from the Latin word *movere*, which means "to move." It is difficult to evaluate a person's motivation until the person does something. **The goal of motivation is to cause people to put forth their best efforts with enthusiasm and effectiveness in order to achieve and hopefully surpass organizational objectives.**[1]

Motivation is concerned with what activates human behavior. Some motives originate from physiological needs such as basic human survival needs like food and water. Other motives stem from psychological needs. For example, **motivation can be thought of as the psychological process that gives behavior purpose and direction.** Some employees have motives that begin with such psychological needs as a desire for recognition, status, self-esteem and achievement.

A manager's basic job may be to have highly motivated employees performing at near peak capacity; however, this will not happen unless two other conditions are met: (1) The employees must have the ability to do the job, and (2) the work environment must be satisfactory.[2] The work environment includes the space, equipment, supplies and support needed to perform a job well. In summary the employees must be motivated to do a job, have the ability to perform the work, and work in a positive environment without any shortage of necessary resources. The lack of any one of these three conditions leads to less than desirable performance.

Theories of Motivation

Perhaps the most widely used theory of motivation, and certainly the oldest, provides reward for good performance or behavior and punishment for bad. In today's organizational world reward can be pay increases, bonuses, promotions, titles, special "perks," "attaboys," and more. Examples of punishment are bad evaluations, demotions, missing a pay increase, transfers, bad work assignments, and the ultimate punishment—loss of job. Most modern motivational theories include rewards as a motivating factor, either in monetary form or psychological. But punishment is rarely mentioned as a basis for motivation since most researchers believe that punishment has no long-lasting positive effect on the improvement of performance.

---

[1] David Schwartz, *Introduction to Management* (New York: Harcourt Brace Jovanovich, Inc., 1980), p. 465.
[2] Victor H. Vroom, *Work and Motivation* (New York: John Wiley and Sons, 1967).

Punishment used as a motivator has a short-term effect but creates resentment and low morale if used excessively. On the other hand when psychological rewards are handed out for outstanding performance, employees respond positively and the effect is more lasting.

Traditional Theory

Traditional theory of motivation evolved from the work of Frederick W. Taylor (refer to Chapter 1). Taylor, called the "Father of Scientific Management," made many contributions to management. One of his most important was the development of the Taylor Differential Piece Rate Incentive Plan around the turn of the century (1900). Taylor believed in rewarding employees who performed above the work standard. His plan established two wage curves for the payment of employees' wages (see Figure 10-1). When an employee's performance exceeded the work standard, his or her pay was calculated using the higher wage curve. If the employee produced less than the standard, the wage was calculated using the lower wage curve. Taylor believed that paying a highly productive employee the same wage as a less productive one would lead to a decrease in the former's performance and result in overall low performance by the employees. Thus, the need to reward performers who produced above the work standard. One basic assumption Taylor made was that money was a motivating factor when directly related to individual employee performance. If the potential financial reward was great enough, employees would produce more.

Most motivation theories used around this time (1900) were based on monetary rewards tied directly to job productivity or output. The nature of workers and more complex issues did not surface until well into the century.

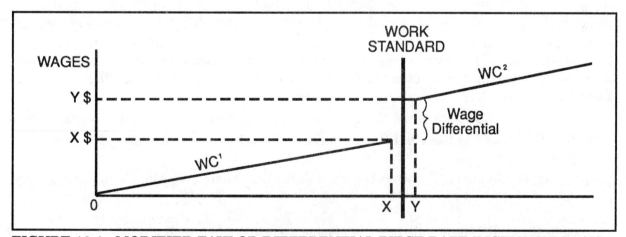

FIGURE 10-1: MODIFIED TAYLOR DIFFERENTIAL PIECE RATE INCENTIVE PLAN

Maslow's Need Hierarchy Theory

The most familiar motivation theory is Abraham Maslow's Need Hierarchy Theory. This theory is studied in a wide variety of academic disciplines, such as sociology and behavioral psychology, as well as in management. In 1943 Maslow presented a paper, which has been reprinted by the American Psychological Association, in which he listed thirteen propositions that he believed would have to be included in any theory of human motivation. His proposition seven appears to be the foundation of his hierarchy theory:

> Human needs arrange themselves in hierarchies of pre-potency. That is to say, the appearance of one need usually rests on the prior satisfaction of another, more pre-potent need. Man is a perpetually wanting animal. Also no need or drive can be treated as if it were isolated or discrete; every drive is related to the state of satisfaction or dissatisfaction of other drives.[3]

The term "pre-potent" is used here to mean a more dominant or stronger, more preeminent need.

Maslow's Need Hierarchy Theory consists of five levels of needs that must be satisfied. As each level of needs is met, the individual is able to focus more attention on fulfilling the higher level needs. Most people move up the hierarchy as they attempt to satisfy unmet needs. These five levels are Physiological and Survival Needs, Safety and Security, Love (also referred to as Social Needs), Ego and Esteem, and the need for Self-actualization.

Maslow's proposition number seven states that the appearance of one need usually rests on the prior satisfaction of another, more pre-potent need. Managers sometimes believe this means one focuses on one level of needs until it is fully satisfied; then moves upward. Maslow never constrained this theory that closely. He said that the lowest unmet need receives the majority of attention while other needs receive less attention. A manager therefore would understand that the basic physiological needs of an employee would have to be fully satisfied before the safety need becomes a motivating factor and so on up the scale. Society and the environment act with an individual's need structure to affect human behavior. If an individual, such as a celebrity or world-class athlete, is operating at self-actualization level but for some reason fears assault or invasion of privacy (a lower level safety need), that safety need becomes pre-potent and receives the most attention.

The thrust of Maslow's theory is that a satisfied need is no longer a motivator. When a need is satisfied, at once other and higher needs emerge and become the motivating factors.

Figure 10-2 shows Maslow's Need Hierarchy. Here is a brief explanation of each level:

Physiological and Survival Needs. These needs include the satisfaction of hunger, thirst, sleep and other basic bodily needs.

Safety and Security Needs. When physiological needs are met, safety and security needs become dominant. Safety needs include a safe work environment; security and safety from threats and criminal acts; protection and economic security.

Love (Social) Needs. According to Maslow's Theory, when both physiological and safety needs are satisfied, the need for affiliation and a sense of belonging becomes preeminent. These are such emotional needs as the desire for social acceptance, love and affection, and friendship.

---

[3] A. H. Maslow, "A Theory of Human Motivation." Copyright 1943 by the American Psychological Association. Reprinted by permission in *Critical Incidents in Organizational Behavior* by Francis J. Bridges and James E. Chapman (Englewood Cliffs, N.J.: Prentice-Hall, Inc., 1977), p. 195.

Ego and Esteem Needs. If the three lower level needs are gratified, the need for esteem arises. Esteem relates to self-respect which comes from being accepted and respected by others. Good self-esteem also occurs when people view themselves as worthwhile individuals. A person at this level strives for the high regard of others.

Self-actualization. This is considered the highest order of need once all other individual needs have been satisfied. Self-actualization has been interpreted in many ways: realizing one's full potential; doing what one most wants to do with one's life; and feeling good about what you have accomplished with the resources at hand. This is the only need that cannot be completely met. Maslow believed one will always strive to become better and achieve more.

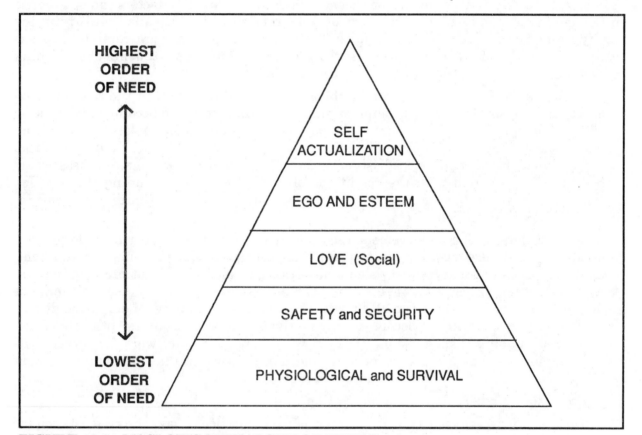

FIGURE 10-2: MASLOW'S HIERARCHY OF NEEDS

Value of Maslow's Theory for Managers

The value of Maslow's Theory to managers is that it emphasizes people's needs and allows managers to work toward providing employees the means to satisfy these needs and become more productive. Since management's task is to activate the desired human behavior to achieve goals, every manager must know each employee well enough to determine the needs and the need level that will trigger the most positive motivation.

This theory is of great value in a general sense, but it does not apply universally to all people at all times. Current research demonstrates that the lower level needs (Physiological and Survival and Safety and Security) may be in sequential order; but beyond that, people may be motivated separately or simultaneously by several needs which are not necessarily in the order of Maslow's Hierarchy.

Motivation-Maintenance Theory

The **Motivation-Maintenance Theory** developed by Frederick Herzberg and associates has also been called the **Dual-Factor Theory** and the **Motivation-Hygiene Theory**. The basis for this motivation theory is that all work-related factors can be grouped into one of two categories. One category of work-related factors is called **maintenance or hygiene factors or job dissatisfiers**. The second category of work-related factors is called **motivation factors or job satisfiers**. To avoid confusion, students should think of the factors as **job satisfiers and job dissatisfiers**.

In the 1950s Herzberg presented a theory of motivation based on the results of extensive, in-depth interviews with approximately 200 engineers and accountants working in the Pittsburgh, Pennsylvania area. The participants were asked to describe job situations in which they felt exceptionally bad or exceptionally good about their jobs. From these interviews Herzberg developed lists of job dissatisfiers and job satisfiers. Job dissatisfiers tended to be associated with the conditions or environment surrounding the job. Job satisfiers were those factors associated with the work itself (see Figure 10-3) and included factors that motivated employees.

Job satisfiers, such as achievement, recognition, the work itself, opportunity for growth and advancement, are motivator factors. Factors associated with the work environment, such as job security, salary, supervision and working conditions, do not promote motivation, but they can prevent it from occurring. These dissatisfier factors (the maintenance or hygiene factors) must be given all the attention necessary to prevent employee dissatisfaction. Employees will not become highly motivated, however, unless both sets of factors are reasonably satisfied. No matter how well the maintenance work factors are satisfied, employee needs are recurrent and take many forms so that managers are constantly faced with the demand for more and more.

Professor Herzberg explained motivation this way:

The motivator factors are a direct derivation of the connections I have observed between the quality of motivation and hygiene and the quality of job performance. The basis of the idea is that motivators are the factors that meet man's need for psychological growth, especially achievement, recognition, responsibility, advancement, and opportunity. [Hygiene] factors are concerned with the job environment—conditions and treatment surrounding the work, specifically company policy and administration, supervision, relationships with others, salary, personal life, status, and security. Their underlying dynamic is the avoidance of pain within the work environment. Motivators are concerned with using people well and, when combined with a good hygiene program, with treating people well. The result will be motivated performance.[4]

---

[4] Frederick Herzberg, "The Wise Old Turk," *Harvard Business Review*, September-October 1974, p. 71.

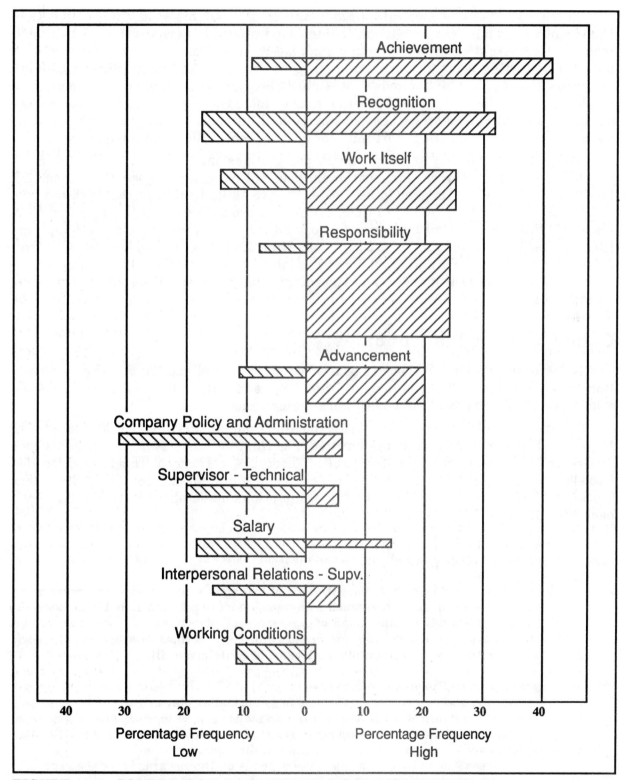

FIGURE 10-3: COMPARISON OF SATISFIERS AND DISSATISFIERS

The wider the box the longer the duration of the attitude. Reproduced from The Motivation To Work, Frederick Herzberg et al. John Wiley and Sons, New York, 1959.

Herzberg's theory of motivation has many critics, but his study and publications about motivation have encouraged much additional research. Perhaps the most valuable result of Herzberg's research to practicing managers is the emphasis placed on the work itself as a starting point for generating employee motivation. Today **job enrichment** programs, based on the Motivation-Maintenance Theory, have been introduced to increase employee motivation on the job. **Job enrichment** includes upgrading a job; increasing a worker's job-related challenges, responsibility and autonomy; and providing jobs that have meaningful work with opportunity for growth, recognition and advancement.

Any manager holding any supervisory position has the opportunity to **enrich** the jobs of his or her employees. Job enrichment does not require an expenditure of money; however, it requires a manager to use some creative skills to change the work environment. For example, an employee in marketing and promotions may be delegated more responsibilities with added authority to work on a special project with the temporary title of Director until the project is completed. After the project is finished, proper recognition should be given for a job well done! The job has been enriched, the employee feels good about the accomplishments, and the recognition provides the incentive for future outstanding work.

Other Motivation Theories

A few other motivation theories bear some mention and explanation. Each motivation theory provides additional insight for managers into the nature of human behavior and shows how motivation influences work performance.

Theory X and Theory Y. In 1960 Professor Douglas McGregor of Massachusetts Institute of Technology wrote a book entitled, *The Human Side of Enterprise.* In his book McGregor developed a motivation theory called Theory X and Theory Y. This theory identifies two styles of managing based on the manager's view of human nature: Theory X or autocratic and Theory Y or participative. The assumptions made about human behavior in each style include these:

Assumptions for Theory X:
- The average human being has an inherent dislike of work and will avoid it if he or she can.
- Because of this human characteristic of dislike of work, most people must be coerced, controlled, or threatened with punishment to get them to put forth adequate effort toward the achievement of organizational objectives.
- The average human being prefers to be directed, wishes to avoid responsibility, has relatively little ambition, and wants security above all.

Assumptions for Theory Y:
- Work is a source of satisfaction and is as normal as play or rest.
- Threat of punishment is only one way to induce people to work, and it is not usually the best way. People who are committed to achieving the organization's objectives will display self-motivation and self-direction.
- A person's commitment to objectives depends on the rewards he or she expects to receive when goals are achieved.
- Under the right conditions, the average person will both accept and seek responsibility.

- The abilities to think creatively, to innovate, and to solve problems is widely, not narrowly, distributed among people.
- The intellectual abilities of most people are underutilized.[5]

McGregor's assumptions about human behavior in the workplace have been challenged as being too extreme to account for all situations and all human behavior. The popularity of the Theory Y approach, however, did encourage managers to practice more participative management, become more concerned with employee morale, and to concentrate on enlarging and enriching the jobs of employees to add challenge to the work and make it more rewarding.

The popularity of participative management today is a direct result of McGregor's Theory X and Theory Y and the publicity given it years ago. The technique of getting employees more involved in subjects which directly affect them is potentially valuable to employees, to the managers, and to the organization.

Preference-Expectancy Theory. Victor Vroom published his preference-expectancy theory in *Work and Motivation*, a book published in 1964. Vroom suggests that employee motivation relates to **preference** and **expectancy** on the job. **Preference is what a person wishes to have happen. Expectancy is the subjective probability of what will happen if certain behavior patterns are followed.**[6]

Employees often have to make rational choices, based on their perception of a situation, to achieve rewards. For example if an employee thinks that working hard and working long hours will bring a significant pay increase, then he or she will be motivated to do this. An athlete trying to earn a spot on the starting team will perform as well as possible to get that reward.

Reinforcement Theory. The late B. F. Skinner of Harvard University was the leading proponent of behavior modification as a motivational tool.

Basically, behavior that leads to a positive consequence (reward) tends to be repeated, while behavior that leads to a negative consequence (punishment) tends not to be repeated.[7]

Positive reinforcement practices include rewards such as a promotion, better pay or transfer to a better job. Skinner believed that rewards or positive reinforcement was the best motivational stimulus to change behavior. Negative consequences or punishment can likely lead to undesirable behavior.

A manager who practices positive reinforcement is generous with earned praise, encouragement and employee participation in problem-solving and decision-making that affects them.

Many other motivation theories exist. Students may want to investigate David McClelland's Need-Based Theory or Rensis Likert's work at the University of Michigan on participative management. Likert's work will be referred to later in this chapter.

---

[5] Douglas McGregor, *The Human Side of Enterprise* (New York: McGraw-Hill Book Company, 1960), pp. 33-34, 47-48.

[6] See Victor H. Vroom, *Work and Motivation* (New York: John Wiley and Sons, 1964).

[7] See B. F. Skinner, *About Behaviorism* (New York: Random House, 1976).

Classifying Motivation Theories

Motivation theories tend to be classified as either **content theories, process theories,** or **reinforcement theories**.

Content theories such as those proposed by Maslow, Herzberg and McGregor focus on the needs within individuals that cause them to act in certain ways. **Process theories** such as Vroom's expectancy theory concentrate on rewards that individuals will possibly receive if they behave or work in a certain way. **Reinforcement theories** associated with B. F. Skinner and others base motivation on consequences of past action influencing future actions.

From a review of all types of motivation theories, some common threads emerge that can be valuable to practicing managers. See Figure 10-4 for a list of the most important.

- The Employee's skills match the requirements of the job
- There is open communication between the employee and the manager (boss)
- The work is challenging and stimulating
- Participation is encouraged in problem-solving and decision-making
- Managers provide positive feedback (recognition)
- Employees are allowed some autonomy or independence of action
- There is opportunity for personal growth
- There is opportunity for promotion
- Compensation, monetary and psychological, is fair as it relates to employee performance
- Jobs are secure (steady employment and benefits)
- Good working conditions and necessary resources exist

FIGURE 10-4: COMMON FACTORS THAT TEND TO PROMOTE MOTIVATION

The points in Figure 10-4 do not include everything that stimulates individual motivation in the workplace. People's wants and job needs differ, and they may change over time. Also, management works with employees who bring personal problems into the work situation. Personal problems can affect motivation and job performance of employees despite good quality management. The changing environment of the organization may affect employee motivation. A typical scenario today is then a foreign investor purchases an American organization, resulting in an air of uncertainty about the future among employees and management. These and many other conditions complicate the subject of motivation for managers. It is often easier to see the results of motivation than it is to explain how motivation works.

MORALE

The American Heritage Dictionary defines **morale** as "the state of mind of an individual or group in regard to confidence, cheerfulness, and discipline.[8] Management theorists have a slightly different view of morale.

David J. Schwartz defines high morale as "the confident, resolute, often self-sacrificing attitude of a group that has strong faith in its leadership and believes organizational goals can be achieved."[9] Rue and Byars define (organizational) morale as "an individual's feeling of being accepted by, and belonging to, a group of employees through common goals, confidence in the desirability of these goals, and progress toward these goals."[10] The latter definitions refer to morale as an intangible factor that relates to a group of employees, not to an individual. Perhaps the most useful way to view morale is as the mental and emotional state of an individual or a group relative to the tasks or functions they perform at any given point in time. This definition incorporates the total feeling of enthusiasm, worth and confidence that an individual or group feels while allowing one to know that this attitude can be fleeting. A common way to express group morale is as *esprit de corps* where a group of employees feels a common sense and degree of purpose and confidence in the future. A classic example of team members' having *esprit de corps* occurs when two baseball teams make it to the World Series. All team members have a common sense and degree of purpose and confidence in themselves. Personal rivalries and differences are put aside, and group morale is high!

Organizations are interested in the subject of employee morale because of the possible relationship to performance and outcome. Other questions that need answering are these: (1) Do highly motivated personnel have high morale? and (2) Does satisfaction with a job or a situation equate with high performance?

Morale and Performance

There is a belief among practicing managers that high productivity results from high morale. There may be a tendency for morale and productivity to correlate positively over the long-run, but there are many exceptions to this generalization. A common case of low morale and high productivity often appears among remaining employees after an organization begins layoffs and personnel cutbacks due to economic difficulties. Fear of dismissal, which does not lead to high morale, will cause these employees to perform better and take their work more seriously.

There is general agreement that high morale in a work group will decrease absences, tardiness, turnover and accidents; however, morale is an intangible factor and is difficult to measure objectively. Determinants that can stimulate high morale include positive recognition of a group's efforts; organizational goals that align with the goals of the group; group participation in the decision-making process; and interesting work assignments. A famous research project that focused attention on morale and productivity is the Hawthorne Studies.

---

[8] "Morale," *The American Heritage Dictionary* (New York: Dell Publishing Co., Inc., 1983), p. 444.

[9] David J. Schwartz, *Introduction to Management* (New York: Harcourt Brace Jovanovich, 1980), p. 481.

[10] Leslie W. Rue and Lloyd L. Byars, *Management, Theory and Applications* (Homewood, IL: Richard D. Irwin, 1989), p. 381.

The Hawthorne Studies

The Hawthorne Studies represent the beginning of the **Human Relations Movement** in management. **Human relations** is the way managers relate to their employees. When employee performance is at a high level because of the way managers interact with their subordinates, we say there is good human relations in that organization. When employee performance and morale are low, we say there is bad human relations.

The Hawthorne Studies began in 1924 at the Hawthorne Plant of the Western Electric Company in Cicero, Illinois and ended in 1932. The original researchers conducted experiments that produced some unexpected results. For example, they lowered the level of lighting in the workplace, expecting productivity to decline. Instead productivity increased. In 1927 Elton Mayo, Fritz Roethlisberger and William J. Dickson, psychologists from Harvard University, were called in to continue the studies. Mayo and his associates conducted hundreds of experiments over the next five years. They improved the working conditions of female employees by scheduling rest periods, company lunches and shorter work weeks. The researchers found that productivity increased. Then, when they eliminated all improved working conditions, the researchers found that productivity continued to increase.

After much analysis the researchers concluded that other factors, beyond the physical environment, affected worker productivity. The other factors that stimulated performance were the human aspects of the job. The women were being paid attention and felt important. They were working together rather than being isolated, and they were allowed to participate as part of a congenial work group.

Hundreds of other studies and thousands of employee interviews were conducted by Mayo and his staff. The same conclusions were drawn that indicated employee performance was affected most by the interpersonal relationships developed on the job, not by the physical working conditions or pay.

Mayo recommended that management study and understand relationships among people; that management get employees to identify with management through participation (interviews, etc.); and that management strive to get group goals of employees aligned with those of management.

Mayo deplored the authoritarian, task-oriented approach that many managers used in that era. Managers who assumed people work only for pay and are self-serving in their interests have what Mayo called the "Rabble Hypothesis."

The findings of the Hawthorne Studies stress the importance of effective supervision on productivity and morale and on lessening human problems in the workplace.[11]

---

[11] See Paul Hersey and Kenneth H. Blanchard, *Management of Organizational Behavior* (Englewood Cliffs, N.J.: Prentice-Hall, Inc., 1977), pp. 53-54.

Motivation and Morale

Motivation is a process that gives behavior purpose and direction. Motivation is based on the satisfaction of human needs. Employees may be highly motivated to perform well in order to be recognized, get promoted or improve their self-esteem; however, this motivation may or may not be accompanied by high morale. It is possible to have highly motivated performers not be in harmony with the objectives of their work group, and therefore be a contributing cause of low group morale. Conversely, it is also possible to have a group of highly motivated employees working together harmoniously with high group morale. There seems to be no direct, continuing correlation between motivation and morale.

Job Satisfaction and Performance

Job satisfaction, unlike the definition of morale, refers specifically to **the state of mind an individual has about his or her work environment.** Morale of the group can affect an individual's job satisfaction just as job satisfaction can have an influence on morale. Managers in the 1990s spend considerable time and effort trying to create job satisfaction among employees. The thesis is that job-satisfied (happy) employees will be better workers. Employees who like their current work situation are considered job-satisfied. Management scholars do not agree on the impact of job satisfaction on performance, but most practicing managers think there is a positive, direct correlation.

Methods introduced to increase job satisfaction in the workplace include job rotation, job enlargement and job enrichment.

Job rotation involves employees' being moved from one job to another periodically to reduce boredom and to increase skills and experience. This approach was popular after World War II in assembly plants where skills might be interchangeable. Today, with operational activities more complex and sophisticated, the options for job rotation are fewer.

Job Enlargement is the expansion of jobs to give the employee a greater variety of tasks to perform with added responsibility. The redesign of jobs is an effort to minimize dissatisfaction among employees who are in boring, repetitive work cycle situations. Critics say that job enlargement may still result in boring jobs and may be interpreted by employees as a management ploy to get more work and greater output using fewer employees. Proponents of job enlargement point out that some employees respond favorably to job enlargement because they can learn and use new skills, have more responsibility, and feel a greater sense of importance in the total scheme of things.

Job enrichment is the process of designing jobs to include motivators (Herzberg) which can lead to more job satisfaction. Motivators include making the work more interesting and challenging, giving workers more freedom or self-direction on the job, and allowing more participation in the planning and decision-making. Students should remember that motivators or job satisfiers are not effective unless the hygiene factors or dissatisfiers are reasonably satisfied as well.

In recent years some organizations have introduced several concepts to enrich jobs and influence the job satisfaction and morale of employees. These techniques include flextime, four-day work weeks and "casual Friday."

Flextime allows selected employees to determine their own daily work schedule as long as they are on the job during certain hours called core time. Core time may be from 10:00 AM until 2:00 PM, but beyond that certain employees can set their own schedule. Many employees, such as working mothers, like flextime.

Four-day work weeks are popular with some organizations if the nature of the work allows this. Employees work four ten-hour days instead of five eight-hour days. This gives the employees a three-day weekend every week and is attractive to many employees; but problems can occur when determining which employee gets which day off.

Casual Friday is also called "dress-down day." In office complexes where employees are required to dress smartly every day, many organizations allow personnel to wear whatever they like on Fridays. Typically, dressing down means employees may wear jeans and a jacket rather than a suit or dress. Casual Friday is very popular in "white collar" work settings, but it has no value in industrial workplaces. It is interesting to note that in other cultures around the world, Friday is considered to be "dress-up" day for working employees. This is true in Puerto Rico and Mexico in the corporate world.

LEADERSHIP

Leadership has been a subject studied and discussed by scholars in various disciplines for centuries. Consider the words of Lao-tsu, a Chinese philosopher who lived about 2,500 years ago:

> To lead the people, walk behind them... As for the best leaders, the people do not notice their existence. The next best, the people honor and praise. The next, the people fear; and the next, the people hate... When the best leader's work is done the people say, "We did it ourselves!"[12]

Do we have a shortage of effective leaders in this country? Most people say we do. Leaders are needed in every type of organization. How often have we heard someone say that our government lacks leadership, or how many coaches and fans watch an athletic contest and say that the missing element is a "team leader?"

Leadership is defined as the process of inspiring or influencing members of a group to perform their tasks enthusiastically and competently.

Formal and Informal Leaders

In the most general terms there are two types of leaders which we will call **formal** and **informal**. Formal leaders are either appointed, elected or volunteer to fill a leadership role in a position that is part of a formal organization structure. Examples are a Chief Executive Officer, appointed by a corporate board of directors; a governor, elected by the people of a state; or an individual who volunteers to chair a fund drive for a church or community project. In each of these cases, the formal leader is part of a formal organization.

---

[12] Reprinted from Andrew D. Szilagyi, Jr., and Marc J. Wallace, Jr., *Organizational Behavior and Performance* (Glenview, IL: Scott, Foresman and Company, 1990), p. 384.

Informal leaders, also called **indigenous** leaders, arise from groups. Informal leaders are not elected nor appointed to the leadership role. Rather, they become leaders because they stand-out in a physical or psychological way. An informal leader may be the one who has the most knowledge about a subject; is the most experienced to lead in a certain situation; possesses a commanding physical presence; is the most articulate in voicing ideas or concerns; or is the most compatible with all group members. Leaders of informal groups are chosen without a vote by the group members.

Leaders and Managers

The words "leader" and "manager" are often used as if they were interchangeable or synonymous. Managers should be, but may not be, effective leaders. Obviously, many effective leaders are not in management. Managers have "employees" who work under their direction and are accountable to them. Managers are totally responsible for the actions of these employees. Leaders have "followers" who are loyal to them as long as they do not become disillusioned with the goals or tactics of the leader. Employees receive pay and benefits for performing work assignments as directed by managers. Followers of a leader receive personal satisfaction and a sense of value from being part of the leader's group as they work toward achieving goals.

Managers who are effective leaders are clearly identified because of employee enthusiasm, loyalty and dedication to reaching the work objectives. Keith Davis expresses the difference between management and leadership as follows:

> Leadership is a part of management but not all of it... Leadership is the ability to persuade others to seek defined objectives enthusiastically. It is the human factor which binds a group together and motivated it toward goals. Management activities such as planning, organizing, and decision making are dormant cocoons until the leader triggers the power of motivation in people and guides them toward goals.[13]

In the simplest terms, a manager who is an effective leader has employees who not only perform as the manager directs them, but do so because they want to work for that manager.

Situational Leadership

Often leaders arise out of a situation or crisis. If an organization is on the verge of going "belly-up," as Chrysler was in 1978, a Lee Iaccoca may appear and take charge to save the company.

Leaders typically emerge during periods of panics, disasters or wars to help restore order and calm the fears of people. Famous leaders such as Churchill, Roosevelt, McArthur, Eisenhower, Patton and others became famous as great leaders because of World War II. Generals Colin Powell and Norman Schwarzkopf became well-known as effective leaders during the Desert Storm War in the Persian Gulf in 1991. Without the period of crisis (and the surrounding publicity) these people might have toiled unnoticed, but equally well, all their work lives. It is the situations these leaders were thrust into that made them historical figures as much as the skills they demonstrated.

---

[13] Keith Davis, *Human Relations at Work* (New York: McGraw-Hill, 1967), pp. 96-97.

Theories of Leadership

Research on the subject of leadership is continuous. A brief description of some of these theories that are important to managers in every field is included.

Trait Theory. Trait theory focuses on what leaders are **like** rather than on what they **do**. Early studies in the 1940s and 1950s attempted to isolate the characteristics common to successful leaders. The results are not too meaningful since personality traits and physical characteristics do not accurately predict leaders in dynamic (constantly changing) situations.

Rensis Likert. Rensis Likert, while with the Institute for Social Research at the University of Michigan, published his research findings about styles of leadership. Likert said that leadership is a continuum ranging from highly autocratic to highly participative. He developed four systems for classifying leaders:

System 1:   Exploitative-Authoritative Leaders are autocratic and motivate through fear and punishment.

System 2:   Benevolent-Authoritative Leaders treat subordinates kindly if employees "play the game." Use both fear and rewards to motivate.

System 3:   Consultative Leaders involve subordinates, encourage input and use rewards to motivate.

System 4:   Participative-Group Leaders purposefully involve members of the group in the decision-making process. They freely delegate authority and use rewards to motivate.

Likert's research indicated that System 4 was the most effective style of management. Managers differ in their leadership styles, however, depending on the situation, types of personnel, time constraints and other factors. Managers may be neither totally participative nor totally autocratic but somewhere in between the extremes.[14]

Other Leadership Theories. Those who wish to study leadership theories in more depth should consider Robert Blake and Jane Mouton's method of classifying leadership styles of individuals using the Managerial Grid;[15] Fred Fiedler's Contingency Approach to Leadership;[16] and the Immaturity-Maturity Theory by Chris Argyris.[17]

Characteristics of Effective Leaders

While the trait theory is not a good predictor of future leadership ability, there are some general characteristics of effective leaders that warrant consideration. Leadership is an intangible quality where seeing the results of any leader determines whether he or she is effective. Leadership is a subject that can be discussed but not taught. Leadership training, which is important to provide an orientation to the subject, rarely, if ever, produces an effective leader. Note the operative word in all cases is **effective**.

---

[14] See Rensis Likert, *The Human Organization* (New York: McGraw-Hill, 1967) and Rensis Likert, *New Patterns of Management* (New York: McGraw-Hill, 1961).

[15] See Robert R. Blake and Jane Syrgley Mouton, *The New Managerial Grid* (Houston: Gulf Publishing, 1978).

[16] See Fred E. Fiedler, *A Theory of Leadership Effectiveness* (New York: McGrow-Hill, 1967).

[17] Chris Argyris, *Personality and Organization* (New York: Harper and Row, 1957).

When one studies and observes, after the fact, what some leaders do to inspire and influence the members of a group to enthusiastically and competently perform their tasks, certain common personal characteristics can be found:

- Leaders have the ability to inspire. Robert Fulmer states that this is the "undefinable ingredient" in leadership which cannot be bought, sold, or built into an individual. If one has it, it can be nurtured and cultivated. If one does not have it, all the leadership training courses in the world cannot make one a leader.[18]
- Leaders have good human relations skills. They respect for people; they have integrity; they stress cooperation and fairness; and they are not afraid to praise people.
- Leaders have good verbal skills. They know how to present facts and ideas effectively and how to persuade others in a confident manner.
- Leaders are totally dedicated to the group's goals. The actions of a leader through hard work and personal sacrifice demonstrate commitment. Leaders set the example for others to follow. Leaders also have the ability to project the group's goals as exciting, important and essential.
- Leaders often are risk-takers who influence others to go beyond normal bounds in achieving objectives. Followers respond to leaders who challenge new horizons without a guarantee of success. Such action usually generates excitement among followers and a feeling of being "special."
- Leaders take full responsibility for whatever happens and totally support their personnel through encouragement, showing an interest in problems, and representing them before higher levels of management.

Factors Affecting Leadership

Many factors affect the opportunity for quality leadership to emerge. For example, if the organization is highly centralized or bureaucratic, there will be less flexibility for individual action and more reliance on following the prescribed course of conduct. Where activities in management are more decentralized, managers have the opportunity to do things their way and exercise leadership skills. Decentralized organizations provide more accessibility to employees and less control over managerial action by higher-level management.

Secondly, groups have personality characteristics. If the majority of the employees in a department are professional and "self-starters," a certain style of leadership, such as participative, might be most effective. If employees are passive and satisfied just to do the jobs and go home on time, the leadership style should be different. Matching group personalities with that of the manager provides the best chance for leadership success. Assessing the personality of a group is important before implementing a leadership style.

[18] Robert M. Fulmer, *The New Management* (New York: Macmillan, 1974), p. 336.

Finally, it is important that all members of a group share in the enthusiasm to work toward common goals. MBO is one program that is designed to create this. If individuals work toward their own objectives contrary to what is good for the whole, there will be excess tension and conflict and an absence of effective leadership. A primary management objective is to have every employee working toward common goals which are important to the employee and to the group. This is called "harmonizing the objectives," and is one of management's top priorities.

Practicality of Leadership Theories

Perhaps the greatest value of leadership theory to practicing managers is to provide more insight into the subject. Leadership theories encourage more research and debate; however, leadership theory does not seem to provide a process to predict accurately effective, successful leaders nor does it provide a basis for training managers to become such leader/managers.

Leadership training can be of value in helping managers become more aware of situations that require leadership and in suggesting alternative ways of leading. Leadership is an art, however, and as Fulmer stated, if a manager does not have the "undefinable ingredient," no amount of leadership training can make one a leader (refer to footnote 18).

Summary

The most common problem managers face is how to get certain employees motivated to do a better job. Highly motivated employees can bring about significant increases in performance and equally significant decreases in problems. Motivation is concerned with what activates human behavior. Some motives originate from physiological needs (such as survival); other motives stem from psychological needs (such as recognition, status and self-esteem).

Many theories of motivation have been developed. The oldest is reward for good performance and punishment for bad performance. The traditional theory is exemplified by F. W. Taylor's wage incentive plan which pays employees who produce above the standard a much higher wage than those who fail to exceed the standard. Taylor assumed money was the primary motivating factor if the potential financial reward was high enough.

Abraham Maslow's Hierarchy of Needs Theory is well known to students. This theory consists of five levels of need: Physiological, Safety, Love, Esteem and Self-Actualization. Maslow said that the appearance of one need usually rests on the prior satisfaction of another starting with the lowest (physiological) needs and moving up the scale. He said that, regardless of any individual's position on the scale, the lowest unmet need would dominate.

Frederick Herzberg developed the Motivation-Maintenance Theory based on job satisfiers and job dissatisfiers. Job satisfiers relate to the nature of the job such as achievement, recognition and the work itself. Job dissatisfiers tend to be part of the conditions that surround the job such as salary, working conditions, supervision and company policy. Dissatisfiers must be adequately satisfied, but they do not promote motivation. Job satisfiers, along with adequate satisfaction of the hygiene or dissatisfier factors, are motivators.

Other motivation theories in this chapter are Douglas McGregor's Theory X and Theory Y, Victor Vroom's Preference Expectancy Theory, and B. F. Skinner's Reinforcement Theory. Motivation theories tend to be classified as either content, process or reinforcement theories.

Morale is defined in several ways. One definition is "an individual's feeling of being accepted by and belonging to a group of employees through common goals, confidence in the desirability of these goals, and progress toward these goals." Morale is an intangible and has an impact on employee performance in many cases. Motivation and morale may or may not have a correlation although there is not a direct correlation.

The Hawthorne Studies represent the beginning of the Human Relations Movement in management. The findings of researchers are significant because these studies demonstrated that factors other than working conditions affect employee performance.

Job satisfaction refers to the state of mind an individual may have about his or her work environment. Job satisfied, "happy" employees tend to be good workers although there is some disagreement on this point. Methods to bring about more job satisfaction in the workplace include job rotation, job enlargement and job enrichment. Job enrichment is the process of designing jobs to include motivators.

Leadership is defined as the process of inspiring or influencing members of a group to enthusiastically and competently perform their jobs. There are formal and informal leaders. Formal leaders are elected, appointed or volunteer but are part of the formal organization. Informal leaders arise from the group and are not elected or appointed. They can be called "indigenous" leaders. Leaders often emerge from crises or disasters such as wars. Such leaders are called situational leaders.

Leadership theories are plentiful including the Trait Theory and Rensis Likert's Theory. Leadership theories encourage more research and debate but do not provide a process to accurately predict successful leaders; nor do they provide a basis for training managers to become successful, effective leaders.

Review Questions

1.   Discuss the meaning of motivation and the three conditions which must exist for employees to become highly motivated.

2.   Highlight the important differences between Taylor's Traditional Motivation Theory and the theories of Maslow and Herzberg.

3.   Theory X and Theory Y are based on assumptions about human behavior. What are these assumptions? Do you think all employees are either an "X" or "Y" type?

4.   Review the common threads that emerge from a study of motivation theories. Can you add to this list?

5.   Define morale and discuss the relationship to employee performance and motivation.

6.   Explain why the Hawthorne Studies mark the beginning of the Human Relations Movement in management.

7.   Distinguish between morale and job satisfaction. What are some of the methods

used to increase employee job satisfaction in the workplace?

8. Define leadership and the major types of leaders.

9. What is the "undefinable ingredient" in leadership? If a manager does not have it, where does one get it?

10. Several factors affect the effectiveness of managerial leadership. Review them and add other factors which you think are important.

Assignments for Personal Development

1. Conduct a small survey involving four or five friends who are employed on a regular basis. Much like Herzberg's study, ask each one to give examples of what he or she most likes and dislikes about his or her job. Review all of the responses and see if what your friends say matches up with Herzberg's job satisfiers and job dissatisfiers. (Remember that all theories have critics and none is "sacred.")

2. Researchers have said that marginal employees only work twenty to thirty percent of their ability whereas highly motivated employees work eighty to ninety percent of their ability. Make a list of five factors or conditions that highly motivate you in your present job. Be prepared to discuss.

Incident

MORALE AND PRODUCTIVITY

For the past five years the Executive Management Committee of Norwood Manufacturing Company had concentrated its efforts on improving the morale of all employees. The consensus of the committee was that if employee morale could be improved, then productivity would increase, leading to more efficient operations and greater profitability. The success of the programs devised to implement this policy astounded everyone including the committee itself. In the five-year period, the general economy was good, company business was excellent, profits were at a record high, and based on annual personnel audits, employee morale was very good and getting better every year.

In bringing about improved morale, the Executive Management Committee had introduced an employee incentive system that gave monetary recognition to good ideas, seniority, outstanding performance, and other achievements; additionally, the committee held monthly employee meetings (never done before on a regular basis) and introduced a company newsletter distributed monthly at no cost to employees. Beyond this, the committee occasionally sponsored safety contests between departments and similar competitions about daily attendance to reduce absenteeism.

However, the current year was disturbing to the Executive Management Committee. Due to a shortage of fuel and other vital materials necessary in manufacturing company products, about 10 percent of the 500 manufacturing employees had been laid off. About five percent of the white collar employees had been laid off and several staff people who retired had not been replaced by new personnel. The company had unprecedented back orders but was not able to meet the demand. Rising prices and shortages were reducing profits drastically.

The committee reviewed the summary of the most recent personnel audit and noted that, compared to previous findings, morale of the employees was at a new all-time low and getting lower. Interestingly enough, productivity per employee was at an all-time high. The committee members wondered if they could have been wasting their time and company money over the years trying to improve employee morale. There did not seem to be any correlation between morale and productivity.

Questions:

1. Should the company do anything at the present time to improve morale? Should they be concerned with the subject ever again?

2. What do you consider the cause(s) of the company's success during the five-year period mentioned?

Suggested Readings

Argyris, C. *Integrating the Individual and the Organization*. New York: Wiley, 1964.

Beggs, James M. "Leadership—the NASA Approach." *Long-Range Planning* 17 (April 1984): 12-24.

Davis, Keith, and John W. Newstrom. *Human Behavior at Work: Organizational Behavior*. 7th ed. New York: McGraw-Hill, 1985.

Herzberg, Frederick. "One More Time: How Do You Motivate Employees?" *Harvard Business Review*, January-February 1968, pp. 53-62.

Magnus, Margaret. "Employee Recognition: A Key to Motivation." *Personnel Journal* (February 1981): 1038-107.

McGregor, Douglas. *Leadership and Motivation*. Cambridge, Mass.: M.I.T. Press, 1966.

Steers, Richard M., and Lyman W. Porter, eds. *Motivation and Work Behavior*, 3rd ed. New York: McGraw-Hill, 1983.

Stogdill, R. M. *Handbook of Leadership*. New York: Free Press, 1974.

Vroom, Victor H. *Work and Motivation*. New York: Wiley, 1982.

CHAPTER 11

THE COMMUNICATIONS PROCESS

After studying this chapter, **you will know**:
- The Importance of Communication
- The Definition of Communication
- Steps in the Communication Process
- Barriers to Effective Interpersonal Communication
- How to Overcome Barriers in Interpersonal Communication
- General Principles of Good Communication
- About Communication in the Formal Organization
- Why the "Grapevine" Can Be a Communication Asset or Liability

Introduction

This chapter provides a basic understanding of the importance of communication for managers in any type of organization. Of particular value to managers are sections in this chapter on steps in the communication process, barriers to effective communication. and general principles of good communication. Also included is a discussion of the informal communication system within the formal organization, called the **grapevine**, which can be an asset or a liability to managers.

Communication is an integral part of managing, and generally the success and efficiency of an organization reflects the effectiveness of its communications.

Communication is central to human activity and interaction. All people communicate whether they are managers, employees, committees, customers, stockholders, or the general public. Management personnel communicate with all of these groups and types of publics in the process of performing their daily jobs.

The Importance of Communication

In earlier chapters we have seen that without managers chaos and confusion would reign, and there would be no organized effort. With managers in place we know that the world is better; individuals have jobs and higher standards of living; and society in general benefits. To be an **effective** manager one must have knowledge of the job and environment, possess a variety of skills, and be totally dedicated to achieving organizational objectives. Perhaps the most important skill a manager needs is the ability to communicate effectively.

Here are a few of the major jobs of managers. Note how important communication skills are to the successful performance of each:

Planning. All managers plan for the purpose of attaining the objectives in the proper period of time, with a minimum of problems, and in the most efficient and effective way. Planning often involves more than one person. Plans have to be approved by higher management; plans are implemented through others; and plans usually impact employees and other individuals and groups both inside and outside the organization. Would you say communication skills are needed to implement plans successfully? The answer is yes. A manager may be a master planner on paper, but he or she can fail miserably in the implementation stage because of poor communication skills.

Decision-making. Managerial decisions flow downward in the organization and generate "actions" which in turn cause "change" in the organization. Managers must effectively communicate the need for action and change if decisions are to be accepted and not resisted by those affected.

Coordinating. A major responsibility of managers is to combine the needed resources, human and otherwise, in the right quantity, of the right quality, at the right place and at the right time to generate efficiency as the goal is reached. Doing this requires effective communication skills as the manager must explain, educate, visualize and harmonize to attain coordination among the employees involved.

Leading. For leaders to have followers they must communicate the objectives of the effort in such a way that followers become enthused, excited and stimulated. If they cannot do this, there will be no followers. Effective leaders must be good communicators whether they are managers or not. Historic leaders such as Franklin D. Roosevelt, Winston Churchill, Adolph Hitler and Martin Luther King, Jr. were master communicators.

Delegating. Assigning work to others is an essential part of management. The job of the manager is not to "do" the work but rather to "get it done" working through others. Can you think of any other management activity that requires greater communication knowhow? If delegatees do not understand exactly what is expected, why it is important, and when the work is to be completed, then the anticipated result must be unsatisfactory performance and failure. Managers are judged on these results.

Controlling. This managerial function appears in all aspects of running an organization. Standards must be established, and the employees affected by them must understand what is expected. Employee performance is measured against the standard, and corrective action is taken if standards are not met. Control programs are essential and work well if employees and departments affected understand the importance of control; if they believe the standards are fair; and if the evaluation and corrective action taken are positive and help both the individual and the organization. None of the desired results occur unless managers communicate effectively in the administration of control programs.

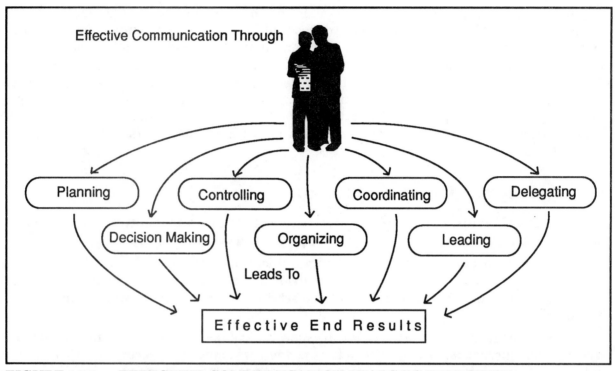

FIGURE 11-1:   EFFECTIVE COMMUNICATION LEADS TO EFFECTIVE END RESULTS

Organizing. Sound organization requires placing qualified employees in the right jobs and balancing the output of work between human resources and physical ones. This generates efficiency of effort. Structuring an organization refers to a clear definition of position authority, responsibility, accountability and communication channels. Lines on an organization chart represent the formal lines of communication. Defects in the organization, especially in the area of communication, are the number one source of daily management problems. To organize soundly requires managers to inform, educate, visualize, train and review employees on a regular basis—all of which demand good communication skills.

In summary, every aspect of a manager's job requires good communication skills, and a considerable amount of a manager's time is spent communicating. American organizations are learning to appreciate the value of effective communication.

D. M. Kersey reports in a study of 1,700 members of the International Association of Business Communicators that effective communication in an organization means higher profits and improved employee relations. He states that communication professionals are becoming instrumental in areas such as customer relations, employee training, benefits delivery and investor relations. Also, communication departments are now more involved in business planning and strategy development.[1]

---

[1] D. M. Kersey, "Faith, Hope, and Clarity," *Management Focus*, Vol. 31, No. 4, July/August, 1984, pp. 4-5.

A second important study which emphasizes the role of effective management communication was conducted by Posner, Kouzes and Schmidt. Their study relates to organizational values shared between managers and employees and the impact such shared values have on job satisfaction, efficiency and employee commitment to organization goals. Their findings indicate that a similarity between organizational values and employees' value systems strengthens both the individuals and the organization as a whole. They recommend that managers use these findings and develop programs to **communicate** organizational values; then, recruit and train personnel who best fit within the corporate value system.[2]

Interpersonal Communication

Communication can be defined as the act or action of imparting or transmitting ideas, information, facts or feelings to a second party.

There are dozens of definitions of communication; however, all communication is two-way. There must be a sender and a receiver. The sender or receiver may be an individual or a group. Communication takes place between individuals; individuals and groups; and from group to group.

Communication is a joint process. If someone speaks, someone listens. If someone writes, someone reads. If someone acts, someone watches. If a second party does not listen, read or watch, no communication occurs. For communication to be **effective** there must be an understanding and response by the receiver. When the response from the receiver is in line with the message transmitted by the sender, the communication is **effective**. If the response from the receiver is not in line with the message transmitted, the communication if **ineffective**. Communication may have occurred, but the response indicates misunderstanding, misinterpretation or simply a refusal to respond as the sender requests. The end result is **ineffective communication**.

The Communication Process

When one seriously studies the activity of transmitting ideas, information, facts and feelings to a second party or group, it becomes clear that a communication **process** exists. The communication process consists of a series of steps that are in sequential order. They are the steps that every effective communicator goes through (knowingly or not): idea origination; the message; channel selecting and encoding; transmission; receiving; decoding, and feedback.

Idea Origination. Ideas are the source of planned communications. If a manager has some ideas about the cause of low employee morale, he or she may wish to communicate these ideas to the supervisors at a group meeting. It is important that the sender consider ideas carefully before developing a message. Ideas should have legitimate value and warrant the time and effort it takes to communicate them effectively to a second party. If it passes this test, a decision will be made to communicate.

---

[2] B. Z. Posner, J. M. Kouzes, and W. H. Schmidt, "Shared Values Make a Difference: An Empirical Test of Corporate Culture." *Human Resource Management*, Vol. 24, Fall, 1985, pp. 293-309.

```
          SENDER              RECEIVER

       Writes  <--------->  Reads and Responds

        Talks  <--------->  Listens and Responds

         Acts  <--------->  Watches and Responds
```

FIGURE 11-2: COMMUNICATION IS A JOINT PROCESS

The Message. The message is the formalization of the ideas which the sender wishes to convey. The message in its physical form may be transmitted by words, written or spoken, or by body language of the sender (nonverbal). Messages must be framed carefully to minimize misunderstanding by the receiver.

Channel Selection and Encoding. Selecting the right channel for transmitting a message is a key to effective communication. Common channels are writing, speaking, electronic media equipment, and nonverbal physical actions. In the old West, Indians used smoke signals to communicate danger, tribe movements and warnings. The channel selected also must be compatible with symbols selected for encoding. Specific channels used to transmit messages might be face-to-face meetings, written letters, fax messages, computer printouts, telephone calls and many others.

Encoding refers to the symbols or gestures a sender selects to transmit a message through the desired channel so that the receiver decodes it properly. Forms of expression may be charts, tables, facial looks, purposeful anger, words and written summaries.

Transmission. Transmission of the message through the selected channel is the next step in the communication process. This is the **physical activity** that takes the encoded ideas to the receiver. Occasionally problems occur in transmitting messages, such as a memo being lost in the delivery of interoffice mail; however, transmission tends to be the easiest of steps in the communication process because no interpretation is required.

Receiver. The receiver or receivers are the persons to whom the message is directed. If the message does not get to the intended receiver, no communication takes place.

Decoding. Decoding is the step in the communication process where the receiver translates the sender's symbols and gestures into meaningful thought. If the sender and receiver have similar values, experiences and word interpretations, there is less chance of a communication breakdown. Effective communication occurs when a receiver interprets the message from the sender in the same way as the sender intended.

Feedback. Feedback is a response by the receiver to the sender's message. It may be an acknowledgment that the message has been received, or the receiver may take the action desired by the sender. Feedback reverses the steps in the communication process. The receiver becomes the sender and the sender, the receiver. All steps in the communication process are followed by the receiver, now the sender, to transmit response to the original sender's message.

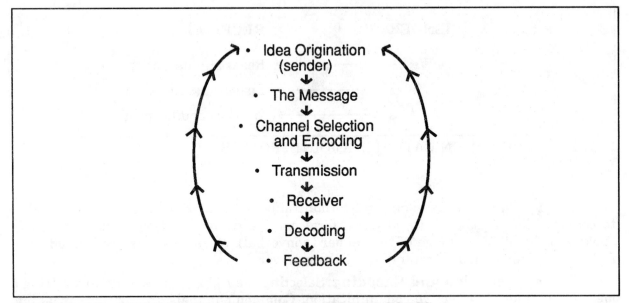

FIGURE 11-3: STEPS IN THE COMMUNICATION PROCESS

Barriers to Effective Interpersonal Communication

Studies about causes of communication breakdown list dozens of reasons. Each of these reasons can be a barrier to effective communication. Reasons run the gamut from the receiver not trusting the sender to prejudice and physical conditions. Figure 11-4 shows some typical barriers to effective interpersonal communication.

For our purposes six of the most common barriers to effective interpersonal communication will be discussed. They pertain to semantics, resistance to change, perception differences, listening, credibility and noise.

The Semantics Barrier. Semantics problems occur because people may have a different meaning or understanding of the words used in written or verbal communications. **Semantics** is the science or study of word meanings. When a sender uses a word with one meaning in mind and the receiver interprets the word differently, the intended message becomes distorted. The word "table" for example has over 100 meanings in the English language. Additionally, words may take on a different meaning depending on how they are expressed by the sender to the receiver in person.

A sender should carefully choose the words that go into a message to minimize the risk of misinterpretation by the receiver.

The Resistance to Change Barrier. It is almost a natural phenomenon for people to resist new ideas, new ways of doing things, or anything that might change the status quo of an organization. Frequently resistance to change by an individual or group becomes a barrier to effective communication. If the receiver does not like the ideas in the message, he or she may reject it totally, only accept the parts of the message they like, or interpret and apply the ideas in a way that will not upset the existing environment. Careful planning, educating and selling new ideas or changes to the parties involved helps to break down resistance to change. **Empathizing** with the receiver while you plan your communication is important. Putting yourself in the receiver's place or imagining you will be the receiver of the message helps a sender plan the communication better. Often this will remove the resistance to change as a significant barrier.

The Perception Difference Barrier. Often a message is communicated to a receiver who interprets the message in a totally different way from that intended by the sender. The receiver's perception of the information is quite different from that of the sender. Differing perceptions occur because individuals have different values, experiences, education, expectations and personalities. Often receivers perceive only information that matches their expectations. Also, they see and hear only what they want to see and hear.

A group of managers may brainstorm an overall organization problem and individually recommend action that mostly benefits their own functional areas. They do not perceive the importance of problems in other areas. Notice that in court several witnesses may be brought in to testify about what they have all observed. Each one's perception of what occurred may be quite different.

The Listening Barrier. Listening is the responsibility of a receiver in the communication process. This requires a receiver to be alert, attentive and to concentrate totally on the message being directed toward him or her. The responsibility of the sender is to make sure the receiver is really listening, not just appearing to be listening. In the process of delegating work to employees managers must make sure that employees correctly understand what they are being asked to do. Sometimes managers have employees repeat back what they have been told to check the receiver's interpretation and make sure the message was heard and understood as sent. Failure of a receiver to listen to a sender is a common barrier to effective interpersonal communications.

The old story is God made us with two ears and one mouth so that we could listen twice as much as we talk! How many of your friends talk twice as much as they listen?

Some receivers fail to listen effectively because they may be day dreaming, not interested in the subject, do not really understand the message, are bored, or are planning after-work activities. It is important to be certain you have the receiver's attention.

Good listening habits can be developed if one wants to improve. Several suggestions are give the speaker your undivided attention; be patient and let the speaker finish before you say anything; make sure your questions and comments are on the subject; do not be on the defensive; and repeat back or summarize what the speaker has said.

The Credibility Barrier. Problems of credibility arise when the sender is not trusted. If receivers doubt the knowledge base, the integrity, or the past performance record of the sender, credibility diminishes. It is difficult for subordinates to respond enthusiastically to messages received if the sender's credibility is in doubt.

A major case involving institutional credibility is reported by D. A. Safer. He reported that the American automobile industry in 1985 had every reason to believe that national public opinion would support their position on Japanese auto imports. The industry's statements and subsequent contradictory actions, however, encouraged the public to question the accuracy and sincerity of its statements, creating a credibility gap.[3]

---

[3] D. A. Safer, "Institutional Body Language," *Public Relations Journal*, Vol. 41, No. 3, March 1985, pp. 26-28, 30.

Perceived credibility by receivers is based primarily on the sender's honesty, competence, enthusiasm and objectivity.[4] The sender may or may not possess these characteristics. It is how the receiver perceives the sender that matters.

The Noise Barrier. Noise is a word used in the communication field that denotes any factor that causes confusion, distortion, or disturbs communication. Examples of "noise" are poor lighting, lack of privacy for conversations, hand written (hard to read) memos, noisy equipment, the drone of ringing telephones, or emotionally upset employees. Most "noise" or interference occurs during the encoding and decoding stages of the communication process.

Overcoming Barriers in Interpersonal Communication

A manager's effectiveness depends significantly on his or her ability to communicate. The transfer of information whether by word or actions is effective if the receiver understands the message just as the sender intended and if the desired action is initiated.

Managers will be better communicators if they are aware of all the barriers that can hamper the communication process. They will be better communicators if they know how to overcome these barriers. Organizations have a responsibility to train their managers to be more effective communicators. For example, Xerox Learning Systems has developed a training program to help people prepare persuasive talks. Their program suggests that the most important rule for a speaker is to know the audience. They teach six steps that can enable a speaker to prepare a presentation that will meet audience needs:

1. Setting objectives
2. Analyzing audience needs
3. Developing benefits that address the needs identified
4. Analyzing audience attitudes
5. Rehearsing and adding special touches
6. Following the basic principles of good delivery.[5]

Figure 11-4 lists some of the barriers to effective interpersonal communications. Perhaps the best way to overcome many of these barriers is for a manager to develop a set of communication values. Values may be referred to as standards or principles to influence personal conduct. If a manager keeps his or her communication values, standards or principles in mind when planning to communicate, many of the barriers will be overcome.

Years ago, John F. Mee, a well-known management professor and author at Indiana University, developed a set of communication principles. These principles, reproduced in Figure 11-5, are as valid today as they were then. Managers can benefit by reviewing all these principles. Here we will elaborate on several of the most significant principles.

---

[4] Jack L. Whitehead, Jr., "Factors of Source Credibility," *Quarterly Journal of Speech*, 54 (February 1968), 59-63.

[5] J. J. Franco, "Speaker, Know Thy Audience," *Training and Development Journal*, Vol. 39, No. 6, June, 1985, pp. 20-21.

> Sender Lacks Credibility
>
> Poor Listening Habits of Receiver(s)
>
> Semantics Problems — Differences in Word Meanings
>
> Predisposition of Receiver (The Closed Mind Syndrome)
>
> Status Differences Between Sender and Receiver(s)
>
> Noise — All Disruptive Physical Factors
>
> Climate in the Work Place
>
> Prejudice and Deep-Rooted Feelings and Emotions
>
> Perceptual Differences Between Sender and Receiver(s)
>
> Information Overload — Too Much Information At One Time
>
> Resistance to Change

FIGURE 11-4: BARRIERS TO EFFECTIVE INTERPERSONAL COMMUNICATION

No One Communication Technique Will Meet All Needs. Creative communicators know that to insure effectiveness they may need to transmit information in a variety of ways. A manager who delegates a work assignment to a subordinate may do so both verbally and in writing to minimize the possibility of any misunderstanding. Students in a classroom will listen to a professor lecture and take notes on the key points while also tape recording the lecture to review later. In these examples the receivers are using more than one channel to insure communication effectiveness. Perhaps no company is more famous for the effectiveness of its advertising than Coca Cola, the most widely recognized corporate name in the world. Notice how many channels of communication Coca Cola uses to advertise (transmit its message) products.

Action Speaks Louder Than Words in Communication. Managers communicate as much by their actions as they do by their words. Can you imagine a department head strongly enforcing the fifteen minute coffeebreak rule for employees, but personally enjoying a twenty or thirty minute "break?" It helps to overcome barriers to effective communication if verbal or written communications are reinforced by managerial action. If a manager says one thing but does another, employees eventually ignore the verbal communication and imitate the action. Furthermore, management loses credibility.

Know Your Subject. A person's ability to communicate tends to vary directly with the person's understanding of the subject being communicated. This principle is a **truism**. Before transmitting information to a second party a manager should do his or her homework. Always research the subject fully before developing your message and before determining the channel for transmitting it. Knowledge about a subject allows a manager to communicate with enthusiasm, confidence and clarity. Receivers such as listeners quickly catch a speaker who does not seem to know what he or she is discussing. Lack of detail, incomplete information, or unclear information become major barriers to effective communication.

1. No one communication technique will meet all needs. A communication program uses many techniques, methods and channels.

2. Confidence is a basic principle of communication. An employee who suspects that he or she is being sold a "bill of goods" will resent the communicator's intrusion and will not be receptive to the message.

3. Action speaks louder than words in communication.

4. Each communication program needs to be tailored to fit the needs and wants of the individual human organization.

5. Planning with regard to any major managerial decision should include planning for communicating it to those who will carry it out and those who will be affected by it.

6. Generalized of "canned" communications cannot form the core of a communication program. Communications which are directed to everyone will probably fail to meet the specific need of anyone. "Canned" communication should be used only when it is complementary to the central theme.

7. Establish good daily communication. If employers communicate solely as a defense against attack, then employees may turn elsewhere for information. Or even worse, they may create in their own imagination answers which will be worse than the truth.

8. A person's ability to communicate tends to vary directly with his or her own understanding of the subject to be communicated.

9. Management's effectiveness with communication tends to vary directly with its belief in the importance and value of adequate communication.

10. Respect for downward communication channels tends to be in direct proportion to the extent to which the supervisor receives and transmits information before the subordinate gets it elsewhere.

11. Development of good communication relationships takes time. They cannot be built in a day — or a year — but they can be improved regularly.

FIGURE 11-5: CARDINAL PRINCIPLES OF EFFECTIVE COMMUNICATION

Source: *Personnel Handbood*, edited by John F. Mee (The Ronald Press Company, New York, 1951).

Plan Your Communication. Planning with regard to any major managerial decision should include planning for communicating it to those who will execute the decision and those who will be affected by it. As we learned in earlier chapters, planning is an activity of today that pertains to the future. Communication, like planning, is initiated to achieve certain end results. Planning your communication requires a determination, in advance, of the ideal end result. A manager then reviews alternative ways to communicate to reach the ideal. Involved in the planning effort is a review of facts, options, risks (barriers), and knowledge of the intended receivers. Communicating too hastily without thinking or planning carefully can lead to disappointing end results. Empathizing with your intended receiver is a valuable step in the communication planning process.

Communication and the Formal Organization

Communication within the framework of the formal organization is as important as communication between individuals. The effectiveness of communication in the formal organization relates to the philosophy of higher management, the culture, whether the organization is highly centralized or decentralized, the communication networks, and much more.

Philosophy of Higher Management. Higher management controls and influences everything in an organization. If the general attitude of top management is to support openness; to practice and encourage participative management; decry rigid rules; follow an "open door" policy; and encourage a team spirit in approaching problems, then communications will flow freely. This is often the practice in relatively small organizations. Also, this philosophy may be apparent in research organizations, some colleges and universities, and where individual employees are viewed as professional type workers. Usually this type of organization is decentralized in structure, and communications flow upward, downward, and laterally without worry about violating the chain of command (scalar principle).

In other types of organizations, the philosophy of top management may be to maintain tight control over all aspects of the organization. If so, the communication process likely will be more formalized according to the networks depicted on the organization chart. Organizations like this are usually highly centralized in structure, more bureaucratic in practice, and follow strict adherence to the chain of command. The branches of the United States military would be prime examples.

Culture. Organizational culture has a direct impact on communication within the formal organization. Several meanings of **culture** are included here:

1. Observed behavioral regularities when people interact, such as the language used and the rituals around deference and demeanor
2. The norms that evolve in working groups
3. The dominant values espoused by an organization
4. The philosophy that guides an organization's policy toward employees and/or customers
5. The rules of the game for getting along in the organization
6. The feeling or climate that is conveyed in an organization by the physical layout and the way in which members of the organization interact with customers or other outsiders.[6]

Notice that the meanings of culture include the words behavior, norms, interactions, rituals, values, rules, feelings, and climate. All of these words or subjects can be part of or have an effect on the communication process.

Centralized and Decentralized Organizations. A centralized organization refers to the decision-making, authority, responsibility, and control being held closely by top management. This would be a vertical organization with relatively smaller spans of control under lower level managers. Communication would follow prescribed channels upward and downward and sometimes laterally if approved first by higher level managers.

---

[6] E. H. Schein, *Organizational Culture and Leadership* (San Francisco: Jossey-Bass, 1985), p. 6.

DOWNWARD	UPWARD
Reprimanding Employee	Submitting Ideas—Suggestion Box
Company-wide Meeting	Quality Circle Report
Benefits Change in Pay Envelope	Committee Recommendation
Announcement Over Public Address System	Response During Employee Appraisal Session
Employee Handbood	Survey Feedback
Delegating Work	Filing a Grievance
Training a New Employee	Exit Interviews
Scheduling Production	Accident Report
Laying Off Employees	Informal Meeting with Boss
Distribution of Bonus	Signing a Petition

FIGURE 11-6: EXAMPLES OF VERTICAL COMMUNICATION

In contrast, the decentralized organization pushes decision-making, authority, responsibility and control downward as much as possible. Lower level managers assume much more of the responsibility and have more authority to decide and control their parts of the organization. This would be a horizontal type structure. Communication tends to flow more freely upward, downward and laterally in this framework. Part of the openness is due to the improved status of lower level managers who have more responsibility and feel more important to the organization. Lower level managers make more decisions and must communicate more often to larger numbers of subordinates.

Communication Networks. Communication networks refer to the flow of information. Networks can also be called communication systems. The most common networks or systems are downward, upward and lateral. Downward and upward communication combined is called **vertical** communication. The simplest example of vertical communication would be between a supervisor and one employee. The supervisor tells the employee what to do (downward communication) and the employee acknowledges understanding what to do (upward communication.

Downward communication originates from higher levels of management and flows downward to lower levels. Downward communication can be an announcement to all employees over the public address system or the posting of important information on the bulletin board. Normally downward communication follows the chain of command (i.e., flows downward one level at a time without skipping any level) unless information is transmitted to all employees at one time. Downward communication tends to be faster than upward communication because of the status and authority associated with the sender. Downward communication is most effective when information is transmitted directly and personally to individuals, small groups and departments. It is least effective when the channel selected for transmission is indirect and impersonal. Examples of this are notices in the paycheck envelope, employee handbooks, and any form of "canned" communications directed to employees at lower levels.

Upward communication becomes effective if higher level managers encourage employees to communicate with them. Upward communication can be suggestions; ideas; responses to questions; reports on work completed, sales made and job problems encountered; and much more. Two major problems hinder the effectiveness of upward communication. One is the fear of employees that higher managers will not welcome their comments, suggestions or ideas, or that they will be misinterpreted in a negative sense. The second problem is that employees are not eager to communicate problems or bad news upward to higher managers.

Upward communication can be valuable to higher management in the following ways:

1. It can demonstrate the effectiveness of downward communication.
2. It can provide information on the progress and achievements of employees below.
3. It can transmit employee suggestions and ideas for improvement.
4. It can send signals to management above concerning employee morale and job satisfaction.

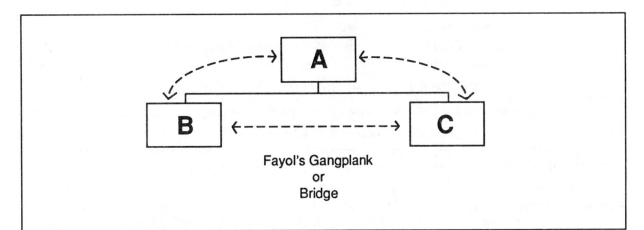

FIGURE 11-7: COMMUNICATION: UPWARD, DOWNWARD, AND LATERAL

Lateral communication traditionally was not acceptable because it violated the scalar principle (chain of command). If "A" is the boss and has two employees, "B" and "C" reporting to him or her (see Figure 11-7), would you allow "B" to communicate formally with "C" without going through "A?" The answer is no since "A" should give permission to "B" to communicate with "C" and since "A" is going to be held totally responsible for what happens under his or her jurisdiction (including actions taken by "B" and "C").

It took the publication of Henri Fayol's famous book, *General and Industrial Management*, in 1916 in France for managers to look at the value of lateral communication. Fayol advocated allowing "B" and "C" to communicate directly to save time, paperwork and for convenience. This direct communication link between "B" and "C" has been called Fayol's **bridge** or **gangplank**.

Lateral communication works effectively and can be justified if the parties involved have been instructed by higher management to do so; if such a responsibility is in the employees' job descriptions; or if it has become a traditional and expected work practice for employee "B" to communicate directly with employee "C." A second justification is that employee "B" or "C" or both keep manager "A" above informed about the direct communication between them.

Lateral communication probably is more common between managers than between nonmanagers. The advantages involve more than savings in time, paperwork and convenience. Lateral communication is vital to coordinating efforts and resources between mutually dependent departments. Also, lateral communication is necessary for a matrix organization structure to function effectively.

- Cannot Be Seen on Organization Chart
- Communication Network Changes Daily/Hourly
- All Employees Are Part of the System
- "Chief Grapes" Are the Key Players
- Has No Conscience! Cannot Differentiate Facts or Truth from Rumors and Lies
- Available for All to Use — Give Input & Get Output
- Follows No Formal Channels of Communication
- Can Be an Asset or Liability to Management

FIGURE 11-8: CHARACTERISTICS OF THE GRAPEVINE

The Grapevine

The grapevine is not a formal communication system; however, it does overlap and intertwine with the formal system. The grapevine is the communication system of the informal organization. Neither the informal organization or the informal communications system (grapevine) are seen on the formal organization chart.

The mystery of the grapevine is that it is invisible yet real; that it is permanent yet elusive; and that it is remarkably efficient in transmitting information even though its communication network changes often—perhaps many times each day. Anyone who has worked full time in the same organization for a few months is well aware that there are "chief grapes" in the grapevine who thrive on moving information around the organization.

How important is the grapevine to managers? It is extremely important because it is a communication system that should be made into an asset instead of a liability. Managers should realize that every employee is part of the grapevine whether they wish to be or not. Managers should understand that the grapevine is accessible to everyone in the organization for input or output. Further, managers should realize that the grapevine has no conscience: It cannot separate the truth from lies nor can the grapevine identify rumors (as different from facts).

Information transmitted via the grapevine follows no formal channel of communication. Plotting information along the grapevine on an organization chart would show a zigzag pattern of lines and crossovers before you traced the origin of the information.

From a management standpoint, the grapevine can be an asset if you wish certain information circulated quickly throughout the organizaton. For example, mention to one employee that raises next year will be around five percent! Also, the grapevine can be a managerial asset if managers tune into it once in a while and listen to what employees are saying and doing. Often this can be a good source of information for evaluating job satisfaction or morale of the employees. In addition, information may be obtained that foretells of employee unrest or dissatisfaction with a situation or issue.

External Communication

Some mention should be made of the importance of an organization's external communication. We have discussed interpersonal communications, formal communications within the organization and the grapevine. Management must view external communication and its effectiveness as equally important.

In the business world today, both profit-seeking and nonprofits communicate through the use of direct mailings, advertising and public service announcements on radio and television, newspaper ads and public relations articles (also called features), and by lending their names to worthwhile events such as charity drives and relief efforts. Major firms often relate externally to the public through public relations departments or agencies. The purpose of the public relations firm or department is to create the proper public image of the organization. Providing information to the public can generate more public support, more demand for a product or service, more donors or more customers.

Organizations should develop strategy for externally communicating effectively in light of their communication objectives. This means a concerted, planned effort at getting the right message to the right public at the appropriate time. Planning and organization are required, and a goal or objective must be firmly established and communicated effectively within the organization.

It appears that more organizations will face scrutiny in the future because of a demanding and well-educated public. Such a climate makes the effectiveness of any organization's external communication programs more crucial. Planned external communication programs can provide a major "payoff" for organizations that provide quality information in an effective manner.

Summary

Perhaps the most important skill a manager should possess is the ability to communicate effectively. Some of the major jobs of managers that require effective communication skills are planning, decision-making, coordinating, leading, delegating, controlling and organizing.

Communication is defined as the act or action of imparting or transmitting ideas, information, facts or feelings to a second party. Communication is always two-way. There must be a sender and a receiver. Communication is a joint process: If someone writes, someone reads; if someone speaks, someone listens; if someone acts, someone watches.

For communication to be effective there must be an understanding and response by the second party. When the response of the second party is in line with the message transmitted by the sender, the communication is **effective**.

The communication process consists of a series of steps that are in sequential order. They are idea origination, the message, channel selection and encoding, transmission, receiving, decoding and feedback.

Typical barriers to effective interpersonal communication are lack of sender credibility; poor listening habits of the receiver; semantics problems; predisposition of the receiver; status differences between sender and receiver; noise; prejudices and more. There are ways to overcome communication barriers. One is for a manager to have a philosophy of communication which consists of standards, values or principles which guide the manager when planning to communicate. One important principle is that a person's ability to communicate tends to vary directly with his or her own knowledge of the subject to be communicated.

Communication within the framework of the formal organization is as important as communication between individuals. The effectiveness of communication in the formal organization relates to the philosophy of higher manager; the culture; whether the organization is highly centralized or decentralized; and the communication networks.

Communication networks refer to the flow of information. The most common networks or systems are downward, upward and lateral. Downward and upward communication combined is called **vertical** communication.

The grapevine is the communication system of the informal organization. Neither the informal organization nor the grapevine appear on the formal organization chart. The mystery of the grapevine is that it is invisible yet real; permanent yet elusive; and that its communication networks change often but it is efficient in transmitting information.

Every employee is part of the grapevine. Managers should view the grapevine as an asset and use it for the good of the organization.

Now, American organizations face a challenge to identify themselves to the public they serve. Therefore, external communication has become more important, and organizations must develop strategies for effective external communication.

Review Questions

1. What is the importance of communication to the management function of planning? To organizing? To implementing? To controlling?

2. Name the steps in the communication process. Where do most of the communication problems occur in the process? Why?

3. Why is the semantics problem such a barrier to effective communication?

4. There are many other barriers to effective communication. Name and explain at least five more.

5. A number of communication principles are mentioned in this chapter. Which one do you think is of greatest importance to a practicing manager? Justify.

6. The "grapevine" is the communication system of the informal organization. Are you familiar with five or six characteristics of the grapevine? Do you know how managers can make the grapevine an asset instead of its being a liability?

Assignments for Personal Development

1. Identify the organization in your geographic area that appears to be most effective in carrying out its planned external communication program. Outline why you think this is so. Include examples of advertising, brochures, written releases, personal appearances, etc.

2. Review all the written, formal internal communication in your organization. Examples would be the company newsletter, employee handbook, notices posted on the bulletin board, etc. How many of these are examples of "effective" communication? How many might be improved significantly?

Incident

WHICH WAY TO GO?

Harry Smith was a charter member of a new, prestigious suburban athletic club. The Club was open to the public but had a limit on its membership. Owner/investors poured several million dollars into the creation of physical facilities that provided many sporting opportunities for its members with the exception of golf. Harry enjoyed the use of the facilities but notices that confusion existed in the administration of programs. None of the employees, including the managers, seemed able to make a decision without checking with someone higher up.

Last week two of the major owners asked Harry to take leave from his job as a vice president at a large urban bank to become Executive Director of the Club for at least a year. If he liked the job, he could keep it permanently; and if not, he could go back to the bank at the end of the year. They told him they had enough clout to get him the "leave," and they needed help badly. The major problem they described to him was a lousy organization with everyone doing their own thing without anyone knowing what anybody else was doing.

Harry promised to consider the offer seriously if they would let him study operations for a few days. They readily agreed.

After three days of observation and interviewing, Harry concluded many things were wrong with the administration of the Club. There was no leadership; poor or nonexistent planning, and the organization was chaotic. The most immediate problem Harry found, however, was the lack of an effective communication system which could provide pertinent information to and from all employees. Improving the formal communication program would be his first priority after he accepted the job.

Questions:

1. If you were Harry Smith, new Executive Director of the Club, which communication system would you advocate and try to implement? Why? (See **Notes on Communication**.)

2. Give an example of another type of organization where you might advocate the opposite approach and explain why.

NOTES ON COMMUNICATION:

Traditional American managers believe in the value of formal communication channels that follow the lines on the organization chart. The communication channels or networks would be upward, downward (together called vertical) and lateral. These managers understand the virtue of organization principles such as unity of command; the scalar principle, and the principle of delegation. To some degree they may practice participative management and even the "open door" policy, but never at the expense of "stabbing" the formal communication channels.

Other American managers find that in the 1990s the old communication systems don't work very well. Following the principles mentioned above and never violating the chain of command, for example, stifles quick action, problem solving, and organization flexibility. These new management thinkers consider communication "openness" vital to dynamic organizations. They believe that today's environment requires organizations to adjust to change quickly and to view employees as growing valuable resources. Such managers also believe in a team approach to solving problems. Traditional communication networks are viewed as obsolete. There is merit to both these approaches.

Suggested Readings

Bosmajian, H.A., ed. *The Rhetoric of Nonverbal Communication*. Chicago: Scott, Foresman, 1971.

Ebenstein, Michael, and Leonard I. Krauss. "Strategic Planning for Information Resource Management." *Management Review* 70 (June 1981): 21-26.

Goldhaber, Gerald M. *Organizational Communication*, 4th ed. Dubuque, Iowa: Wm. C. Brown, 1983.

Grikscheit, Gary M., and William J. E. Drissy. "Improving Interpersonal Communications Skill." *MSU Business Topics*, Autumn 1973, pp. 63-68.

Lesikar, Raymond. *Business Communication*. Homewood, IL: Richard D. Irwin, 1972.

Micheli, Linda, Frank V. Cespedes, Donald Byker, and Thomas J. C. Raymond. *Managerial Communication*. Glenview, IL: Scott, Foresman, 1984.

Swift, Marvin H. "Clear Writing Means Clear Thinking Means..." *Harvard Business Review*, January-February 1973, pp. 59-62.

CHAPTER 12

ORGANIZING WORK EFFORT OF INDIVIDUALS AND GROUPS

After studying this chapter, **you will know:**
- What job design is
- Factors that affect job design
- Job design methods
- How to implement job design
- The types of groups to manage
- The value of work groups to the organization
- About special groups
- How individuals and groups are a source of creativity
- The importance of change and how to implement it

Introduction

The implementation of plans and programs through individuals and groups is the focus of this chapter. The manager of the 1990s must understand the importance of designing jobs properly so that employees receive job satisfaction and will, in turn, increase productivity. Increasing productivity is the key to sustained success and economic growth.

Managers must also understand the importance of formal and informal groups and how to manage them effectively. Of special significance in this chapter is a discussion of task forces and committees.

Perhaps nothing is more important in this chapter than the material on creativity. The 1990s will be remembered as the decade of accelerated creativity because of the economic competitiveness throughout the world. All organizations need to adopt a philosophy of purposeful creativity, i.e., **making progress on purpose rather than by accident**.

Finally, the important subject of "change" is discussed with suggestions about ways to implement change and overcome some of the traditional barriers to change and the natural tendency of people to resist change.

Organizing Jobs

American businesses, governmental agencies and other nonprofit organizations have been startled in recent years by an apparent lag in worker productivity, reduced efficiency of output, and increased foreign competition. Many industries, formerly dominated by American manufacturers, have been overwhelmed by foreign competitors. The nature of the American economy has changed along with the characteristics of American employees. Today, there is a renewed interest among American managers in the individual employee and the specific job he or she performs. This interest is justified by the premise that the more satisfied an employee is on the job, the more positively that employee will respond. The end result will be greater productivity and improvement in the efficiency of output.

Some management experts have suggested that waste in time, effort and monies in the typical business organization might reach as high as twenty (20) percent. In the typical nonprofit organization, it has been suggested that this figure might be as high as thirty (30) percent (in government agencies, large educational institutions and certain social agencies). There is no doubt that most organizations could improve performance and generate greater efficiency if management approached the task in a more professional way.

The beginning point for improving overall organizational effort is the design of individual jobs.

Job design is the process of specifying the tasks to be performed; the work methods to be used in performance; and the relationship of that job to other jobs in the organization for the purpose of improving the quality and quantity of work.

There are three steps in job design: First, individual tasks are combined into specific jobs. The jobs are then assigned to qualified employees, and all work activity is coordinated to achieve efficiency of effort.

Current interest in job design stems from work specialization. Historically, the United States became a great economic power because of the principle of division of labor (work specialization) as advocated by Adam Smith and Thomas Jefferson and applied by Eli Whitney. The result of division of labor was mass production of standardized products at low unit costs. Mass production drastically improved the standard of living of workers in this country; however, after nearly one hundred years of benefits from its application, American employees, managers, organized labor and researchers now question the continued value of work specialization in relation to greater productivity and increased efficiency.

A common view of repetitive work is that it is dull and dehumanizing with the end result of alienating the individual employee from the workplace. Thus, there is new interest in job design for the purpose of improving the quantity and quality of work while providing greater job satisfaction to the employee. Many approaches to job design are available to managers. Nearly all these approaches are aimed at reducing the need for job specialization.

Factors Affecting Job Design

Job design is a product of many factors. The greatest impact on structuring any job comes from job depth and job scope, the type of available employees, economic restrictions, union limitations, and the management philosophy of the organization.

Job Depth and Job Scope. Before designing or redesigning a job, a manager should determine how specialized the job is or should be. Determining the **job depth** and **job scope** is one approach. **Job depth** refers to the individual employee's flexibility to control his or her work performance. If the job must be performed in a set sequential fashion, then job depth is low. If the employee has the flexibility to determine the order of work and the work pace and make many decisions affecting job performance, then job depth is high. Obviously, if job depth is high, there is less specialization of work.

Job scope refers to how specialized and narrow the work activity is. If an employee concentrates on doing a single task repeatedly, job scope is low. If the employee's job involves doing five or ten different tasks, job scope is broader no matter now much repetition there is.

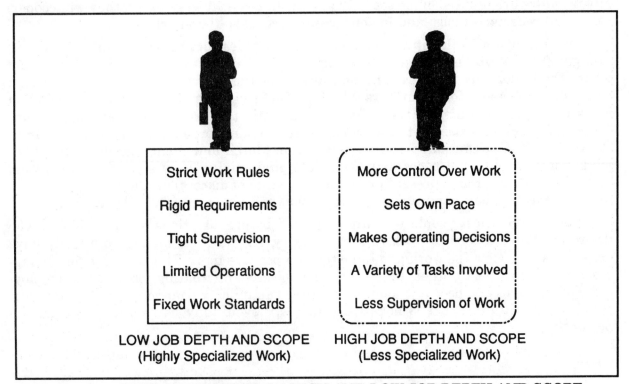

Strict Work Rules

Rigid Requirements

Tight Supervision

Limited Operations

Fixed Work Standards

LOW JOB DEPTH AND SCOPE
(Highly Specialized Work)

More Control Over Work

Sets Own Pace

Makes Operating Decisions

A Variety of Tasks Involved

Less Supervision of Work

HIGH JOB DEPTH AND SCOPE
(Less Specialized Work)

FIGURE 12-1: CHARACTERISTICS OF HIGH AND LOW JOB DEPTH AND SCOPE

Job specialization varies inversely with the degree of job depth and job scope. Low job depth and low job scope produce the most specialized job. As job depth becomes higher and job scope broadens, specialization decreases. Figure 12-1 illustrates the characteristics of high and low job depth and scope.

Types of Employees. The availability of labor is a major factor in designing jobs. If an organization is located in a large city, the labor pool will usually include many potential employees who can be trained to operate machinery or perform job duties with a minimum of supervision. Such employees can perform high quality work with less specialization of tasks. Where the available labor force is less skilled or the supply more limited, jobs may need to be designed with a high degree of specialization and more repetition of limited tasks. Of concern to management in both these cases is the degree of supervision required which is a consequence of job design.

Economic Restrictions. Resources available to a manager, both for personnel as well as equipment and facilities, may dictate job design. Restricted budgets and space limitation directly affect the flexibility of a manager in designing jobs. A manager's intentions may be idealistic, but a lack of funding to initiate change can limit the design of a job. Further, if facilities and equipment are old and nearly obsolete, job design can be severely restricted.

Union Limitations. Union philosophy often conflicts with management's thinking about job design. If the union-management contract specifies work standards which in turn set pay rates, the option for redesign of jobs will be limited. In recent years, however, many unions have cooperated with management in redesigning jobs because of competitive pressure and fears that more jobs would be lost without such cooperation. Usually if unions are assured of job security and no decrease in wage rates, they will cooperate in the redesign of jobs, and in some cases encourage the effort.

Organization Philosophy. Managerial philosophies vary among organizations. But, in organizations where managers view employee job satisfaction as a major priority and where the philosophy includes genuine concern for the individual employee, job design is directly affected. Most managers who hold these views believe that job satisfaction leads to greater productivity, less absenteeism, little turnover, and overall higher efficiency. While results such as these have occurred in many organizations, some researchers see a different cause-and-effect relationship. March and Simon conclude that high job satisfaction does not necessarily stimulate productivity. They state that motivation to produce "stems from a present or anticipated state of discontent and a perception of a direct connection between individual production and a new state of satisfaction.[1]

Fortunately most people who are employed by organizations are individuals who desire and have chosen to work in that industry. Higher level managers already have employees who view the work and industry in a positive light. This is a plus for managers who have as part of their philosophy the objective of creating job-satisfied employees. On the contrary, poor managerial practices can quickly change an employee's positive attitude into one that is negative which will eventually be reflected in marginal performance.

---

[1] James G. March and Herbert A. Simon, *Organization* (New York: John Wiley & Sons, Inc., 1958), p. 51.

Job Design Methods

Managers may use any of several job design methods. The specific method chosen will be influenced by all the factors affecting job design and how the manager weights them in his or her deliberation. Some of the more widely used job design methods are time and motion analysis, job rotation, job enlargement, the sociotechnical approach, and job enrichment.

Time and Motion Analysis. This method of designing jobs, also called **job engineering**, originated with the scientific management movement pioneered by Frederick W. Taylor and Frank Gilbreth (see Chapter 1). Time studies are made of repetitive work cycles, and motion analysis is conducted to improve the way tasks are to be performed. From these two types of studies a work standard and the correct way to perform the job are established. This approach leads to improved efficiency of output but also creates intense specialization of work. A significant disadvantage of this method is that the individual employee must adapt to the machine, leaving little room for individuality or creativity in the workplace. Jobs designed using time and motion analysis have low job depth and scope and often lead to employee job dissatisfaction. This employee discontent is generally thought to come from frustration over workers' having little input about standards and work methods; however, William Gomberg stated years ago that worker participation in the setting of production standards does not necessarily lead to a more peaceful and productive relationship.[2]

Job Rotation. To maintain employees' interest in work, some managers introduce a job design method called job rotation. Employees, including managers, are moved from one job to another. Job rotation often reduces the boredom of a task and stimulates interest in the new work. The rotation can also be from a day work schedule to an evening work schedule and can include a new job as well as new associates, supervisors, etc. Job rotation also has the advantage of cross training employees to insure more depth at each job in case of an emergency.

Job rotation or cross training not only is a form of good planning and insurance in case key employees leave, get ill or are promoted; but it also provides employees a new perspective about total operations. Cross training adds value to the individual as well as provides benefits to the organization.

Job Enlargement. Job enlargement is a design method that adds more responsibilities to a worker's existing job. Instead of three or four functions, the worker's job may be increased to ten or twelve functions. Theoretically, depending on the nature of the job, the worker's sense of importance may be greater. The goal is to reduce boredom and increase output and job satisfaction. Job depth and scope will be higher. This method may work well in organizations where machines do not control the output and where individual initiative is encouraged. Employees who aspire to advance within the organization willingly accept additional duties.

Sociotechnical Approach. The sociotechnical approach to job design is a method in which both the technical system and its related social system are considered. From

---

[2] William Gomberg, *A Trade Union Analysis of Time Study* (Englewood Cliffs, N.J.: Prentice-Hall, Inc., 1955), pp. 25, 271-272.

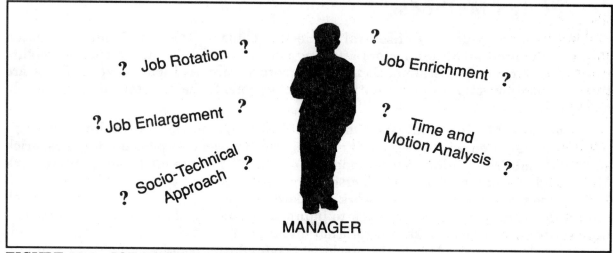

FIGURE 12-2: JOB DESIGN METHODS

the workplace a group or team of employees is formed and given total responsibility for achieving job goals.

This approach emphasizes the social values in the workplace, sometimes called the work climate, and stresses mutual respect between management and the employees. Decision-making is a joint endeavor. One popular example of this approach is quality control circles, which solicit workers' ideas regarding changes.

It does not automatically follow, however, that jobs designed on the basis of both social and technical aspects increase productivity, raise morale and/or generate higher efficiency. As Haynes and Massie noted:

> There are no simple generalizations on the superiority of group endeavor. The problem for management is to determine whether the task at hand is one for which group endeavor will in fact carry benefits which exceed the costs.[3]

Job Enrichment. Job enrichment is a job design method that originated from the work of Frederick Herzberg on factors affecting motivation. Herzberg's hygiene/motivator theory of motivation established factors that motivate employees and factors that maintain them (hygiene factors) but do not motivate them. Herzberg identified motivating factors as achievement, recognition, work itself, responsibility and advancement.[4]

In a practical sense job enrichment is the design of a job which psychologically benefits the employee by allowing greater self-direction, more opportunity to perform interesting work, and added responsibilities. The employee has more control over the job and sinks or swims based on the results.

Without question, job enrichment increases job depth. High employee motivation, a higher quality of performance, greater job satisfaction, less absenteeism, and much lower turnover result from this approach to job design.

---

[3] W. Warren Haynes and Joseph L. Massie, *Management: Analysis, Concepts, and Cases*, 2nd ed. (Englewood Cliffs, N.J.: Prentice-Hall, Inc., 1969), p. 151.
[4] Frederick Herzberg et al, *The Motivation to Work* (New York: John Wiley and Sons, 1959).

While enriching jobs may benefit the employees involved, the organization must gain also. There are always specific costs associated with job enrichment, such as equipment and layout changes, salary increases, training costs, etc. Realistically, organizations that introduce job enrichment programs wish the value of benefits from such programs to far exceed the costs of implementing them. These cost savings or increased revenues are generated by the greater efficiency and increased output and other factors previously discussed.

Perhaps the most unique example in America of a company that has designed every job from top to bottom to be enriched is W. L. Gore and Associates, Inc., headquartered in Newark, Delaware. The term job enrichment is not used by sponsors (managers) in this organization, but the nature of each job perfectly matches the definition of job enrichment.

W. L. Gore and Associates, Inc., was founded in 1958 by W. L. Gore, a former researcher with E. I. DuPont de Nemours.

The company's sales currently exceed $700 million with over two dozen plants located throughout the United States. Of the five basic product groups, Gore-Tex fabrics is the best known to the general public. Gore-Tex produces a waterproof yet "breathable" fabric for making tents, outdoor clothing and other such equipment.

W. L. Gore and Associates, Inc., is unique because no one has a job title of "manger." Every employee is an "associate," and Mr. Gore describes the un-management company as a "lattice organization."

Unlike traditional "pyramid" management structures with carefully defined chains of command, the lattice organization contains no titles, no orders and no bosses. "Associates" (employees) are allowed to identify an area where they feel they will be able to make their best contribution. Then, they are encouraged to maximize their individual accomplishments.

Mr. Gore says, "People manage themselves. We organize ourselves around voluntary commitments. There is a fundamental difference in philosophy between a commitment and a command."[5]

Implementing Job Design

Once jobs have been designed, managers must carefully select the most qualified employees to perform the job. The selected employees must possess the desired qualifications; they must understand job content; they must understand methods of performance; and they must be motivated to do the job. When employees are selected to fill certain jobs, it is helpful if managers tell them why they were selected, the importance of the work, and how their work will relate to other jobs, departments and the ultimate consumer.

It is easier to establish this **role clarity** with new employees if the manager has developed **job descriptions** and **job specifications**.

---

[5] Lucien Rhodes, "The Un-Manager," *Inc.*, August, 1982, p. 34.

A **job description** is a written statement of all the duties and responsibilities to be performed on a particular job. [See Figure 12-4]

A **job specification** is a written statement of the personal qualities an individual should possess to perform a particular job (such things as skills, abilities, knowledge, etc.). [See Figure 12-5]

Job descriptions and job specifications are developed after performing a **job analysis**.

Job analysis is the collection of data about a job through observation, interviewing, questionnaires, charting, and other means. The purpose of job analysis is to provide factual, objective data about the major duties and responsibilities involved in performing the job; the tools and equipment used in doing the job; the physical activities involved; the skills, knowledge and abilities required; and to include a description of the work environment. From this collected data, called **job analysis**, job descriptions and job specifications are developed.

Job specifications are important in the selection of the right employees to fill particular jobs. Equally important is the use of job descriptions to clarify the work role of the employee selected to fill the job.

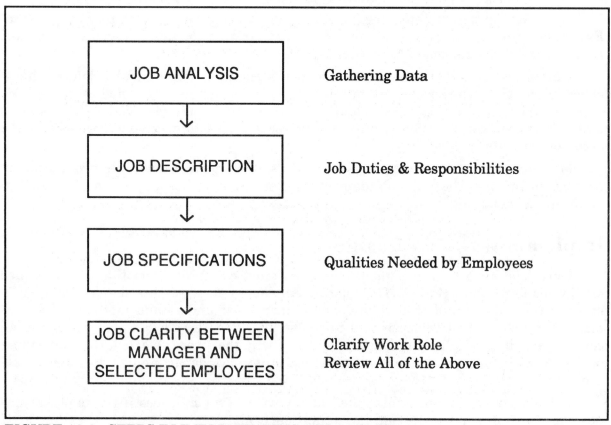

FIGURE 12-3: STEPS IN IMPLEMENTING JOB DESIGN

IDENTIFICATION

Computer Programmer Job Title	*Nonexempt* Status	*007.167* Job Code
April 10, 1981 Date		*Olympia, Inc.—Main Office* Plant/Division
Arthur Allen Written By		*Data Processing—Information Systems* Department/Section
Juanita Montgomery Approved By		*21* *2,480* Grade Points
Programming Supervisor Title of Immediate Supervisor		*22,500-25,850-29,200* Pay Range

SUMMARY

Performs studies, develops and maintains program concerned with employee benefits, focusing specifically on life, medical and hospitalization, accident and disability, and retirement insurance for all divisions of Olympia.

RESPONSIBILITIES AND DUTIES

1.0 Serves as a member of the Employee benefits team of programmers.
    1.1 Updates, modifies, and designs new applications in such areas as enrollment, premium costs, premium collections.
    1.2 Maintains existing programs that constitute employee health and retirement benefits program for employees of Olympia.
    1.3 Develops reports on the status of existing program for which responsible.

2.0 Recommends needed redesign studies.
    2.1 Reviews proposed changes in legislation.
    2.2 consults with user representatives on proposed changes in existing benefit: programs, constraints, and potentially relevant developments.
    2.3 Discusses with other programmers and software specialists use of most suitable application programming technology.
    2.4 Identifies impact of program changes on existing computer programs.
    2.5 Recommends to supervisor changes that should be made in applicable software.

3.0 Carries out study projects.
    3.1 Investigates feasibility of alternate design approaches with a view to determining best solution within constraints set by available resources and future demands.
    3.2 Explores desirability of various possible outputs, considering both EDP and non-EDP costs, benefits, and trade-offs.
    3.3 Identifies types and designation of inputs needed, system interrelationships, processing logic involved.
    3.4 Develops programming specifications.
    3.5 Informs supervisor of progress, unusual problems, and resources required.

4.0 Designs internal program structure of files and records and reviews its operation.
    4.1 Determines detailed sequences of actions in program logic.
    4.2 Codes, tests, debugs, and documents programs.
    4.3 Writes and maintains computer operator instructions for assigned programs.
    4.4 Monitors existing programs to ensure operation as required.
    4.5 Responds to problems by diagnosing and correcting errors of logic and coding.

FIGURE 12-4: SAMPLE JOB DESCRIPTION

Source: Richard I. Henderson, *Compensation Management: Rewarding Performance*, 4th ed. (Reston, Virginia: Reston Publishing Company, Inc., 1985), p. 202

CLASS TITLE: Systems Project Leader

CHARACTERISTICS OF THE CLASS:

Under direction, is responsible for work of considerable difficulty in supervising a project team in the plan, design, and implementation of a major data processing project.
Incumbents are responsible for supervising a team of programmer/analysts in the design, installation, and implementation of a system and functions with complete independence within the framework of the assignment. This level is distinguished from the EDP Programmer/Analyst III by having respon-sibility for planning, designing and implementing a total project and may assign responsibility at the job level to EDP Programmer/Analyst III. This level is distinguished from the EDP Systems Project Manager who has the responsibility for managing several project teams.

EXAMPLES OF DUTIES:

Supervises and participates as a member of a project team in systems design and implementation; plans and design automated processes determining applications and computer requirements, conducting feasibility studies, scheduling projects and implementation of activities; coordinates the development and implementation of projects working with users and DP personnel to maintain schedules, to identify/resolve problems, and to maintain effective communication with users and DP management; assists users in planning and the development of new systems and maintenance, modification and enhancement of existing systems to identify/resolve problems, assure that sched-ules are being met, provide better service, and maintain effective communication links; prepares written instructions/descriptions for use in developing user procedures and programming specifica-tions; supervises the activities of programming staff in the development of coded instructions for digital computer processing and may perform programming functions as required; plans and develops test data files, testing sequence and reviews test results for adherence to programming and operations standards.

KNOWLEDGE, ABILITIES AND SKILLS:

Considerable knowledge of electronic data processing equipment capabilities; considerable knowl-edge of application systems design techniques and procedures; considerable knowledge of project organization, management and control; good knowledge of the principles and techniques of programming and digital computers; good knowledge of the principles of supervision; some knowledge of statistics. Ability to analyze data and situations, reason logically, draw valid conclu-sions and develop effective solutions to systems problems; ability to design procedures for processing data with digital computers; ability to prepare comprehensive reports; ability to analyze and evaluate the progress of the system being developed; ability to speak and write effectively.

MINIMUM QUALIFICATIONS:

Two years experience equivalent to an EDP Programmer/Analyst III

FIGURE 12-5: SAMPLE JOB DESCRIPTION/SPECIFICATION COMBINATION

Source: Robert L. Mathis and John H. Jackson, *Personnel*, 3rd. ed. (St. Paul: West Publish-ing Company, 1982), p. 160.

Organizing Groups

Management faces the on-going challenge of running an efficient organization. To meet this goal, full utilization of employee potential is essential. Four steps aid the manager in maximizing use of employees:

Step 1:   Design jobs effectively and fill them with qualified personnel.

Step 2:   Group similar jobs together to form departments.

Step 3:   Coordinate the activities of machines and employees into harmonious group effort which generates efficiency.

Step 4:   Structure all departments into an effective and efficient working "whole" (the ideal end result).

In the process of organizing, managers have many options for action. For example, managers have choices about job design, about structuring the organization, about employee selection, and about what groups, if any, they wish to use to achieve the ideal end result.

Groups play an important role in most organizations. Boards of Directors, committees, task forces, and teams are some examples. Groups can be formal or informal. Members of formal groups can be elected, appointed or volunteer. Members of informal groups have the freedom to enter or exit at will. Understanding the types of **groups** and the roles they can play to benefit overall organizational effort is important to a manager.

Identifying groups. Many types of groups have been identified in management, but there is no standardization of terms. Groups have been called formal, informal, functional, task forces, permanent or standing, ad hoc, committees, boards, commissions, teams, projects, directors and more. For the purposes of this text, groups will be identified as **formal** or **informal** with attention given to specialized groups, such as committees, which affect management practices.

A group is *two or more individuals who through interaction and mutual dependency work together to achieve common goals.*

Formal Groups. Formal groups are created purposely by management to achieve specific objectives. Employees in a payroll department would be an example. Specialists from functional departments assigned to work on a special project (see Matrix Organization in Chapter 7) would be another. Management sometimes establishes task forces to work on a complex organizational problem. When the work is completed, the task force is dissolved. A task force is a formal group and can also be called an ad hoc committee. Some organizations also have standing (permanent) committees which function continuously (although membership may change periodically).

Informal Groups. Informal groups emerge spontaneously, created by the members themselves for the purpose of sharing some common interest. The interest may be personal, social, recreational or work-related. Employees on a softball team or the gang that eats lunch together each day are examples of informal groups.

Informal groups are part of the informal organization which has its own leaders and its own communication network, known as the "grapevine." The informal organization never appears on the formal organization chart, but it has a significant presence just the same. Management must consider the informal organization and use it to advantage in performing daily management functions.

```
FORMAL GROUPS CREATED BY MANAGEMENT

                Board of Directors
                  Departments
               Standing Committees
                  Task Forces
                 Project Teams

INFORMAL GROUPS CREATED BY MEMBERS

                  Lunch Gang
                  Car Poolers
                Office "Cliques"
                 Softball Team
              Disgruntled Employees
```

FIGURE 12-6: EXAMPLES OF FORMAL AND INFORMAL GROUPS

Value of Work Groups to the Members. Whether the work group is formal or informal, the members may receive benefits in the following areas from belonging:

Social satisfaction can be obtained through interaction with group members. Sharing problems or joys of mutual interest; discussing common objectives; listening to other opinions; and developing camaraderie with colleagues can be sources of social satisfaction.

Safety needs in the form of job security may be realized by membership in a group. This is the case when an employee joins a union. As a group, members are stronger in a confrontation with management than they would be as individuals. Departments often protect members from other departments in a period of crisis or conflict.

Self esteem and dignity are often increased through group participation and involvement. Realizing new goals through team effort or acquiring new skills from on the job training can increase a feeling of self-worth and importance.

Value of Work Groups to the Organization. Groups become the foundation of organized effort within the organization. Work groups provide these major values to the organization:

The Synergistic Effect. Grouping employees in an orderly way, when proper skills and equipment are in place, allows the output (end result) to be far greater in value than the output of isolated individuals. Group formations begin the process of increasing the efficiency and productivity of work effort.

Value in decision-making. Managers can use groups as participants in decision-making. New ideas and approaches may come from within the group that will be more readily accepted by the group if the decision affects them. Also, members' knowledge of a subject may be greater than that of management when the problem directly involves them. Additionally, group recommendations often provide new alternatives for management to consider.

Orientation and socialization of new employees. Groups often provide the means for orienting new employees to the workplace. Explaining work expectations, job requirements, standards of conduct, the philosophy of management which is actually practiced, and even helping the new employee learn the job are all of great value to the organization. The act of introducing new employees to older workers and making them feel comfortable in the work environment helps the new employee adjust more quickly to the workplace.

Special Groups

Task Forces. Task forces are created by management to concentrate their time and talents on specific problems determined by management. Often the members of a task force are drawn from different subunits or functional areas to address a problem that is interdepartmental. Once the work of the task force has been completed, the group is disbanded.

An early example of task forces is found in England during World War II. The British government set up teams of specialists to work on complex operational problems important to the war effort. Because of a shortage of skilled scientists/researchers from specific areas, the groups were composed of individuals with different backgrounds and skills. This multi-disciplinary approach to solving complex operational problems proved highly successful, and a new management field, called **operations research,** was begun.

Task forces are used in organizations today for these purposes:

1. Make recommendations to management;
2. Reach decisions and initiate action under the authority of higher management;
3. Draw conclusions and implement the results in individual areas of managerial influence.

Task forces are also called **ad hoc** or temporary committees, but the designation "task force" with its implication of action and authority (power) may be preferred, if management wishes to convey a sense of urgency about a problem.

Two common examples of using "task forces" are these: a Mayor appoints a "task force" to raise funds for building a multipurpose arena to serve the needs of a city; a "task force" may be established by university officials to double the endowment funds over a five-year period.

Committees. An old adage, reprinted on plaques and various business-related bric-a-brac says this:

> If something is urgent, do it yourself.
> If you have time, delegate it.
> If you have forever, form a committee.

Unfortunately, this is what committees signify to many people. Service on a committee is often viewed as a world-class waste of time and energy. This does not have to be the case, however, if management applies the guidelines suggested here to the formation and administration of committees.

Committees are either **standing** or **permanent**, or they are **ad hoc** or **temporary**. Since **ad hoc** or **temporary** committees are similar to task forces in operation, this discussion will concentrate on **standing committees**. Suggestions for improving use of all committees applies to both types.

ADVANTAGES	DISADVANTAGES
1. "Two heads are better than one" when dealing with major organizational problems.	1. Committees compromise findings.
2. Functional specialists from different areas provide expertise.	2. Committees can generate conflict where none existed before.
3. Committee decisions or recommendations may be more readily accepted by members.	3. Committees are time consuming and therefore expensive.
4. Diverse membership communicates information quickly.	4. Committees do not pinpoint responsibility on any one individual.
5. Creation of a committee stresses the importance of the work.	5. Committees can be viewed as a tool to avoid individual managerial responsibility.
6. Committee decisions are shared by the group rather than being the action of one person.	6. Talent of committee members may be better used on other activities.
7. Committee involvement often motivates members.	
8. Membership on a committee provides opportunities for training, growth, and the acquisition of more knowledge.	

FIGURE 12-7:   ADVANTAGES AND DISADVANTAGES OF COMMITTEES COMPARED

1. Members not qualified to serve
2. Dominated by people with rank and title
3. Objectives not specified by higher management
4. Members' interest not stimulated by higher management
5. Chairperson is incompetent
6. Absenteeism
7. Committee work viewed as unimportant
8. Incompatibility of members
9. Meets too often or not often enough
10. Members receive no reward or recognition
11. Committee membership is too large

FIGURE 12-8: SOME CAUSES OF COMMITTEE FAILURE

A committee is *a formally appointed group of two or more people to consider and satisfy some organizational need.*

Standing committees are permanent. While membership on the committee rotates periodically, the committee and its function stay. Standing committees play an important role in all types of American organizations. Standing committees run the United States Senate; trustees often formulate policies and goals of some private American universities; boards of directors oversee the management practices of business firms; and a finance committee may review all budgets and expenditures of management above a certain dollar limit. Standing committees function at all levels of an organization, i.e., an employee safety committee.

Although there are conflicting views about the worth of committees, most managers agree that committees can play a valuable part in meeting certain organizational needs. Advantages and disadvantages of committees are summarized in Figure 12-7.

Managers often view the pros and cons of forming a committee before they act. There are many potential advantages and disadvantages to the use of committees, but the committee form of organization structure is widely used.

Committees should be formed as needed, constructed properly, administered correctly, and rewarded fairly for the contribution made by the members. Figure 12-8 lists some of the causes of committee failure which must be overcome if committees are the prove effective. In Figure 12-9 major suggestions for improving committee effectiveness are listed. After reviewing these suggestions, you can evaluate your next experience on a committee.

Summary Comments about Committees. Committees should be groups that management can use effectively for the good of the total organization. Individuals who have served on committees should feel that the experience was educational, pleasant, personally rewarding, and important. They should look forward to serving on another committee in the future.

Effective committees benefit everyone. Managers should plan the formation of committees as carefully as they plan budget expenditures.

Using committees poorly is expensive, time consuming, and a detriment to the morale of employees involved. Poor committee implementation is as bad a management practice as the improper use of any other resources, such as equipment and inventories.

Management of Group Behavior. The previous discussion has concentrated on committees as groups whether they are task forces, standing committees, project teams, boards or other designations. Managers have a responsibility to manage groups as well as they do individual employees.

One of the most important research studies regarding group behavior was conducted by Bernard Berelson and Gary A. Steiner who published an inventory of scientific findings about human behavior in 1964. In effect, these findings (reproduced as an extract in Figure 12-10) are principles of behavior of individuals as members of a group. Managers may gain more meaningful insight into group interaction and individual behavior within groups after reviewing these points. They are valuable tools to the student of management who seeks to understand group behavior better.

Step I: **Have Competent Members**

Make certain that committee members are qualified, competent and motivated to serve on the committee and that they can deal effectively with the specific objectives assigned to the committee. Committee members can be appointed, elected, or can volunteer. Regardless of job title, salary level, and length of experience in the organization or how the committee is selected, the committee will not function well with incompetents as members. Remember, thoroughbreds run in the Kentucky Derby — not mules!

Step II: **The Committee Must Be Properly "Charged"**

Someone in higher management who carries authority and has the respect of the committee members should "charge" the committee. The "charge" should include why the committee has been formed; the importance of the work; the importance of the individuals selected; and the time-table for completing the assignment. The "charge" should include not only the act of entrusting the committee with their duty, but also energize them.

Step III: **Select or Elect a Competent "Chairperson"**

The "chair" of a committee is the key to success in implementing the committee's work. The "chair" needs to be an effective **manager** who can plan, organize, implement, and control committee activities. The "chair" delegates, sets time schedules, coordinates work, recognizes accomplishments, follows-up on assignments and much more. The "chair" also must be an effective **leader** who can instill enthusiasm among the members, develop loyalty within the group, and generate high morale and motivation during the committee's existence.

Step IV: **Recognize/Reward Committee Accomplishments**

Once the work of the committee has been completed or the work of the committee has reached a certain benchmark, then recognize the results. Recognition or reward may be in the form of a company-sponsored dinner; a personal letter to each member; a report of the committee's accomplishments in the company newsletter; or a visit by top management to the committee where each member is thanked personally for his or her contribution. Committee members deserve recognition for outstanding accomplishments.

FIGURE 12-9:   STEPS IN IMPROVING THE EFFECTIVENESS OF COMMITTEES

Individuals and Groups as a Source of Creativity

It is well known that individuals and organizations become more creative in a time of crisis. In World War II, the United States created the atom bomb to end the war with Japan. During the oil and gasoline crisis of the 1970s, any number of alternative fuel sources sprang to life for cars and homes. When you have a flat tire on a dark road in the middle of the night and the flashlight batteries are dead, you will build a small fire to see what you are doing (even if you have to rub two sticks together). **Crisis creativity** is important, but the progressive leaders of industry today do not rely on this kind of creativity to give them the competitive "edge" in their field. Rather, modern managers do not merely react to conflict and problems to find novel solutions and better methods, they are progressive managers who encourage creativity in a proactive way. This can be called **purposeful creativity**, and the distinction is clear!

Purposeful creativity *is a planned, continuous effort by management to encourage creativity*. The end result is new products, improved existing products, greater market share, better methods of operation, more efficient systems of activity, and general improvement in all aspects of running an organization. Managers in these kinds of organizations have adopted a philosophy of **"making progress on purpose"** instead of by accident. Progress is made by designed effort not simply by reacting to organizational needs and conflict.

To achieve purposeful creativity, managers must establish a climate for individual and group creativity. The following steps lead to such a climate:

1. Top management must totally endorse and continually support the concept of **change** if it will prove beneficial and economical to the organization.
2. A program encouraging creativity (new ideas and new ways of doing things) must be introduced with full support of management and complete understanding by the employees.
3. Individual employees and groups must be given the opportunity to learn more about the creative process. This should include training sessions, literature and exercises that stress idea generation.
4. A formal organization should be created to administer the creative/idea program properly on a continuous basis. This effort, composed of full-time employees or administered by a committee, should develop a system of idea encouragement; a procedure for reviewing submitted ideas; a manner for recognizing selected ideas; and a reward program for employees whose ideas are implemented.
5. Finally, there should be a program to implement the best of the ideas. Often this requires a mix of functional specialists under the direction of an administrator who coordinates all aspects of the new activity.

Many ideas submitted by individuals or groups will not have practical value. But some will, and the important point to remember is that the effort must be formally recognized and the participants encouraged to continue to think creatively.

Innovation and Implementation. *Creativity* is the generation of new ideas. *Innovation* is the practical application of new ideas. Obviously, ideas without implementation lead nowhere. Years ago children with worn out roller skates often took the wheels and nailed them on a plank of wood to make a homemade scooter. Finally someone had the "idea" of naming these skateboards, making them sleek and colorful, and selling

---

Extract A

HUMAN BEHAVIOR: AN INVENTORY OF SCIENTIFIC FINDINGS
Bernard Berelson and Gary A. Steiner

A1. The more people associate with one another under conditions of equality, the more they come to share values and norms and the more they come to like one another.

A3. The more interaction or overlap there is between related groups, the more similar they become in their norms and values; the less communication or interaction between them, the more tendency there is for conflict to arise between them. And vice versa: the more conflict, the less interaction.

B1. The small group strongly influences the behavior of its members by setting and/or enforcing standards (norms) for proper behavior by its members—including standards for a variety of situations not directly involved in the activities of the group itself.

B2. The less certain the group is about the right standards, the less control it can exercise over its members.

C1. In most groups, there is a rough ranking of members, implicit or explicit, depending on the extent to which the members represent or realize the norms and values of the group: the more they do, the higher they rank.

C9. In general, there is an alternation within groups, especially those having tasks to perform, between communications (interactions) dealing directly with the task and communications dealing with emotional or social relations among the members—the former tending to create tensions within the group and the latter tending to reduce them and achieve harmony.

C10. Both the effectiveness of the group and the satisfaction of its members are increased when the members see their personal goals as being advanced by the group's goals, i.e., when the two are perceived as being in harmony.

C11. The more threatened the individual members feel (i.e., the more they think they will personally lose something by the group's performance), the more concerned they become about being accepted in the group and the less effective the group as a whole becomes, with regard to both efficiency of performance and satisfaction of the members.

C12. The more compatible the members are, in norms, skills, personality, status, etc., and the more the procedures of the group are accepted and understood, the more effective and satisfying is the performance of the group in its tasks.

C13. Active discussion by a small group to determine goals, to choose methods of work, to reshape operations, or to solve other problems is more effective in changing group practice than is separate instruction of the individual members, external requests, or the imposition of new practices by superior authority—more effective, that is, in bringing about better motivation and support for the change and better implementation and productivity of the new practice.

FIGURE 12-10: EXTRACT ON BEHAVIOR OF INDIVIDUALS WITHIN GROUPS

Source: Bernard Berelson and Gary A. Steiner, *Human Behavior: An Inventory of Scientific Fincings* (New York: Harcourt, Brace and World, Inc., 1964), pp. 325-360, as reproduced in Haynes and Massie, *Management*, pp. 173-74.

them as wonderful new toys. Commercializing this product resulted in millions being sold annually because an "idea" was implemented.

The Creative Process and Sources of Ideas. Ideas come to all people at odd times and in strange places. Many highly creative people keep a notepad or recorder handy at all times to jot down their ideas as they come. Most employees are not this creative, but each is more creative than imagined. The role of the manager is to encourage employees to use their full creative potential.

A common sense creative process, as applied to an individual, is as follows:

1. Identify the subject to resolve
2. Research the subject
3. Review all information over a period of time
4. Project alternative ways to achieve objective
5. Test alternatives
6. Select and implement an alternative.

The first step in the **planning process** (see Chapter 5) is to generate ideas. Managers should take the best of these ideas, put them in tangible form, and make them working objectives. To say that all good ideas will come only from the employees or the managers is misleading. Many good ideas can be generated by customers, clients, vendors, competitors, and other sources. A company determined to "make progress on purpose" does not overlook any source of new ideas.

Stimulating Creativity. The three best known techniques for stimulating creativity are brainstorming, synectics, and the nominal group process.

Brainstorming[6] was developed by Alexander F. Osborn, who at the time was a principal with the New York advertising agency of Batten, Barton, Durstine & Osborn. The technique has enjoyed wide use for over twenty-five years. Brainstorming attempts to generate many ideas in a relatively short period of time. A small group of seven or eight people are brought together, presented a problem, and asked to recommend solutions to the problems (spontaneously). It does not matter how absurd the solutions may be. The purpose is to generate a large quantity of ideas about a problem in an unrestricted setting in a brief period of time. From the large number of proposed solutions, perhaps one or two may work once refined.

Synectics[7] means "holding together continuously." The technique, developed by William J. J. Gordon, is somewhat similar to brainstorming except participants in the group may have different specialized backgrounds and the experienced leader carefully explains the problem to be discussed. As participants recommend solutions, the leader encourages them to think more creatively about the problem and to develop more nontraditional approaches to the problem. The leader structures the discussion suggesting direct analogies be applied in consideration of a solution to a problem. For example, how sea gulls glide over the ocean might be valuable in overcoming some of the problems of ultralight airplanes.

---

[6] Alexander F. Osborn, *Applied Imagination: Principles and Procedures for Creative Problem-Solving*, 3rd ed. (New York: Scribners, 1963).

[7] William J. J. Gordon, *Synectics: The Development of Creative Capacity* (New York: Harter, 1961).

Synectics is a group process where all participants get involved in evaluating solutions and the leader "holds together" all of the ideas and recommended solutions which are used in the final determination of a solution.

Nominal group process[8] is a technique developed by Andre Delbecq and Andrew H. Van de Ven for the purpose of developing creative alternatives to problems. The process begins when a problem is clearly explained to the group. Then, each group member, working alone, prepares a list of ideas or possible solutions to the problem. Following this, each member of the group presents his or her ideas or solutions to the problem to the other members. These ideas are recorded. After all members have made their presentations, an open discussion follows and each idea or recommendation is evaluated. Next, the members vote privately on each other's ideas and rank the ideas in order of importance. The results are announced to all and a brief discussion follows. Lastly, a final secret vote is cast by each member and the group's preference is determined.

The nominal group process technique, unlike brainstorming and synectics, does not generate an open discussion of ideas. Much of the work within the group is done privately by each member, and there is a limit placed on participants' verbal interaction. Still, this process, like the others, generates many good ideas and creative solutions to problems.

TECHNOLOGICAL	ENVIRONMENTAL	INTERNAL
Machines	Laws	Policies
Equipment	Taxes	Procedures
Processes	Social trends	Methods
Automation	Fashion trends	Rules
Computers	Political trends	Reorganization
New raw materials	Economic trends	Budget adjustment
	Interest rates	Restructuring of jobs
	Consumer trends	Personnel
	Competition	Management
	Suppliers	Ownership
	Population trends	Products/Services sold

FIGURE 12-11: TYPES OF CHANGES AFFECTING ORGANIZATIONS

Source: Leslie W. Rue and Lloyd L. Byars, *Management Theory and Application*, Fifth edition (Homewood, IL: Richard D. Irwin, 1989), p. 504.

---

[8] Andre L. Delbecq and Andrew H. Van de Ven, "A Group Process Model for Problem Identification and Program Planning," *Journal of Applied Behavioral Science* 7, No. 4 (July-August, 1971), 466-492.

Managing Change

Every type of organization today is confronted with change. Managers must be able to cope with changes if they are to be successful. Also, managers must understand that employees' resistance to change is a normal or natural reaction unless the fear of change is removed before it takes place. Figure 12-11 shows the types of changes affecting organizations.

Primarily changes which affect organizations can be classified as **technological, environmental** and **internal.** Introducing and using the computer is an example of technological change. An example of environmental change would be federal laws that opened opportunities for women. Internal changes are common such as adjusting to budget cuts or adapting to a new boss. Any type of change can greatly affect a manager's job.

Resistance to Change

Overcoming employees' resistance to change is another job of all managers. Understanding the major barriers to change can prove helpful.

The most common reasons employees resist change are these:

1. **Employees fear the unknown.** They are not sure what the consequences of the change will be nor how it will affect them.
2. **Economic threats.** Employees are not certain about the impact of change on their jobs and income.
3. **Personal inconvenience.** Changes may require employees to work at a new location or fill a newly created job. In either case, it is a personal inconvenience.
4. **Personal relationships changed.** Change can alter interpersonal and social relationships and create resistance from the employees affected.

In the majority of cases change is introduced by managers. Therefore, managers must understand the kinds of change and the major barriers to change. Also, managers must plan on how to introduce change and minimize resistance to it. Rue and Byars present suggestions for reducing resistance to change in Figure 12-12. All of these suggestions are sound and involve employee participation. Whenever possible, change should be planned well ahead of implementation. Employees who will be affected must not only be involved but must understand the value of the change; be educated to the purpose of the change, and be sold on the need for the change. Sudden changes introduced without following the above suggestions will automatically create employee resistance.

Build trust.
Discuss upcoming changes.
Involve the employees in the changes.
Make sure the changes are reasonable.
Avoid threats.
Follow a sensible time schedule.
Implement in the most logical place.

FIGURE 12-12: SUGGESTIONS FOR REDUCING RESISTANCE TO CHANGE

Source: Rue and Byars, *Management Theory and Application*, p. 506.

Summary

American managers have a renewed interest in the American employee and the jobs they hold. This concern has been spurred by declining productivity and efficiency in some industries and increased foreign competition. Justification for management's interest in employees and their jobs is based on the premise that the more satisfied an employee is on the job, the greater productivity and efficiency of output will be.

The starting point for improving overall organizational effort is the design of individual jobs. Job design is the process of specifying the tasks to be performed, the work methods to be used in performance, and the relationship of the job to other jobs in the organization for the purpose of improving the quality and quantity of work.

Factors affecting job design are job depth and job scope, types of employees available to work, economic restrictions, union limitations, and company philosophy.

Many job design methods are available to the manager. Specifically the method selected will be the result of considering all the factors affecting job design. The job design methods are time and motion analysis, job rotation, job enlargement, sociotechnical, and job enrichment.

Implementing job design and clarifying the work role of the employee are made easier if the manager develops job descriptions and job specifications.

Groups play an important role in most organizations. Groups can be formal or informal. Understanding the types of groups and the roles they can play to benefit overall organizational effort are important to a manager.

A group is defined as two or more individuals who, through interaction and mutual dependency, work together to achieve common goals.

Formal groups are created purposely by management to achieve specific objectives. Informal groups emerge spontaneously, created by the members themselves, for the purpose of sharing some common interest.

Members of groups may receive great benefits from being part of a group. Some are social satisfaction, safety needs being realized, and an increase in self-esteem and dignity. Work groups also may be of value to the organization by providing help in decision-making, by orienting and socializing new employees to the organization, by creating the synergistic effect in the workplace. In addition, special groups such as task forces and standing committees provide assistance to managers. Task forces are formed by management to concentrate their time and talents on specific problems. Once the work of the task force has been completed, the group is dissolved. Standing committees are permanent groups even if members change over time.

Committee effectiveness can be improved by having competent committee members, having the committee properly "charged," having a competent chairperson who is a good manager/leader, and by recognizing or rewarding a committee after its work has been completed.

Individuals and groups are also a source of creativity in an organization. Creativity can be identified as **crisis** creativity or as **purposeful** creativity. Purposeful creativity is a planned, deliberate effort by management to encourage creativity to improve existing products, create new ones, increase market share, improve methods of operation, increase efficiency of activity and improve all aspects of running an organization. To achieve purposeful creativity managers must establish a climate for group and individual creativity.

Often creativity stimulation techniques are used to generate ideas and solutions to problems. The three best known techniques are brainstorming, synectics and the nominal group process.

Managing change is another important management responsibility. Changes which affect organizations the most are classified as technological, environmental and internal. The most common reasons employees resist change are fear of the unknown; economic threats; personal inconvenience, and changes in personal relationships. Whenever possible changes should be planned well ahead of implementation and include employee involvement.

Review Questions

1. Explain each factor that affects job design. Which of the factors do you consider the most important?

2. Which of the job design methods is an offshoot of Frederick Herzberg's hygiene/motivation theory? Explain.

3. How important is job analysis to the development of job descriptions and job specifications? Discuss.

4. Distinguish clearly informal groups from formal groups. Identify how each type of group is formed and for what purposes.

5. Crisis creativity and purposeful creativity both generate new ideas and solutions to problems. How do these differ? Give examples of each.

6. Can you name the three best known creativity stimulation techniques? Discuss the steps in each technique.

7. Name and classify the major types of change.

Assignments for Personal Development

1. Select a job that is considered mundane or dull (such as that of a clerk or secretary). Write a plan to enrich the job through job enlargement.

2. Imagine you are a Sanitary Department Director for a mid-sized city and the Mayor notifies you that a ten (10) percent budget cut is imminent. Outline how you would implement the budget cuts. How would you involve your staff of assistant directors, maintenance personnel, users of the services and the community in general?

Incident

THE DYSFUNCTIONAL COMMITTEE

Hazel Upshaw was one of twelve committee members appointed by the President. The committee's purpose was to generate suggestions about how to market more effectively and creatively the company's line of merchandise. Hazel had been on the committee for three months, and nothing had come forth from the committee. They met once a month and did nothing more than gossip and complain about the management. She thought being on the committee was a total waste of time. The chair of the committee was inept but worked overtime to stay popular with committee members.

Just yesterday, each committee member received a memo from the President announcing the transfer of the chair to a new job located elsewhere which removed the chair from the committee. At the conclusion of the memo, the President recommended Hazel Upshaw to become the new chair. He also charged the committee to become productive quickly, or the committee would be disbanded.

Questions:

1. Give Hazel some suggestions for improving committee effectiveness.
2. What is the role of a committee? Does committee action ever replace the duties and responsibilities of higher management?

Suggested Readings

Aries, Elizabeth. "Interaction Patterns and Themes of Male, Female, and Mixed Groups." *Small Group Behavior*, 7 (1976), 7-18.

Dion, Kenneth L., Robert S. Baron, and Norman Miller. "Why Do Groups Make Riskier Decisions Than Individuals?" In *Advances in Experimental Social Psychology*, Vol. 3. Ed. Leonard Berkowitz. New York: Academic Press, 1970, pp. 305-77.

Hackman, J. Richard, and Neil Vidmar. "Effects of Size and Task Type on Group Performance and Member Reactions." *Sociometry*, 33 (1970), 37-54.

Homestead, Michael S. *The Small Group*. New York: Random House, 1981.

Napier, R. W., and M. K. Gersjemfeld. *Groups: Theory and Experience*. Boston: Hoghton Mifflin, 1973.

Schweiger, David M., William R. Sandberg, and James W. Ragan. "Group Approaches for Improving Strategic Decision Making: A Comparative Analysis of Dialectical Inquiry, Devil's Advocacy, and Consensus." *Academy of Management Journal* 29 (March 1986): 51-71.

Wanous, John P., and Margaret A. Youtz. "Solution Diversity and the Quality of Group Decisions." *Academy of Management Journal* 29 (March 1986): 149-58.

GLOSSARY OF KEY TERMS

A

Acceptance Theory of Authority: Holds that the employee, the subordinate or the influencee determines whether the manager has any authority or not. Evolved from the work of Chester I. Barnard.

Accountability: The responsibility of an employee to his or her supervisor. Sometimes called "reportability."

Affirmative Action Plan: Special programs to eliminate inequities in the status of women and minorities.

Age Discrimination in Employment Act of 1967 (amended 1978 and 1986): This act prohibits employers from discriminating in employment against individuals on the basis of age.

Agency Law: Deals with the relationship in which one person, the **agent**, acts for or represents another, the **principal**, by the latter's authority.

Antitrust Laws: The primary laws are the Sherman Antitrust Act (1890) and the Clayton Act (1914). Laws were passed to encourage free and open competition in business.

Apprenticeship Training: An ancient form of training that is prevalent in skill trades today. Often related to the union whereby a skilled craftsperson teaches the trade to an individual for several years.

Art of Management: Refers to an individual manager's style of managing. Also is the application of the sum total of knowledge and experience gained to bring about desired results.

Assessment Center: The purpose is to predict management potential of participants through a variety of techniques such as in-basket exercises, role playing, incident analysis, and simulation.

Audit: Usually thought of as a method of control with financial matters. Audits can include other activities in the organization as well.

Authority (Manager's): When associated with managers, authority is the right to act officially.

B

Basic Process in Management: Identifies the main jobs of all managers as planning, organizing, implementing and controlling.

Brainstorming: Takes place when employees or a group are encouraged to present solutions or ideas about a problem off the "tops of their heads." The purpose is to present a large quantity of ideas in a short period of time.

Breach of Contract: A failure to perform a duty imposed under a contract.

Budget: A financial forecast or plan that projects expected income and expenditures over a given period of time.

C

Certainty: When a manager knows exactly what will happen when a decision is made.

Civil Rights Act of 1964 (amended 1972 and 1978): Title VII of this Act prohibits discrimination in employment on the basis of race, color, religion, sex or national origin in organizations that conduct interstate commerce.

Classical Organization Theory: Importance is placed on organization structure or the hierarchy. Principles of organization have been developed to provide guidance to practicing managers.

Codes: Guidelines that are standards of professional practice or behavior.

Collective Bargaining Agreements: Agreements include the governing terms and conditions of employment for workers in their respective organizations and industries.

Committee: A formally appointed group of two or more people to consider and satisfy some organizational need.

Communication: The act or action of imparting or transmitting ideas, information, facts or feelings to a second party.

Conceptual Skill: The ability of top-level managers to provide overall direction to the entire organization.

Constitutional Law: The Constitution contains statutory provisions and judicial interpretations concerning important social, economic and political issues.

Contract: An agreement between two or more parties that is enforceable under the law. It can be written or oral.

Control (Controlling): A management function designed primarily to insure that performance is according to plan.

Control Process: Any control process involves these three steps: (1) setting standards; (2) appraising conformance to the standards, and (3) taking corrective or remedial action if the standards are not met.

Controlling Controls: Refers to an effort to prevent an organization from having too many control programs if they cannot be justified or cost-effective.

Coordination: Refers to the blending, matching or synchronizing of individual and group effort.

Court System: Refers to the two basic legal systems in the United States: the federal system and the state system.

Creative Decision-Making: Where participants in a group are encouraged to think creatively about solutions to a problem without advanced preparation.

Criminal Law: Defines criminal conduct and prescribes the punishment to be imposed on a person convicted of engaging in such conduct.

Culture: The dominant values, feelings and beliefs that evolve in working groups.

Customer Departmentation: An organization structured around identifiable customer groups.

D

Data Processing: The capture, processing and storage of data.

Decision-Making: Involves selecting a course of action from alternative choices.

Decoding: The step in the communication process where the receiver translates the sender's symbols and gestures into meaningful thought.

Defamation: May be **libel** (in writing) or **slander** (spoken words) that tend to harm the reputation of another as to lower him or her in the estimation of the community or to deter third persons from associating or dealing with him or her.

Delegation: The assignment of authority and responsibility to a person or group of people at the next lower level in the organization.

Demography: The statistical study of human population with emphasis on size and density, distribution and vital statistics.

Departmentation: Denotes the grouping of jobs by functions, products, location, customers, time, sequence and numbers. Departments may refer to divisions, plants, sections, branches, bureaus, regions or other synonyms.

Disciplinary Action: Can be a verbal or written reprimand, a suspension or a demotion.

Division of Labor Principle: Refers to breaking work down into basic component tasks and emphasizing specialization of effort.

Documentation: Any written statement concerning the employee's work performance or behavior on the job.

Due Process: A course of legal proceedings which have been established in our system of jurisprudence for the protection and enforcement of private rights.

E

Encoding: The symbols or gestures a sender selects to transmit a message through the desired channel so that the receiver decodes it properly.

Environment of Management: The sum of all the social, cultural, economic and physical factors that influence the lifestyle of an individual, organization or community.

Equal Pay Act of 1963 (amended 1972): Prohibits wage discrimination on the basis of sex when the jobs require equal skills, effort and responsibility and are performed under similar working conditions.

Ethics: Generally considered to be a set of moral values or principles that influences behavior of individuals or societies.

External Constraints: The environmental constraints that affect managerial actions and originate outside the framework of the organization.

F

Fair Labor Standards Act of 1938: This law set minimum wages (amended many times since), overtime pay and child-labor standards.

Federal Court System: Consists of the Supreme Court, 12 Courts of Appeals, 91 district courts, certain specialized courts and administrative agencies.

Final-stage Control: The activity of reviewing the results of the final product or service.

Flextime: Allows selected employees to determine their own daily work schedule as long as they are on the job during certain hours called **core time**.

Forecasts: An effort by a manager to anticipate future occurrences in light of current information and predictions.

Formal Leaders: Individuals who are appointed, elected or volunteer to fill a leadership role in a position that is part of the formal organization.

Formal Organization: A group of people working together toward common objectives with a clearly defined hierarchy.

Functional Departmentation: The nature of the work defines the units of the organization.

Functional Foremanship: Exchanges multiple accountability for intense specialization to support the work of individual employees. Developed by F. W. Taylor.

Functional (Specialized) Staff: A special kind of staff position or department that is given limited line authority under certain conditions.

Functions of Management: The main activities of a manager which include planning, organizing, implementing and controlling.

Functional Plans: Are plans classified by their use or function such as marketing or finance plans.

G

Gantt Control Chart: A visual control chart used in measuring output against expectations along a time axis.

General Management Problems: Any kind of organizational problem that includes people as part of the problem.

Gordon Technique: Developed by J. J. Gordon as a creative problem-solving technique. The leader describes the problem with one word which becomes the starting point for discussion which leads to ideas that have practical application to the problem.

Graicunas' Theorem: V. A. Graicunas developed a mathematically sound theorem in 1933 which says as you add employees to an organization, you do so arithmetically, but the organizational relationships increase geometrically.

Grapevine: The communication system of the informal organization.

Group: Two or more individuals who through interaction and mutual dependency work together to achieve common goals.

Group Decision-Making: When several individuals, such as a committee, mutually agree on a decision.

H

Hardware: Includes the computer and its physical components such as the printer, screen and keyboard.

Hawthorne Studies: A series of studies at the Hawthorne Plant of the Western Electric Company (Illinois) from 1924 to 1932. Studies showed that psychological and social conditions in the workplace had more influence on increased productivity than did changes in the physical environment of the workplace.

Human Resource Planning (HRP): Includes two steps: (1) a projection of the future human skills and talents that the organization will need to meet its strategic objectives; and (2) the formulation of a detailed plan to recruit and staff the jobs so that the organization can satisfy its strategic objectives.

I

Implementing: Putting the plans and programs of management into action working through employees.

Incoming Controls: A type of control activity at the beginning of a work process to screen or prevent problems from occurring.

Informal Group: Emerges spontaneously, created by the members themselves, for the purpose of sharing some common interest.

Informal Leaders: Also called **indigenous leaders**. They are not appointed nor elected to a leadership role, but arise out of a group because they stand out in a physical or psychological way.

In-process Control: Takes place when manufactured goods are subjected to quality checks during the manufacturing process.

Internal Constraints: The environmental constraints that affect managers and originate from within the organization.

Intuitive Approach to Decision-Making: Making decisions based on hunches, feelings and intuition.

J

Job Analysis: The collection of data about a job through observation, interviewing, questionnaires, charting and other means.

Job Depth: Refers to the individual employee's flexibility to control his or her work performance.

Job Description: A written explanation of all of the duties and responsibilities of a job.

Job Design: Process of specifying the tasks to be performed; the work methods to be used in performance; and the relationship of that job to other jobs in the organization for the purpose of improving the quality and quantity of work.

Job Enlargement: The expansion of jobs to give the employee a greater variety of tasks to perform with added responsibility.

Job Enrichment: The process of designing jobs to include motivators (Herzberg) which can lead to more job satisfaction.

Job Rotation: Employees, including managers, are moved from one job to another to maintain an employee's interest in work.

Job Satisfaction: Refers to the state of mind an individual may have about his or her work environment.

Job Scope: Refers to how specialized and narrow the work activity is.

Job Specification: Details the human traits, education, experience and skills an individual must have to qualify for a particular job.

L

Labor Law: Dictates the rules and regulations that govern the relationship between labor and management, defining the rights, privileges, duties and responsibilities of each.

Labor-Management Relations Act of 1947 (Taft-Hartley Act): Act was an amendment to the Wagner Act of 1935 and was designed to balance some aspects of the Wagner Act. The Act lists the rights of unions and management and establishes the 80-day cooling off period if a strike endangers the national health and safety.

Leadership: The activity of inspiring or influencing members of a group to enthusiastically and competently perform their tasks.

Line and Staff Structure: A line organization structure that has added staff specialists or staff departments.

Line Functions: Activities that directly relate to the achievement of the primary objectives of the organization.

Line Structure: Organization structure built around the activities essential to the attainment of the primary objectives of the organization.

Long-run Plans and Objectives: Normally plans and objectives beyond one year or more are called long-run.

M

Management: The achievement of predetermined objectives working through others (employees).

Management By Objectives (MBO): A program where managers and their employees jointly decide on the employees' objectives. Plans are made for achieving these objectives which become standards against which employee performance is evaluated.

Management Is the Significant Difference: A concept that emphasizes that managerial decisions originate actions which bring about change; thus, creating the difference between competing organizations.

Management Information Systems (MIS): A computer-based network that integrates the collection, processing and transmission of information.

Maslow's Need Hierarchy Theory: Based on the assumption that individuals are motivated to satisfy certain levels of need from the lowest to the highest.

Matrix Structure: Organization structure based on the mathematical concept of matrix. Individuals from different functional areas are assigned to work on a specific project.

Methods: Guidelines that specify an exact way to do a particular task.

Modern Organization Theory: Studies the organization as a system of interdependent variables.

Morale: The state of mind of an individual or group at a given moment about basic job needs, wants and desires.

Motion Economy Principles: When applied eliminates wasted motion and lessens fatigue.

Motivation: Comes from the Latin word *movere* which means "to move." The goal of motivation is to cause people to put forth their best efforts with enthusiasm and effectiveness in order to achieve and hopefully surpass organizational objectives.

Motivation-Maintenance Theory: Developed by Frederick Herzberg. Theory is based on all work-related factors being grouped into one of two categories: **maintenance factors** which will not encourage motivation but can prevent it and **motivators** which, when combined with maintenance factors, can encourage motivation.

N

Neoclassical Organization Theory: Modifies classical theory by expanding into the behavioral sciences with emphasis on the importance of individual behavior, motivation, coordination and leadership.

Negligence: An unintentional tort that focuses on an individual's conduct or actions.

Nominal Group Process: Techniques developed where a group's purpose is to develop creative alternatives to problems.

Nonprogrammed Decisions: Are decisions that apply to unusual problems or situations that are nonroutine.

O

Objectives (Goals): When formalized, become what the organization or individual are trying to achieve.

Occupational Safety and Health Act of 1970 (OSHA): OSHA mandates that employers provide their employees with a healthy and safe work environment that is free from recognized hazards which cause or are likely to cause death or serious physical harm.

On-the-job Training (OJT): A common form of training occurring daily under the direction of an experienced employee or the immediate supervisor.

Operational Plans: May be single-use or standing plans. They are plans that are detailed in content. Single-use plans are not likely to be repeated. Standing operational plans exist to guide managerial actions when organizational activities repeat.

Organization: A group of people who work together toward common objectives with a clearly established hierarchy.

Organizational Handbook (Manual): Sometimes called a policies and procedures manual. Contains, in writing, much of the same information given the new employee orally during orientation.

Organization Structure: The hierarchy or framework within which the activities of an organization take place. It defines the relationships within the organization among work units and clearly indicates the lines of authority, responsibility, accountability and communication.

Organizational Guidelines: The "red tape" that managers introduce to influence employees' behavior as they work toward achieving the stated objectives. Examples of "red tape" are rules, policies, procedures and much more.

Organizational Morale: Defined as the confident, resolute and often self-sacrificing attitude of a group that has strong faith in its leadership and believes organizational goals can be reached.

Organizing: Managerial effort to assign work and allocate resources; then, arrange the work and resources in such an orderly way that a group's effort generates the desired end result in the most efficient and effective manner possible.

Orientation: Orientation of new employees is a process of integrating the employees into the organization, work group and job.

P

Performance Appraisal: Compares the employee's actual work against the work standard or the objectives of the job for that employee.

Personal Philosophy of Management: Consists of an individual manager's fundamental beliefs, basic concepts, convictions and firm ideas about management and his or her behavior as a manager.

Personal Skills: Skills needed most by first-level and middle-level managers. Examples are being an effective leader and communicator.

Peter Principle: Originated by Laurence Peter, a concept that managers tend to be promoted to their level of incompetence.

Planning: An activity of setting goals and objectives; then, developing the detailed methods of achieving them within the specified time period, with a minimum of problems, in the most efficient and effective way feasible.

Planning Process: A series of steps to follow and subjects to discuss and review in establishing and finalizing a plan.

Policies: Guidelines that are flexible, subject to interpretation and are introduced mainly to influence managerial action.

Preference-Expectancy Theory: Based on the work of Victor Vroom who suggested that employee motivation relates to preference on the job (what a person wishes to have happen) and expectancy (the subjective probability of what will happen if certain behavior patterns are followed).

Problem-Solving: Involves determining the proper response to a situation which is considered to be nonstandard or not acceptable.

Procedure: A logical sequence of steps or jobs arranged in a particular manner to achieve the desired end result.

Procedures: Guildelines that consist of job tasks or steps which must be taken in chronological order to achieve a specified end result.

Product Departmentation: The organization is structured around major products or products of a similar nature.

Programmed Decisions: Those decisions that are repetitive and routine.

Programmed Training: A process of studying material and being tested at periodic intervals to confirm satisfactory progress.

Programmer: A person who writes instructional programs that tell the computer what to do.

Purposeful Creativity: A planned, deliberate effort by management to encourage creativity on a continuing basis.

Q

Quality Control Circles (QCC): Originated in the U.S. and became popular in Japan. QCC involve a small group of individuals who meet on a regular basis to discuss and resolve quality problems.

Quality of Work Life: Refers to the way in which work provides an opportunity for an individual to satisfy a wide variety of personal needs.

R

Rational Approach to Decision-Making: Based on the application of the scientific method to general management problems to draw conclusions, make recommendations and/or decisions.

Reckless Misconduct: A tort action that is characterized by intent on the part of the defendant to commit the act but no intent to harm the plaintiff by the act.

Recruitment: A program to attract people with the desired skills, experience and talent to apply for job openings.

Regulations: Guidelines issued authoritatively by higher management or government for employees to follow. One example would be safety regulations issued by OSHA.

Reinforcement Theory: B. F. Skinner was the leading proponent of behavior modification as a motivational tool. The essence is that behavior that leads to a positive consequence tends to be repeated.

Responsibility: An acceptance of accountability for doing a particular job.

Risk: A condition under which a manager can predict future occurrences and assign relative probabilities to them.

Risks: Events or occurrences that managers should be able to foresee with reasonable accuracy and plan for so that if they do occur, the loss or damage can be minimized or offset.

Rules: The strictest and most narrow type of "red tape." Guidelines that demand certain employee action with no room for interpretation.

S

Scalar Principle: Refers to authority in an organization. Authority originates at the top and flows downward throughout the hierarchy one link or level at a time without skipping any level.

Science of Management: The application of the scientific method to general management problems leading to problem-solving and decision-making (also called the Rational or Subjective Decision-Making Approach).

Scientific Method: Includes seven steps and is used by managers today when analyzing general management problems leading to a recommendation or decision.

Search Committee: A group of people from different functional areas appointed by someone in higher administration to perform the functions of a personnel department to recruit, screen, interview and recommend applicants to fill positions in the organization.

Selection: The process of reviewing the qualifications of applicants for specific jobs and hiring those that appear most qualified to do a particular job.

Semantics: The science or study of word meanings.

Short-run Plans and Objectives: Usually refers to plans and objectives of one year or less time.

Skills Inventory: Contains information about the job skills of all employees.

Social Responsibility: Acting in the best interest of society in general.

Social Security Act of 1935: This act established a federal tax on payrolls and provided retirement and disability benefits to employees covered.

Software: Refers to the program which includes the instructions to a computer to perform certain tasks.

Span of Management (Control) Principle: States that there is a limit to the number of employees a manager can effectively supervise.

Staffing: The acquisition and placement of qualified employees in jobs that fully utilize the talents and skills of the individual.

Staff Functions: Activities that indirectly relate to the achievement of the primary objectives of the organization.

State Court System: In general, each of the 50 states has a three-tiered court system, with a trial court level, appellate court level and supreme court level of review.

Strategic Management: The process of managerial decision-making and implementation of plans that directly affects the quality of performance and survival of an organization in the long-run.

Strategic Planning: The process of determining an organization's long-run goals and objectives in compliance with its mission and formulating the proper plan of action (strategy) that will guide efforts to achieve the desired end results over the long-run.

Strategic Plans: Plans developed and designed to achieve the broadest objectives of the organization (sometimes called Master Plans).

SWOT Analysis: A planning tool that lists an organization's internal strengths and weaknesses and external opportunities and threats.

Synectics: A creative problem-solving technique that involves participants; fantasies about how a particular problem could be solved if there were no constraints.

Synergistic Management Concept: A manager's mission to direct the use of resources in such a way that, over a period of time, the end result in value is far greater than the starting value of the combined resources.

Synergy: The combination of factors in which the end result is greater than the sum of the parts: $2 + 2 = 5+$.

Systems Analyst: A person who investigates potential computer applications and determines the types of programs needed.

T

Task Forces: A special group created by management to concentrate their time and talents on specific problems determined by management.

Technical Skills: Refers to knowledge of operations, processes, specifications and details of an organization's operations.

Test Reliability: Exists when the individual taking the test scores about the same on the test when taken a second or third time.

Test Validity: Occurs when performance on the job closely relates to performance on the tests.

Theory X and Theory Y: Developed by Douglas McGregor who made certain assumptions about human behavior in the workplace. The theory identifies two styles of managing based on the manager's beliefs about human behavior: Theory X or autocratic and Theory Y or participative.

Therbligs: The word coined by Frank Gilbreth to define basic units of motion common to most jobs.

Time and Motion Analysis: A method pioneered by Frederick Taylor in which time studies are made of repetitive work cycles and motion analysis is conducted to improve the way tasks are to be performed. From these studies a work standard is established (also called Job Engineering).

Time Standards: Refers to the amount of time allotted for reaching your objectives. Time standards set at a level of excellence means the time standard set is well above average.

Title IX of the Education Amendments of 1972: A federal statute that mandates: "No person in the U.S. shall, on the basis of sex, be excluded from participation in, be denied the benefits of, or be subjected to discrimination under any educational program of activity receiving Federal financial assistance."

Tort: A private (or civil) wrong or injury, other than a breach of contract, suffered by an individual as the result of another person's conduct.

Total Quality Management (TQM): A program designed to control quality and improve all aspects of an organization's activities using statistical techniques, employee teamwork, joint problem-solving and open communication on a continuous basis.

Total Responsibility: The concept that a manager is absolutely and totally responsible for everything that happens, good and bad, from his or her position in the organization downward.

Traditional Theory of Motivation: Based on money as a motivating factor when pay directly relates to employee performance.

Training: A process in which employees acquire new skills and knowledge that will enable them to be more effective in the performance of their jobs.

Trait Theory: Focuses on what leaders are like rather than on what they do.

U

Uncertainties: Events or occurrences that a manager cannot anticipate and plan for so that if they do occur, the organization will either be damaged or benefited.

Uncertainty: A condition which exists under which the manager has little or no information.

Universality of Management Principle: Managers in any type of organization, located anywhere, will engage in the basic process of management as they work through other people to achieve objectives.

V-Z

Vestibule Training: Takes place in a separate work environment that simulates real working conditions.

Windfall: A benefit that accrues to an organization when an uncertainty occurs which could not be anticipated by management.

Zero-Base Budgeting (ZBB): An operating, planning and budgeting process which requires each manager to justify every budget request in detail.

INDEX